JACOBEAN
CITY COMEDY

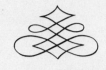

JACOBEAN CITY COMEDY

SECOND EDITION

Brian Gibbons

METHUEN
LONDON AND NEW YORK

First edition published in 1968 by
Rupert Hart-Davis Ltd and
Harvard University Press

Second edition published in 1980 by
Methuen & Co. Ltd
11 New Fetter Lane, London EC4P 4EE
Published in the USA by
Methuen & Co.
in association with Methuen, Inc.
733 Third Avenue, New York, NY 10017
© *1980 Brian Gibbons*
Typeset in Garamond by Red Lion Setters, London WC1
Printed in Great Britain at the
University Press, Cambridge

British Library Cataloguing in Publication Data

Gibbons, Brian, b. 1938 (Oct.)
Jacobean city comedy. – 2nd ed.
1. Jonson, Ben – Comedies   2. Marston, John,
b. 1576 – Comedies   3. Middleton, Thomas –
Comedies   4. English drama – 17th century –
History and criticism   5. English drama
(Comedy) – History and criticism
I. Title
822'.052   PR2638   80-40798

ISBN 0-416-73450-2
ISBN 0-416-73460-X Pbk

CONTENTS

———————————————

TO MY
MOTHER
AND
FATHER

———————————————

PREFACE TO THE
SECOND EDITION

The first draft of this book was written in 1964 and 1965, when I was a research student at the University of Cambridge; when revised it was submitted as a doctoral thesis in 1966. Only slight changes were made to that version – some abbreviation and compression, the cutting of detailed scholarly apparatus – before its publication in 1968 as the first book exclusively devoted to the subject. The first edition assumed in the reader a degree of familiarity with the plays and with the then current critical and scholarly assumptions about them. It was not addressed to a general readership.

All this was a number of years ago. In preparing a second edition for a wider readership I have had two main aims in mind. First, I have brought my account of the plays up to date by revising it, in matters of detail, wherever the evolution of my own views, or subsequent critical and scholarly work by others, has made revision seem appropriate. Second, I have tried to make allowances for the general reader, for whom some of the plays may be unfamiliar, and I have tried to make the literary and dramatic theories of the playwrights clear and accessible. To this end chapters 1, 4, 5, 6 and 9 have been recast and revised in detail. Since this book first appeared in 1968 a number of interesting and valuable articles and editions have appeared, together with some important studies of the broad area of English Renaissance drama. I have compiled an up-to-date bibliography which will help to extend a reader's interest in critical comedy of the Jacobean period.

Although I cannot claim that this book was originally written wholly for amusement, I freely confess to a good deal of enjoyment in its original composition. This revised version remains short; it does not seek to overwhelm by its bulk; and though it is in part a work of literary history, it was always intended to express enthusiasm for its subject.

The University of York   Brian Gibbons
February 1980

ACKNOWLEDGEMENTS

I was immensely helped, when writing the first draft of this study, by the generous advice and criticism of Professor Muriel Bradbrook. To her, and also to Mr Christopher Morris, Professor L. C. Knights, Professor Nicholas Brooke and Professor Bernard Harris, I remain extremely grateful for help and criticism at that time. My thanks also to Professor G. Blakemore Evans, the reader (as I have only recently learned) for Harvard University Press, whose comments and corrections improved the final draft of the first edition; whatever shortcomings and mistakes remained in it are my own responsibility.

I would like to thank Professor Alexander Leggatt for his helpful remarks on my draft of the second edition.

In the second edition I have made every effort to acknowledge debts, where appropriate, to other critics and scholars. If I have inadvertently failed to acknowledge any obligations, I offer apology to those concerned.

I

CITY COMEDY
AS A GENRE

Our Scene is London, 'cause we would make knowne,
No countries mirth is better than our owne.
No clime breeds better matter, for your whore,
Bawd, squire, imposter, many persons more,
Whose manners, now call'd humors, feed the stage:
And which have still beene subiect, for the rage
Or spleene of *comick*-writers.
                    (*The Alchemist*, Prologue 5-11)

The audience at the first performance of *The Alchemist* at the Globe in
1610 probably did not need this reminder. The first decade of the
Jacobean age had witnessed a sudden profusion of comedies satirizing
city life, and these had included major comedies by Jonson, by
Marston, and by Middleton, as well as the bulk of the repertory of the
children's companies at Blackfriars and Paul's. By 1610 Jonson could
probably feel some paternal – if not proprietorial – pride at the
establishment of a new dramatic genre, city comedy. The playwrights
had self-consciously, sometimes aggressively, forged the new form,
distinct in its satiric mode from chronicle plays like Dekker's *The Shoemakers' Holiday*, and scornfully excluding romantic, magical or marvellous elements which figure so strongly in other kinds of Elizabethan
comedy, such as *The Old Wives' Tale*.

In this book I hope to show how city comedy may be seen as a distinct
genre with a recognizable form, style and subject-matter. By emphasizing each play's relationship to the common form, rather than its
place in its individual author's oeuvre, a fresh approach is gained;
moreover, this is the first study exclusively devoted to city comedy *as a
genre*,[1] and this seems to me worthwhile both as a contribution to literary history and as a means to fresh critical appreciation. I believe that

the critical usefulness of providing this context for the study of the individual plays is indeed substantial; as E.H. Gombrich[2] observes:

> if the history of an art is of any relevance to aesthetics, it is precisely because it will help us in these first rough and ready classifications on which all our subsequent understanding may hinge. Granted that a great work of art is so rich in structure that it remains potent even when misunderstood: if we are really out to receive its 'message' we cannot do without all the contextual aids the historian can unearth.

I have traced the emergence of city comedy in some detail, often play by play, because the dramatists, habitually used as they were to working in the complex of Elizabethan drama's inherited conventions, readily assimilated innovations as they appeared, conventionalizing whatever proved both popular and workable. Playwrights who wrote within the genre include gifted original artists who stimulated and modified its growth; there are also the merely imitative hacks who consolidated and conventionalized. Both kinds of playwright may be shown drawing unashamedly on the new satiric style of stage comedy from the moment it becomes recognizable in Jonson's 'humour' plays of 1598 and 1599, and once the conventions of city comedy proper are established by about 1605 they are widely recognized. Jonson, Marston and Middleton reacted to each other's successive plays, reshaping, copying, changing emphases, in response to their developing thought about the subject of the city. The process is a complex and delicate one, partly intuitive, partly deliberate and conscious, as is implied by Jonson's remark that right imitation is 'to draw forth out of the best, and choisest flowers, with the Bee, and turne all into Honey'.[3]

In order to delineate this process clearly a selective emphasis has been necessary, but it has also been my intention that such an approach should provide a fresh critical account of these plays as works of critical realism, and this aim too has demanded a selective emphasis. I have not attempted in this deliberately short book to accommodate everything I have to say about this subject or about all these plays – though I have tried to minimize oversimplification. Yet, in another sense, in writing about drama the critic will always oversimplify. He can only hope to stimulate appreciation of a play when it fully lives in performance, for the depth and texture of that collaborative creation of actors and spectators result from the interplay of many effects, some evanescent – changing shades and tones of colour, light and sound – and some continuous – rhythms of movement, situation and language. The feelings and resonances set up there cannot be detached from the space of time during which actors perform and audiences participate; it would require a critical method with 'a point as subtle as Ariachne's broken woof' to account fully for that experience. On the other hand, the critic can seek for the most sympathetic modern analogy for the kind of theatre offered by mature city comedy in the hands of Middleton and Jonson, and it may be helpful to think of our own experience in the theatre of the modern playwright Bertolt Brecht: for we might recognize, in sympathetically Brechtian productions of plays like *Michaelmas Term* and *The Devil Is an Ass*, more of the theatrical vitality and wit which make city comedy live.

Jonson's central role in shaping city comedy testifies to his original dramatic genius and his stimulating influence on his fellow, and rival, playwrights; but it is not often recognized that his own art drew a lively stimulus from certain congenially ironic fellow playwrights and from the general buoyancy of the market for city comedy; nor should one altogether dismiss the much mocked Thomas Dekker, a resilient maker of plays and city pageants who furnished some priceless raw material. This is not, in short, another book about Ben Jonson alone.

To approach these plays in the context of the developing genre of city comedy involves some adjustment of critical focus, in the first place, since Jonson and Middleton have long been admired for their realism. But in what sense can we use the term realism in relation to Jacobean city comedy, and how far is it important to an appreciation of the plays? T. S. Eliot, in his essay on Middleton of 1927, concedes that Middleton's keen concentration on the spectacle of the interplay of different social classes marks an important development in realistic comedy, but for Eliot this is not part of its significance or value as literature, and furthermore, Eliot declares, Middleton 'has no message; he is merely a great recorder'. Ben Jonson, on the other hand, has been recommended by the professional historian G. Unwin as a cogent and perceptive observer of the social and economic affairs of his time; Unwin declares that 'a study of the leading characters of *The Devil Is an Ass* . . . would be by far the best introduction to the economic history of the period'.[4]

Yet of course the realism of Jonson is not the realism of Zola or Henry Mayhew, and it differs also from the subjective realism of James Joyce. As critical realists Jonson and Middleton seek to shape character and incident in order to bring alive the underlying social and moral issues through the specific and local experience. The dynamic of such art springs directly from the creative dialectic implicit in the dramatist's criticism of life. I hope to show that the dramatists of city comedy articulated a radical critique of their age. They dramatized conflicting forces in the confused development from the England of Elizabeth towards the Civil War. But there is a distinction between dramatizing conflicting *forces* and merely reflecting *manners*. When Middleton presents the situation of a merchant ambitious to become a country gentleman, on the level of comedy of manners this is completely conventional; what makes it serious and significant is that the conventions also have metaphoric richness: the merchant embodies forces of appetite and materialist opportunism which Middleton represents as dominant in Jacobean society (and closely connected to law and lawyers). The realism of the significant plays, I would argue, is essentially in transforming typical elements of city life into significant patterns, expressing consciously satiric criticism but also suggesting deeper sources of conflict and change. It is only in the feeblest derivative comedies in the genre that the presentation of London life can be dismissed as literal-minded exploitation of local colour. The best dramatists are certainly sensitive to the pressures and cross-currents of large-scale political, economic and social change, although their plays continue to utilize traditional elements of didactic form and satiric schema.[5] Here indeed there is a reflection of the whole culture's reluctance to formulate new social or political or philosophical theory to meet new conditions. Not that the Morality tradition in the early sixteenth century lacked alertness to current politics and personalities,[6] or was inhospitable to the satiric impulse – but there was still conservatism in its insistence on the timeless and abstract when personifying issues, however modern their costume might be. So Skelton's interlude has the perennial characters Magnificence, Cloaked Collusion, and Poverty, while in Bale's *King John* the king rubs shoulders with Private Wealth, Usurped Power, and Sedition (though Bale directs that the actors playing these parts are to double as the Pope, Cardinal Pandulph, and a monk).

City comedy does not derive solely from the Morality tradition, it also absorbs the tradition of Roman intrigue comedy in Plautus and Terence, and its descendant the *commedia dell' arte*. Here there is an insatiable appetite for the detailed exact recording of ways in which ordinary men survive in the city. Intrigue comedy, unlike the Morality tradition, shows a minimal interest in social protest or reformist theory, but its prompt enthusiasm for witty deceit as a means to acquire sex and money expresses a direct and basic pragmatism; its stylized image of life has the durable potency of myth, while its stress on detailed, recognizably familiar locations and the texture of contemporary urban life has guaranteed its usefulness to later dramatists of different countries and different periods of history. Though the comic resolutions available in its tradition may move between the poles of jovial fulfilment and bitter mockery, intrigue comedy will always make us recognize the inevitable element of absurdity and oppression in any social order, however desirable it may be for other reasons.

The Morality tradition and intrigue comedy involve basically contra-dictory attitudes to society; combining them in a typical city comedy generates a dialogue in which high-minded theory confronts low-life experience of the city. The essentially ironic nature of the art of drama gives particular impetus to this process, which we see at its best in, for example, Marston's *The Malcontent*, where the Duke's two roles are contradictory, or in *The Alchemist*, where figures of seeming moral authority like Surly or Lovewit are revealed as skilful role-players with an eye always on the main chance. City comedy's founder Ben Jonson was himself a man of paradox and contradiction whose own plays are profoundly dialectical, and the initial approach to city comedy may properly be made by way of Jonson himself. Although at times Jonson insists on a monolithic idea of himself, high and aloof, immune to detraction, addressing odes to himself in which he awards himself the Chair of Wit, he is also capable of a more sensitive and acute critical insight, as in his poem replying to the portrait painter Burlase, who had written of the impossibility of conveying in a portrait the unique living quality of Jonson the man. Jonson compares himself to a gargantuan barrel of wine:

> Why? though I seeme of a prodigious wast,
> I am not so voluminous, and vast,
> But there are lines, wherewith I might be embrac'd.
>
> 'Tis true, as my wombe swells, so my back stoupes,
> And the whole lumpe growes round, deform'd, and droupes,
> But yet the Tun at *Heidelberg* had houpes.
>   (*My Answer. The Poet to the Painter*, 1-6)

Jonson's 'mountain belly' and great thirst were famous, but the image is more than merely visually apt and witty; it reveals Jonson's sense that his strong appetites, his creative yet potentially anarchic comic imagination, were in tension with his classicist's discipline and shaping intelligence. A critic does well to follow the suggestion and appreciate the inner spirit of the comedies as it expresses itself through the form.

The years in which Jonson's career as an original playwright was launched also witnessed the rise of Elizabethan non-dramatic satire, formally acknowledged by the Archbishop of Canterbury who in 1599 banned satires and epigrams, and by the burning of Marston's satiric poems. In this same year the boy actors reappeared on the stage, having been banned some nine years earlier, probably for satiric involvement in the Martin Marprelate controversy, and they at once became associated with the newly fashionable satiric taste. Donne, who had written his five satires before 1598 and was so influential among the Inns of Court poets, became an enduring and positive stimulus to Jonson in his non-dramatic poetry; yet it is important to notice here how very strong was Jonson's ambition to realize also *in the theatre* the formal characteristics of satiric poetry and to give satire's moral and social principles and assumptions dramatic expression. It is in the Prologues and Inductions to his comedies that this ambition announces itself most plainly and aggressively, as for instance in *Every Man out of His Humour*, where Asper says:[7]

> I fear no mood stamp'd in a private brow
> When I am pleased t'unmask a public vice.   (*Induction*, 22-3)

but such assertions are only part of a much more thorough-going modification of the inherited comic form and the expectations of spectators. The satirist demands certain things of his readers which are not required of the reader of lyric poetry. Satiric poetry establishes a distance between reader and subject and between reader and poet, for it invites astringent critical discrimination and the pleasures of glee, disgust, intellectual exercise of wit, rather than sympathetic identification with character, scene and experience. When Jonson set out to write satiric comedy for the stage he was immediately involved in establishing a relationship between the play and its spectators which corresponds to that prevailing between satiric poetry and its readers. Beneath the evident modish ostentation of the Prologue's satiric pose is a genuinely radical programme of innovation. The theatre was to be changed.

Jonson had collaborated with Nashe in 1597 in a play, *The Isle of*

Dogs, which had provoked the authorities (and the fact that no copy of the play survives might suggest that someone took care to see to its total disappearance), but the affair makes plain enough that satiric drama always has natural affinities with the spirit of controversy and has its anarchic and rebellious aspects. In our century 'political theatre' and satiric cabaret in Berlin after the First World War provided a stimulating context for the early dramatic experiments of Bertolt Brecht, in which elements of the Morality tradition are combined with Dadaist and other kinds of experimental theatre, music-hall, and serious modern music-drama, in a series of plays presenting social criticism. To connect Brecht with Jacobean comedy is not of course entirely arbitrary. Brecht's experiments with Epic Theatre in fact derive partially from his admiration for the conditions of the Elizabethan theatre as he imagined it; an arena full of spectators as knowledgeable as those at a modern boxing match and as high-spirited as those at a circus: so unlike those at, say, a Garbo movie. Brecht saw that to bring his kind of life into the modern European theatre he would have to change the audience first. Their complacent expectations were formed by what is typified in, say, the opera of Puccini or the 'well-made' play. The plays of Marlowe and certain other Elizabethans are, on the other hand, rich in conflicting ideas about moral and social ideals. Brecht adapted Marlowe's *Edward II* as well as Shakespeare's *Coriolanus*. It was because of the centrality of these issues and the questioning of traditional or 'official' attitudes in Elizabethan plays that Brecht found them valuable as models and relevant in his campaign to question the modern theatre 'not about whether it manages to interest the spectator in buying a ticket, i.e. in the theatre itself – but about whether it manages to interest him in the world'.[8] The persistent use of parody and satiric caricature was Brecht's first means of altering the relationship between audience and play, later to be misleadingly labelled 'alienation', '*Verfremdungseffekt*'. By 1926 Brecht was able to pronounce categorically on his theory and intentions, as in the following dialogue:[9]

Q Who do you write for?

Brecht For the sort of people who just come for fun and don't hesitate to keep their hats on in the theatre.

Q But most spectators want their hearts to flow over.

Brecht The one tribute we can pay the audience is to treat it as thoroughly intelligent. It is utterly wrong to treat people

> as simpletons when they are grown up at seventeen. I appeal
> to the reason.
> *Q* But . . . you don't make the incidents clear.
> *Brecht* I give the incidents baldly so that the audience can think for
> itself. That's why I need a quick-witted audience that knows
> how to observe . . . the figures are not matter for empathy;
> they are there to be understood.

Yet this rather austere tone of the early years is a misleading guide to
the successful plays of either Brecht or Jonson, where usually a contradictory voice or attitude is provoked by any solemn didacticism.

The juxtaposition of contradictory elements produces a complex
dramatic experience in the Brecht/Weill *Dreigroßchenoper* where the
satiric ironies of Brecht's text and of his allusive, cabaret-style episodic
form, so ebulliently untidy at the edges, are extended and counter-
pointed by Weill's score, which creates an equivocal musical texture
through allusive deployment of many popular and highbrow modes,
and provides an equal, not dominant, medium of expression. The result
is that something of the exuberant wit and attack of Elizabethan theatre
is revived. Brecht's later play *Arturo Ui* exhibits with remarkable
clarity the enduring possibilities of multiple parody as a dramatic
language. In this play a parody mosaic of various theatrical genres, their
conventions and character types, and of other media, such as the
popular press, Nazi propaganda, and Hollywood gangster movies, is
used to identify and attack particular social and political attitudes
through the corrupt artistic modes they employ. At the same time
Brecht's ironic distancing creates from these parodic elements something new and bold, a kind with its own authentic comic identity, its
own integrity as art. Paradox, the most condensed form of dialectic, is
common to the characters created by Jonson and by Brecht, and this
suggests a common ideal: that intellectual issues are to be dramatically
embodied, in order to intensify the life of the play and to resist any
reduction of its ideas to schematic abstraction. Such plays are to be
simultaneously intelligent, humanely serious, and hilarious.

It may be helpful at this point to take a particular Jacobean city comedy
and to recall the characteristic atmosphere and texture of the plays in
the genre. The collaborative venture of Chapman, Marston and
Jonson, *Eastward Ho*, performed in 1605, is highly suitable for this
purpose since it not only satirizes citizens, usurers and gallants, but it

also incidentally offers self-parody of the genre's typical styles of comedy and language.

The action of *Eastward Ho* arises from the conflict of the industrious and idle apprentices of a London goldsmith. The industrious apprentice, fortified by, and continually quoting, Puritan precepts (the banality of which is not disguised) is commended by his master for his honest industry. The goldsmith tells him, with a mouthful of comically predictable clichés, that he expects to see him 'one o'the Monuments of our Citty, and reckon'd among her worthies, to be remembred the same day with the Lady *Ramsey*, and graue *Gresham*' (IV. ii. 70-2). The other apprentice is dissolute and insubordinate, the conventional Interlude prodigal-gallant, complete with feather. He is warned, equally predictably, to 'thinke of huskes, for thy course is running directly to the prodigalls hogs trough, huskes, sirra' (I. i. 98-100). His name is Quicksilver; we can be sure that he is due for gulling and ridicule before the play ends.

Corresponding to the two apprentices are the goldsmith's two daughters; one is humbly earnest and modest, the other vain, empty-headed and licentious. Her snobbish ambition is to 'bee Ladyfied forsooth: and be attir'd just to the Court-cut, and long tayle'. She marries the absurdly foppish and typically destitute knight Sir Petronell Flash; both of them are satirized for their mannerisms and foolish obsessions with dress in a way reminiscent of Jonson's early 'Comical Satyres' of 1599 and 1600 (*Eastward Ho* was written in late 1604). Sir Petronell has lost his country estates to usurers long ago, and he outlines the typical interests of the gallant in Jacobean city comedy with the lamenting survey: 'Tauerns growe dead; Ordinaries are blowne vp; Playes are at a stand; Howses of Hospitallitie at a fall; not a Feather wauing, not a Spurre gingling any where . . . my creditors have laide to arrest me.' (II. ii. 220-2, 259-60). The play's setting in the city of London is accurately achieved with many placing references to street and district names to attract local interest, as in the Coney-Catching pamphlets and the recent plays *Westward Ho* and *Northward Ho* by Dekker and Webster; for similar reasons, lawyers' and usurers' jargon is accurately reproduced.

Security, the usurer, schemes to bring the gallant to his knees – another conventional city comedy element – and the usurer is himself gulled of his money and cuckolded; he acts as unwitting pander to his own wife when she is disguised. Quicksilver's speech to him summarizes relations between usurer and gallant in city comedy:

> Come old *Securitie*, thou father of destruction: th'indented
> Sheepskinne is burn'd wherein I was wrapt, and I am now loose,
> to get more children of perdition into thy vsurous Bonds.
> Thou feed'st my Lecherie, and I thy Couetousnes: Thou art
> Pandar to me for my wench, and I to thee for thy coosenages:
> (II. ii. 11-16)

Sir Petronell and the idle apprentice Quicksilver set out on a voyage to
make their fortunes in Virginia. We are offered a burlesque view of the
supposedly 'worthy' motives and 'adventurous' spirit of Elizabethan
merchant investors and colonizers. Virginia is a paradise of Mammon:

> I tell thee, Golde is more plentifull there then Copper is with vs;
> and for as much redde Copper as I can bring, Ile haue thrice the
> waight in Golde. Why man all their dripping Pans, and their
> Chamber pottes are pure Gold: (III. iii. 25-8)

The evocation of the new world is also an occasion for comment on the
political scene at home in James's London; for in Virginia 'you shal
liue freely . . . without Sergeants, or Courtiers, or Lawyers, or Intelligencers, onely a few industrious Scots perhaps' (ll.40-2). This hit at
James and his favourites is followed by another, uttered this time in a
mock Scots accent, when the two voyagers, still drunk from their farewell party, are washed up on the Isle of Dogs in the lower Thames
(which they suppose to be France) and are greeted with the line: 'I ken
the man weel, hee's one of my thirty pound knights' (IV. i. 178).
James's wrath descended on the three playwrights, and the play was
banned, so Jonson repeated his achievement of 1597 in *The Isle of
Dogs*.

The play's various episodes result in the undignified arrival in the
Counter Prison of the two prodigals, the snobbish daughter and the
usurer, who suffer the formally necessary ridicule and judgement. True
to convention, the play ends on a cheerful note once folly and error are
'corrected'. The goldsmith who has distributed credit and censure
draws attention to the traditional nature of his role, and to the play's
form, by explaining to the audience the didactic meaning of the
exemplum, as if the play were a Moral Interlude. The comic rhymes
and thumping rhythm amusingly parody the old style (it is worth
noting that in 1601 on the Blackfriars stage there had been a revival of
Liberality and Prodigality):

Now London, looke about,
And in this morall, see thy Glasse runne out:
Behold the carefull Father, thrifty Sonne . . .
The Vsurer punisht, and from Fall so steepe
The Prodigall child reclaimd, and the lost Sheepe.

(V. v. 205-7, 209-10)

The hypocritical nature of Quicksilver's repentance, incidentally, is implied simply by the fact that he expresses it in Puritan jargon.

Eastward Ho, then, is characteristic of city comedy in its sturdy dramatic form, its subject-matter, and its style, even if parody and burlesque are unusually preponderant. Its three authors invite their audience to share their conspiratorial glee in the inspired travesty as much as in the straightforward satiric comedy of London life. This self-conscious concern with literary and theatrical fashion, with current affairs and with metropolitan social, political and literary gossip, has often been thought to reflect the interests of supposedly exclusive audiences at Blackfriars and Paul's where the children's companies performed.[10] City comedy as a genre is not restricted by any conjectural 'Coterie' taste; though *Eastward Ho* does exhibit the preoccupations of the early phase of the children's companies' repertory up to 1604-5, it is also an important indication of future trends in the work of Jonson and Middleton – not least in the confident use of London settings.

The plays of the genre may be distinguished from the other kinds of Jacobean comedy by their critical and satiric design, their urban settings, their exclusion of material appropriate to romance, fairy-tale, sentimental legend or patriotic chronicle. The consciousness of literary decorum enabled writers to work in widely different styles for different occasions and audiences. When city comedy playwrights turned to other modes, for instance the Court masque or city pageant, they expected as a matter of course to work in another accepted decorum and within that different genre's set rules. Jonson himself provides a crisp illustration of the point, for when he devised the triumphal 'Londinium' arch for the beginning of James's 1604 London procession, Jonson embodied the spirit of the occasion with proper dignity – Edward Alleyn himself personifying the Genius of the City and, in a speech written by Jonson, arousing the slumbering old Father Thames to welcome the king. Even in so festive a city comedy as

Bartholomew Fair such a spirit could find no straightforward expression; usually, indeed, London pride is subject to sustained irony or
derision in these plays.

As I have already indicated, the satiric impulse in city comedy finds
formal expression through a new combination of inherited traditions:
that of the Morality – and in particular the recent dramatic kinds, the
Estates Morality and the Tudor Interlude – and, on the other hand, a
native tradition of popular comedy fused with classical Roman intrigue
comedy and with the living *commedia dell' arte*. The latter built its
improvised performances on foundations of stock trickery episodes,
lazzi, and stock character types, thus depicting the very form and pressure of folly, roguery and crime in modern dress. City comedy also
inevitably owed a debt to non-dramatic literary traditions, chief among
which are satire and complaint.

The satiric form involves the non-dramatic poet in adopting a pos-
ture of disgust with social and moral corruption and folly. He might
point out examples of these faults to an interlocutor, or directly to the
reader, while surveying the social, urban scene. Satire of this kind, of
course, can often include the traditional invective of the medieval
Church against such general and unchanging evils as the depravity of
women and the corrupt state of worldly ambitions and appetites.
Horatian satire is essentially particular in its targets and precise in its
focus, while Juvenalian satire has a harsher tone comparable to that of
the Church's invective (often called Complaint to distinguish it from
Roman satire).[11] When a satirist like Marston turned from writing
verse to drama he embodied the satiric persona in a dramatic character.
Malevole in *The Malcontent* is the best known example. But before
that play was written Jonson had dramatized not only the satiric
persona but the whole form of Horatian satire, in which the satiric view
takes us through a survey of folly and vice in recognizably familiar
urban locations. In Jonson's *Every Man out of His Humour*,
Cynthia's Revels and *Poetaster* the audience can recognize their own
city of London in the detail and the styles of dialogue, and it was out of
Jonson's experiments in these plays, the 'Comical Satyres',[12] that the
form of Jacobean city comedy evolved.

The writer of a Coney-Catching pamphlet[13] is no less eager to adopt
the persona of authoritative censurer though his concern is restricted to
the trickery of various kinds of urban thief. His literary manner derives
from popular Jest Book narrative prose. Complaint and homily, rather

than Roman satire, provide the source for the moralizing and invective, but the vigour, life and comedy of certain pamphlets probably owe much to traditional 'bitter jesters' who entertained at fairs, revels and on the stage. G. R. Hibbard has noted[14] how Thomas Nashe, the most talented of the pamphleteers, adopted a literary persona akin to that of the Vice of the medieval drama, and points out that Nashe was familiar with the antics of Tarlton, the most famous clown of his age; indeed Nashe's opponents often described him as a 'Tarltoniser', and we can see that Nashe's prose is that of an instinctive dramatist. There are further links between dramatists and pamphleteers, for, like the dramatists of city comedy, the pamphleteers Greene, Dekker and Rowlands deliberately created a kind with form and conventions analogous to drama. In a Coney-Catching pamphlet the author explains to the reader what the tricksters do, and dramatically conceived episodes provide illustrative exempla. Character and incident are conventional; indeed the pamphleteers created the kind by absorbing material from earlier, rather pedestrian writers such as Awdelay and Harman. This material is mixed with Jest Book incident and atmosphere, characters are created in the conventions of Popular dramatic comedy, and much trouble is taken to give local colour by setting episodes in particular streets and districts of London and assigning familiar urban activities to characters. Significantly enough the most convincing pamphlets are those shaped by the dramatist Greene, who took his material at third or fourth hand. The Coney-Catching pamphlet is a minor genre just preceding the beginnings of city comedy; it could not develop further without being absorbed into drama, and this is what in fact happened.

We cannot see the rise of city comedy in full perspective without some consideration of the theatres and companies for which the plays were written and on whose boards they were performed. This is the more important since in a well known study (*Shakespeare and the Rival Traditions*) Alfred Harbage underlined his preference for the 'Popular' style of the adult companies which he distinguished from the satiric 'Coterie' style of drama performed by the boy actors. The adult companies performed on open stages, with spectators in galleries and on the ground surrounding their scaffold. The boy actors by contrast performed in closed, smaller playhouses: Paul's, Blackfriars and Whitefriars. There was probably some difference in acting styles between the boys at Blackfriars or Paul's and the men at the Globe in the early years from 1599 to 1602, where the term 'Coterie' usefully serves to distinguish between adult and boys' companies – though it should not carry any suggestion of deliberate exclusive 'in-group' intimacy or triviality or social snobbery. However from 1602 to 1608 the boys matured physically and professionally, and when Blackfriars was taken over by the King's Men in 1608 Paul's had already closed, and Whitefriars was never successful.

It is probably impossible to define the difference between Popular and Coterie styles, since the former was progressively influenced by experiments in the latter during the years 1600 to 1606. Certainly the repertories of the boys contain many plays marked by artifice and stylization of form and subject, in contrast to the bustling activity and robust style of the adult repertories. Jonson's *Cynthia's Revels*, written for boys in 1600/1601 has simplified, mannered characterization, with much opportunity for parody acting – the boys were noted for this. There are opportunities, similarly, for declamation of set speeches, and the cast is large with no unduly taxing parts. However subsequent plays such as *Poetaster*, *The Malcontent*, *Michaelmas Term* and *The Dutch Courtezan* not only develop a much more flexible and varied dramatic style but contain parts to extend an experienced adult actor – Tucca, Malevole, Quomodo, Franceschina. When *The Malcontent* was transferred from the boys' house to the Globe, where the King's Men performed it, it was modified only in the opening and closing acts;[15] the essential structure, mood, stagecraft and acting roles remained in substance unaltered. This rather undermines the clear distinctions drawn by Alfred Harbage between Coterie and Popular drama. Harbage defined Coterie theatre style as satiric, intellectual and cruelly critical, opposing and rivalling the adult Popular repertory's complacent romance, warm-hearted comedy and spectacular tragedy. Harbage's may indeed be a valid account of Coterie style from 1599 to 1602, but we ought to note that progressively after 1600 many of the plays performed by the King's Men at the Globe shared the satiric and intellectually questioning mood. In fact the King's Men performed nearly every major play in the period irrespective of its style. Even if a playwright was principally a Coterie writer, like Marston, his best work seems to have been acted at the Globe. Despite the fact that city comedy orginated at Blackfriars and Paul's, nevertheless the King's Men performed *Volpone*, *The Alchemist* and *The Devil Is an Ass*. City comedy was never so tied to Coterie style that its development had to cease when the zenith of Coterie popularity passed in about 1606, and in fact the great triumphs of city comedy appeared after Blackfriars was taken over by the King's Men in 1608-9. The genre grew out of a process of creative imitation and cross-fertilization between play-wrights competing both as individuals and as servants of rival compan-ies, Coterie and Popular. Both the untalented conventional writers and those with original creative gifts profited from this situation. They learned from each other, adapting, imitating and absorbing each other's original achievements as they appeared. The genre grew as this process continued to produce fresh art; but it was an art essentially dif-ferent from the genial comedy of *The Shoemakers' Holiday* or *George a Greene the Pinner of Wakefield* or *The Four Prentices of London*.

It will be remembered that L. C. Knights emphasized in *Drama and Society in the Age of Jonson* that the age witnessed the 'taking shape' of the 'capitalist system' which destroyed a 'native tradition' springing from an 'individual and social morality'.[16] I would emphasize rather that the playwrights contrasted the idealized Tudor philosophy of the state, which owed much to Christian doctrine, with a stylized, complaint-derived account of the lamentable evils of 'nowadays'.

The plays of city comedy give the impression of actuality as a result of literary art and dramatic craft, and their selection of material, their point of view, is determined by a critical and satiric mode, not objective or sociological scientific method. Yet the plays deal with Jacobean social and economic conditions, and if there is every reason for treating their account with the caution appropriate to art, there is also much to be gained from reviewing the historical background from as independ-ent a position as possible. Hence something can be learned of their significance as criticism of society, while their independent status as works of art will stand out clearly. I have therefore reviewed relevant areas of Jacobean background in the light of modern professional historical scholarship, which has of course been extremely active in this area. Literary critics can learn from historians that theirs is not the only humane discipline which is subject to changes in intellectual fashion; but it is not necessary to decide ultimately between a Whig or a Marxist approach for my purpose, where 'irritable reaching after fact or reason' serves at least to complicate and fracture simplistic assumptions, such as that the age witnessed a sudden transition from a rurally based organic society to an urban new capitalist state of possessive individualism. There had, after all, been a steady and unchanging stream of invective from the Church throughout the Middle Ages against the Rise of Capitalism, New Men, Usury, and Economic Individualism.

L. C. Knights noticed that the plays presented criticism of society in which 'the diagnosis was moral rather than economic' and he further affirmed that 'the reactions of a genuine poet to his environment form a criticism of society at least as important as the keenest analysis in economic terms'.[17] It is certainly not the aim of this study to assert that there is no relation between the form and mood of Jacobean city comedy and the Jacobean social and moral world; merely that the plays do not present in any useful sense 'a keen analysis in economic terms' nor may they be rashly cited as evidence of actual conditions as if they were the equivalent of Henry Mayhew's *London Labour and the London Poor* or Charles Madge's *Mass Observation*. What they present is a keen analysis in moral terms.

City comedy playwrights were interested in money-lending in the first place as a modern manifestation of the sin of avarice. Of course there was increasing popular recognition that the use of large-scale capital was a science to be feared for its power. Its laws of operation, moreover, might be as menacing in their implications as the laws of political power propounded by the notorious Machiavelli. The usurer is the villain because he embodies a power which is not integrated into the social or political system, which is subversive of hierarchy and divorced from public accountability and from public responsibility. This is the threat posed by Marlowe's Barabas, to both Christian *and* Turk, and this is what makes them unanimous in desiring his liquidation. The plays focus on the nation's private and public value systems as they are brought out in relation to money. They exhibit the limitations of the conceptual understanding of money, but also the complexity of psychological attitudes to it in early Stuart society: something graphically apparent in the careers of the royal actors, James I and Charles I, on a wider stage. Indeed the period's received social theory and its underlying assumptions are frequently shown in the plays to be wooden, naive, or otherwise disconcertingly inadequate – but always under cover of the ironic mode of satiric comedy.

There are some striking hints in city comedy of pressures which are to become dominant later in the century for Thomas Hobbes when working out his social theory. His insistent advocacy in *Leviathan* is, as he stresses, 'occasioned by the disorders of the present time',[18] and his prose itself characteristically enacts the willed imposing of discipline on energies imaginatively felt to be fearfully, but also temptingly, anarchic. In Hobbes we find a profound state of imbalance, a deep fascination with freshly observed modes of aggression. Although the

plays of city comedy evolve no explicit social theory, they partly anticipate Hobbes in presenting an image of the times through opposed ideas
and opposed experiences set in increasingly complex patterns of
interaction; furthermore, while some of these promise the possibility of
resolution or reconciliation through the medium of comedy, others,
interestingly, do not.

II

A FOUNTAIN STIRR'D

CITY COMEDY IN RELATION
TO THE SOCIAL
AND ECONOMIC BACKGROUND

The dramatists were alarmed yet excited by the sciences of power and of money, so self-sufficiently exclusive of influence from morality or tradition. Expectation indeed set all on hazard, and the words of Shakespeare's Achilles find many explicit and implicit echoes in Jacobean drama:

> My mind is troubled, like a fountain stirr'd;
> And I myself see not the bottom of it.
>
> (*Troilus & Cressida* III. iii. 314-15)

It seemed that with luck the manipulator of money might get literally limitless riches. Lord Burghley had faith in Sir Edward Kelly's claim to the secret of transmuting base metal into gold, and actually joined Leicester and others in financing one William Medley, who set up a plant to transmute iron into copper in 1574.[1] Like Sir Epicure Mammon in Jonson's *The Alchemist*, Burghley might have been deluded in thinking alchemy possible, but he was right in supposing that gold could bring him more wealth and experience than his imagination could conceive. Almost twenty years before Jonson's *The Alchemist*, Marlowe had created characters in the grip of voracious appetites for riches and power. *Doctor Faustus* concerns a man's aspiration for limitless knowledge and his use of an instrument of evil, Mephistophilis, to attain it. Jonson's Sir Epicure is partly a parody, partly a comic counterpart of Faustus. Marlowe's Jew of Malta is freed by his non-Christianity, indeed atheism, and his career of money-manipulator, from all moral sanction; his riches and his scientific policy gain him control of Malta – and, by analogy, of any Renaissance nation-state. Barabas the Jew is manifestly capable of sustained success in practical life; it is this which makes his career so disquieting. Nor is it ambition which causes his fall; on the contrary Barabas falls because he rejects the dominion which his empirical methods have brought within his reach. Barabas dies because he relaxes in a society composed of men driven by greed and fear, at war with one another. The Jew's rise and fall may be interpreted in the formulation of Hobbes; his career ceases in death as soon as he falters in his 'restless desire for power after power'.[2] Of course Marlowe's hero-villains are also shown to deserve death; it was still the Elizabethan age, and Marlowe's art is profoundly ambivalent.

Marlowe's hero-villains fall; but their vitality and the power of their appetites invigorate the plays and accord with our sense of the complexity of human nature and the ambivalence in our attitude to them and to similar motives within ourselves. The Jacobean playwrights are similarly ambiguous in their attitude to the money-lender and Machiavel, but nevertheless every usurer is cast as a rogue if not a villain, for above all the usurer is the aggressor in the urban civil war of appetites aroused by money.

Resistance to such a state of affairs is instinctive to the Jacobeans, integral to their Christian upbringing and to the satiric-didactic tradition in which they write. If they acknowledge the exciting possibilities, the expanding world of power and wealth which the scientific method offers, yet their satiric approach focuses on its damaging repercussions in individual lives. Jonson's *Every Man out of His Humour* memorably declares that a hostile and selective attitude marks his work; he shows

> the times deformitie
> Anatomiz'd in every nerve, and sinnew.
>
> (*Induction*, 120-1)

There is from the outset no question of empirical, openminded, balanced observation.

Today not much stir would arise from the reiteration of Francis Bacon's observation:[3]

> that it is a vanity to conceive that there would be ordinary borrowing without profit; and it is impossible to conceive the number of inconveniences that will ensue, if borrowing be cramped. Therefore to speak of the abolishing of usury is idle . . . It appears by the balance of commodities and discommodities of usury, two things are to be

reconciled. The one, that the tooth of usury be grinded, that it bite
not too much; the other, that there be left open a means to invite
moneyed men to lend to the merchants, for the continuing and
quickening of trade.

Here the clarity of the empiric approach reveals itself in the firm
deductions from observation of 'what men do, not what they ought to
do'. Bacon is still discussing money in relation to human behaviour;
others by this date were approaching the subject by treating money as a
machine with its own discoverable laws of operation. They were all
opposed utterly by the doctrine and preaching of the Church.

A steady stream of invective against riches and all their uses poured
from the writers of complaint throughout the Middle Ages. St Jerome,
typically, wrote 'let him deny that avarice is idolatry who is prepared to
describe the selling of Our Lord for thirty pieces of silver as a just act.'[4]
In fact the Papacy itself exploited sophisticated and indeed criminal
financial techniques for centuries, as Richard Ehrenburg's *Capital and
Finance in the Age of the Renaissance* shows, but the doctrine
remained unchanged. R. H. Tawney memorably wrote in *Religion and
the Rise of Capitalism*[5] that

> the social doctrines advanced from the pulpit offered, in their
> traditional form, little guidance. Their practical ineffectiveness
> prepared the way for their theoretical abandonment. They were
> abandoned because, on the whole, they deserved to be abandoned.
> The social teaching of the Church had ceased to count, because the
> Church itself had ceased to think ... in the age of Bacon and
> Descartes, bursting with clamorous interests and eager ideas,
> fruitful, above all, in the germs of economic speculation ... the social
> theory of the Church of England turned its face from the practical
> world, to pore over doctrines which, had their original authors been
> as impervious to realities as their later exponents, would never have
> been formulated.

In Elizabethan and Jacobean outbursts against bloodsucking usury and
the evils of making money beget money, we should beware of the
anachronistic attitude and rhetorical artifice of complaint tradition, and
we should be alert to detect the dishonest mustering of argument by
borrowers and spendthrifts in that great age of litigation. In fact
powerful money-lenders such as Thomas Sutton preferred to prolong
mortgages to the landed aristocracy at 10 per cent rather than foreclose

on property, if it was scattered and hard to administer, and he usually allowed three or four years renewal before he clamped down. Lawrence Stone tells us (in *The Crisis of the Aristocracy 1558–1641*) how Sutton had £45,000 out at interest when he died; earls would address him as 'my verrey lovinge friend'.[6] Though money-lenders may not have foreclosed as savagely as satirists suggest, they had a great deal of business with the aristocracy, many of whom found life at Court cripplingly expensive. Elizabeth's chief courtiers mostly died heavily in debt, Leicester owing £68,500 and Hatton some £64,700.[7] These figures give some idea of the scale of capital transactions involved, and in fact there is a contrast between the ignorance and anachronistic sincerity of those who wrote about the evils of money, and the advancing knowledge and skill of those who actually controlled and used money in large amounts, but rarely wrote about it at all. Hence we find neither Myddleton nor Cranfield troubling to write about money except to scribble in the margins of their account books, when profits were high, the pious exhortation 'Allmighty God be praised'.

Outbursts against usury in the sixteenth century resulted in part from the misunderstood phenomenon of the price rise. The period from 1500 to 1642 may be seen as a single phase dominated by the price rise. In the first forty years of the sixteenth century prices rose by half; by 1560 they had more than doubled; by 1600 they were five and a half times the level in 1500.[8] The cause of this phenomenon was ascribed at the time to the greed of unscrupulous individuals, an ascription which, being preserved in printed literature, dies hard. Inexperience with the phenomenon of a price rise in time of good harvests led to a search for scapegoats and reiteration of the old doctrine of just price. This declared that in time of plenty everything reverted to a price determined by natural law; money itself was thought to represent the intrinsic value of the metal it contained. Statutes against rigging markets and enclosures show the prevalence of the search for scapegoats, though in 1574 a Frenchman, Jean Bodin, produced a theory rejecting the just price. Bodin discovered that prices represent the relationship between the money available and the goods available. If goods become scarce while purchasing power remains constant, prices will rise. Similarly, if the supply of goods remains constant but supplies of money increase, the value of the money will drop and prices rise. Bodin argued that the vast increase in minted bullion (brought by Spain to Europe from America) was the cause of the price rise.

It has been argued by certain modern theorists that the upward but divergent paths of agricultural, industrial and labour prices in this period in England are in fact evidence of population pressure; indeed that a growing population was an important, if not the most important, general cause of inflation at the time. Food production, it is argued, could not keep up with demand, so prices rose, while an increasingly buoyant labour market kept wages from rising at the same rate; but the flexibility of industry, being greater than that of agriculture, allowed it to respond more readily to demand, so producing a dissimilar rate of price rise. Still, the problem is complex, for though the influence of population increase is acknowledged – in England the population increased from 2.2 million in 1500 to 3.75 million in 1600, an increase of 70 per cent, according to an estimate in 1970[9] – price rises are also likely to have been affected by short-run but violent pressure from bad harvests (there were some disastrous ones in the 1590s) and by government action in spending heavily on military campaigns, or debasing the coinage in spectacular terms, as under Henry VIII. Such factors could distort price-rise patterns independently of pressure from population growth. R. B. Outhwaite[10] points out that since the sixteenth-century price rise has been called the greatest specie-based inflation of which we have record, it seems unlikely that this could have occurred 'without an increase in the monetary stock, and it is improbable that the latter had no connection with the inflow into Europe of Spanish-American silver'.

European trade was sufficiently busy to ensure that a price rise in one place would soon have extensive effects. In England, where commercial life was dominated by the export trade in raw wool and cloth, a price rise would soon be sensed throughout all ranks of society, from the king who took customs revenues to the merchants and the producers – on the largest monastery ranches as well as the smallest pinfolds – down to the carriers and sailors. Henry VIII had a disastrous effect on prices between 1544 and 1551 when he debased the coinage, because newly minted shillings were treated as a quarter the value of old minted, the former containing 25 per cent silver, the latter 90 per cent; but even after the Duke of Northumberland restored the coinage in 1560 prices continued to climb.

The unabated violence of the price rise had a thoroughly disturbing effect on the social life of England throughout the period 1500 to 1642. On the land, the price rise turned what had once been a good income into a liability. Landlords became poorer, their tenants prospered in a rising market. For the landlord the choice was between raising rents or taking control personally to profit from the yield. The increase in the profitability of land gave added impetus to what became, as a result of Henry VIII's dissolution of the monasteries, the most fluid land market since the Norman Conquest.

Plainly this was to affect the situation of tenants. A widespread redistribution of property – monastic lands, crown lands, the land of nobility or gentry reorganizing or disposing of their estates – obviously must have resulted in rent-raisings and evictions, especially in the case of tenants-at-will who had little legal standing. However, not all landlords were harsh, and many in the North preserved earlier conditions even at the cost of personal impoverishment. Where land was bought to make a quick profit obviously rents would be raised, enclosures ruthlessly carried out and evictions effected. However, most of the monastic lands actually went to landowners who merely added them directly to what they already had and farmed them as before. Rents rose in the second half of the sixteenth century but so did prices. Land sales and enclosures continued in the seventeenth century but the enclosure movement had a history stretching back before the Dissolution, on monastic lands as well as private.[11]

In place of the view presented in the literature of complaint and satire, then, we must substitute an account more complex and less romantic. The picture of rapacious extortioners depopulating the countryside and impoverishing those who clung on – particularly the 'old' nobility and gentry who had given Christian hospitality, and their faithful tenants – is too bad to be true. It has been estimated that in a county where enclosures were made, not more than 30 per cent of arable land, or 4 per cent of all land, was affected in this period.[12] The inexorable shift to higher, more economic rents in the early seventeenth century undermined the loyalty of tenants on big estates, slowly but surely; for changing patterns of life drew the aristocracy and gentry increasingly to London, caused their territorial possessions to shrink and their influence over tenants to weaken. Ties of sentiment lasted in many cases for more than the next two centuries, but political and religious issues became increasingly alive to tenants as the reign of James I continued.

The greatest landlord was in fact the monarch; though his income was fixed, he also had the highest expenditure in the land, and therefore had most to lose by inflation. The Tudor governmental budget was unfortunately based on this fixed income, from which all ordinary expenses were supposed to be paid. How far this income had become inadequate by Elizabeth's reign is revealed by the fact that her ordinary revenue stood at £200,000 per annum, yet it cost her £126,000 to send men to the Netherlands in 1585.[13] As a result in the six war Parliaments between 1585 and 1601 she was forced to ask for subsidies, but even with them, and higher income from raising rent on crown lands, she was forced to find more capital by selling off crown lands like her father before her. The significance of this steady royal impoverishment during the price rise may be clearly seen in the struggle between James I and Parliament, and becomes crucial in the struggle between Charles I and Parliament. The House of Commons was aware that the king's power and dominion contrasted with his progressive pauperization; they appreciated the connection between capital and power.

The more literal connection between capital and power in this period manifests itself in the expanding raw material and manufacturing industries. The dissolution of the monasteries released from ecclesiastical control large areas of coal and metal bearing land. The growth of towns, especially London, created a big demand for coal (though the immediate impetus behind the expansion of the coal industry was the imminent exhaustion of the native timber supply) and the expansion of the coal industry encouraged the expansion of the salt, metal mining and metal working industries. In both coal and salt industries heavy investment was necessary. J. U. Nef in his study *The Rise of the British Coal Industry* tells us[14] that 'there were probably not more than fifty men in Elizabethan England with sufficient wealth to finance, single-handed, the largest colliery of the day even had they been able to realise all their assets'. In his article 'Technology and Industry 1540 − 1640' published in the *Economic History Review* in 1934, Nef describes the striking rate and size of developments in technology; such new techniques backed by increased capital investment caused annual trade in waterborne coal alone to increase from 51,000 tons in 1541 − 50 to 1,280,000 tons in 1690. In the Durham coalfields for example coal seams practically abandoned in the 1550s could be reached easily by the early Jacobean period with the use of new pumping equipment. Of course mining was a highly speculative venture. Workings failed, expenditure was heavy, it was hard to calculate the break-even point in a new working, harder still to guess how long it would be profitable. Capital clearly played a vital part in the development of the industry from 1500 onwards.

These facts are an essential balance to the view offered by satirists that industry was a stamping-ground for immoral, voracious profiteers alone. So we read J. U. Nef's account of how 'the first shaft rarely struck coal. In sinking, the capitalist was guided in Elizabethan times ''by the judgement of those that are skillful in choosing the ground for that purpose''. Even in the most extensively exploited district the miners sank many useless shafts. Boring rods . . . were too crudely constructed to determine whether to mine at all.'[15] Adventurers had to be prepared to spend from £100 to £1,000 or more before reaching seams, and on the Northumberland coast every attempt before 1640 to start large-scale mining failed completely. The demands on the determination and, notably, the capital of mining adventurers were clearly great. We may pursue this matter further by considering how the Sunderland salt pans were finally developed with success, in the face of typically severe sixteenth-century industrial conditions.

One John Mount, backed by a group of influential Court officials who obtained an exclusive patent in 1566, undertook to buy out the small men and install a number of expensive iron pans, all to be operated as a unified enterprise. He failed for want of capital. During the 1590s groups of merchants from London, King's Lynn and the North took up the project. They installed up-to-date equipment in a nearby mine – including one machine costing £2,000 alone – and this mine supplied the salt pans with fuel. The capital was raised through merchants and the Earl of Huntingdon, who bought shares in the venture.[16] The good planning which ensured control of fuel supplies at an economic cost, installation of good equipment, and sufficient geographical proximity of the two enterprises to allow co-ordination, resulted in success. Yet it is worth noting that the venture was only possible because capital was available and had been secured at the outset. It is doubtless true that the history of Tudor and Stuart industry affords many cases of fraud, and disastrous mismanagement of capital and labour. Still, on the eve of the Civil War Britain was producing over four times as much coal as the whole European continent.[17]

The importance of skilful handling of capital was manifest in other mining industries – iron ore, zinc ore used in brass founding, and alum used in cloth dyeing. The role of industry in the national economy was of course still very considerably less important than agriculture; but it was growing throughout the period. To trace the development in processing iron ore is to see the progressive demands for heavier investment, to become aware of the crucial function of capital in sixteenth-century England.

The earliest processing technique with iron ore was to produce blooms of pig iron which were then hammered into the required shapes. Blast furnaces were imported from Europe to produce cast iron, but their fuel was wood, and no success attended the many experiments in adapting the furnaces to coal. Yet the first iron cannon was cast at Buxted in England in 1543, and by 1590 there were a hundred forges and iron mills. Aristocrats were prominent investors in new techno-logical developments such as slitting mills and tinplate mills; Bevis Bulmer patented a new iron cutting machine in 1588 and two years later the first slitting mill was brought over from Liège. Earlier, in 1565, Sir Henry Sydney tried to manufacture steel. Sydney's venture involved bringing fifty-five Flemish technicians to set up forges in Sussex and Kent, supplied with ore brought by sea from his own Glamorgan estates, financed by himself, his receiver general and (of course) a London merchant.[18] Ironically enough the effect of European wars stimulated the expansion of English metalworking industries so that British sailors began to complain about the efficiency of Spanish cannon, actually made in Britain and exported. Such technological developments required capitalization.

The long-term importance in the economic history of Britain of investment in such industries suggests that the attention given to the successes of Elizabethan privateers at sea may be misplaced. Drake's voyages were certainly sensational. Here is the description in Hakluyt[19] of Drake's capture of the treasure galleon *Cacafuego*:

> about sixe of the clocke we came to her and boorded her, and shotte at her three peeces of ordinance, and strake down her Misen, and being entered, we found in her great riches, as jewels and precious stones, thirteene chests full of royals of plate, foure score pound weight of golde, and six and twentie tunne of silver.

The glamour of Drake's prizes is a marked contrast to the grimy, slow and wet process of extracting wealth from Durham mines, or the obscure and diverse results of trading agreements and gradually expanding export markets. Yet S. T. Bindoff declares roundly that

> it is impossible to regard the exploits of Drake and his fellow gangsters as anything but a curse on the economic life of the age. At a time when the country was short of capital for peaceful enterprise they diverted considerable quantities of capital to sterile or destruc-tive ends. When international credit was making patient headway in

the face of ignorant hostility they dealt its delicate mechanism wanton and damaging blows. They pandered to the fatal lure of gold and silver when economic thought was beginning to grow out of its agelong preoccupation with the precious metals.[20]

The clarity of this argument picks out the important part played in economic life by the merchant. Of course to understand the term 'merchant' in its modern sense of intermediary between producer and retail distributor is to have little idea of the seventeenth-century connotations of the term, when merchants were involved in the whole chain of production and distribution processes, financing and accounting. An idea of the merchant's co-ordinating function in the cloth trade, and of the essential function of the capital he provided, can be gained from a petition made during the Jacobean period, and cited in Unwin's *Industrial Organisation in the Sixteenth and Seventeenth Centuries*.[21] The petitioner explains:

> there is in England 39 English shires and of these but 12 that use any quantity of clothing and of these 12 but 5 that have any store of woolle of their owne breeding . . . the places of the growing and the places of the converting are as far distant as the scope of this kingdom will give leave. The woolles growing in the counties of Worcester Salopp and Stafford are spent partly in Worcester and a great part of them in the counties of Gloucester Devon and Kent and much of them in Southampton. The woolle of the counties of Lincoln Northampton Rutland Leicester Warwick Oxon and Buckingham are thus dispersed. One sort of it is carried into the North parts to Leeds Wakefield Halifax Ratsdale . . . some to the farthest parts of Essex and Suffolk. Some woolles growing in Norfolk are brought three score miles or more to London and from thence carried eight score miles and more into N. Wales and there draped into clothe and soe sent back againe and soulde in London . . . because in those places those sorts of woolle will be improved to the greatest advantage for the King and commonwealth.

This makes crystal clear the vital function of the middleman and financier. The merchant experienced in floating loans and with access to capital was a prominent figure in industrial development, as we saw in the history of the Sunderland salt pans; often the same merchant whose main income was from the production and distribution of cloth bought shares in privateering voyages now and again, jockeyed for rights of sale with other merchants when a spice laden carrack was brought captive up the Thames to London, acted as agent in London for foreign business interests, and might dabble in mortgages, land speculation or land-owning, or even invest in a blast furnace in the forest of Dean, when he was not combining governmental and private business on trips to Europe.[22] The activities of such rich merchants included the provision of services now provided by banks (the term 'banker' was coined during the seventeenth century) although the Jacobean and Caroline money market lacked the resources demanded by government needs, that is to say, it was too small and under-organized to provide large sums to be repaid at low interest rates over long periods.[23]

When the Antwerp bourse was destroyed by the Spanish in 1576 Britain's chief trading outlet was closed. War with Spain closed further outlets all down the west coast of Europe and trade stagnated. Merchants knew of no other outlets until the maritime discoveries of the preceding half-century were developed for trading purposes. Capital was attracted to these by the potential for large profits, even though the high risk resulted in many heavy losses. Yet Bindoff[24] observed that 'few investments have yielded such a stupendous dividend as the £72,000 which floated the East India Company out onto the stream of time.' The recovery of trade in the peace which followed the Spanish wars resulted in general prosperity on the eve of the Civil War, with developing trading outlets in Russia, the Levant and the Orient for staple products and for the swiftly developing manufacturing industries.

R. H. Tawney[25] wrote that

> to a great clothier, or to a capitalist like Pallavicino, Spinola or Thomas Gresham who managed the Government business in Antwerp . . . usurious interest appeared, not bad morals, but bad business. Moving, as they did, in a world where loans were made, not to meet the temporary difficulty of an unfortunate neighbour, but as profitable investment on the part of not too scrupulous businessmen, who looked after themselves and expected others to do the same, they had scant sympathy with doctrines which reflected the spirit of mutual aid not unnatural in the small circle of neighbours who formed the ordinary village or borough in rural England.

The facts of the financial operations in trade and industry in continental Europe charted by Richard Ehrenburg in *Capital and Finance in the*

Age of the Renaissance indicate how sophisticated and complex were those systems of credit and capital, whereas Lawrence Stone, in *The Crisis of the Aristocracy*, charts a corresponding English situation where rates of interest were near *double* those of mercantile communities such as Holland and Genoa; even though English interest rates dropped from 12-15 per cent in 1550-70 to 8 per cent in 1624, they remained far higher than Holland's.[26] Such high interest rates obviously must have slowed economic growth and show that popular strictures against money-lending could only help to obstruct the development of easier credit facilities. Obstructions to new credit and capital systems merely damaged trade and industry, with little corresponding improvements to 'usury'.

Though it is true that the huge capital required to set up and sustain manufacturing industry in mass production was not in demand until the mid-eighteenth century, yet the full industrial revolution was an acceleration of developments, and a logical extension of methods, explored and utilized by sixteenth and seventeenth-century industrialists, stockbrokers and capitalists. It is inappropriate to describe mid-sixteenth-century England as an 'organic society' merely 'threatened' by capitalism. The network of European stock exchanges already functioning in the early Tudor period was a sophisticated and complex machine. Certainly it is also true that business life at this period must have been harsher because the law was less extensive and less efficiently executed, government control less competent and, like financial knowledge, theory and skill, often ill informed or crude in particular instances. Risk and reward in business can be high enough to deter the scrupulous hand and the tender conscience. Was it gullibility, stubborn grit, expertise or foolhardiness that attended investment in a venture which had already failed once, in the middle of what most merchants thought was an irrevocable state of depression? For this was what the group did when they invested in the Sunderland salt pans. To set up, in those days of experiment in the still little known sciences of geography, navigation, business management and capital investment, companies such as the Muscovy and East India Company doubtless required plain good luck; risk and danger were severe. It was not only great merchants who invested, but small ones like the one from Exeter studied by W. G. Hoskins, who had money in 'adventures abroad' both 'in the Isles' and in Spain.[27] Lawrence Stone's lively biography shows Pallavicino as a man who behaved criminally in financial affairs and prospered,[28] but A. H. Dodd's account[29] of the more strategically

important Myddleton's achievements in varied fields, despite the
slowness of communications, the inefficiency and inadequacy of theory
and factual data – of the kind now found in economic statistics, for
example – is illuminating as an account of the real difficulties of
commercial and governmental management in the period.

Successful merchants and capitalists were of course frequently
blamed for social upheaval and the decay of 'the old order'. L. C.
Knights recalled[30] that Sir Simonds D'Ewes was disgusted at the fact
that Lionel Cranfield 'started up suddenly to such great wealth and
honour from a base and mean original'. Knights implied that the
popular quotation from Ulysses' speech on 'degree' (*Troilus and
Cressida* I. iii) might aptly be invoked. But D'Ewes is merely invoking
a familiar 'nowadays' lament from Complaint tradition, often used
completely disingenuously, as Sylvia Thrupp shows (in *The Merchant
Class of Medieval London*, chapter VII), if not unrealistically:

> Families of the fourteenth and fifteenth centuries actually knew very
> little about their ancestry. They had few deeds or seals antedating the
> twelfth century, few hereditary arms ran back any further, and there
> were no early portraits. There is no genealogical information on the
> medieval rolls of arms. The pedigrees of which people boasted were
> passed on orally through the memories of the aged, a process which
> allowed fairly free play to the imagination. In the late fourteenth
> century several friends of the first baron Scrope testified on hearsay,
> without having seen any written record professing to prove it, that
> he was descended from great gentlemen of the time of the Norman
> Conquest.

It is certainly unwise to suppose that D'Ewes sees Cranfield as a new
kind of bourgeois-capitalist entrepreneur in a chivalric society. The
Elizabethan and Jacobean social structure is better understood in terms
of ranks. Movement up or down the scale occurred constantly but the
rights, functions, and habits of each rank remained largely unaltered. If
a knight was promoted to the nobility he was treated as a noble and his
acquaintances had to adjust themselves to his new dignity and prestige.
G. R. Elton has summarized the situation[31] by observing that the upper
ranks of sixteenth-century England included men without titles as well
as those with them; traffic between titled and untitled was brisk because
the principle of primogeniture forced younger sons downward (even
sons of gentlemen down to tradesmen, as in the case of Quicksilver in
Eastward Ho), while the crown could and did promote up into the ranks

of gentry and nobility. We may recall the king's speech in *All's Well That Ends Well*:

> 'Tis only title thou disdain'st in her, the which
> I can build up . . .
>   If she be
> All that is virtuous, save what thou dislik'st,
> A poor physician's daughter, thou dislik'st
> Of virtue for the name; but do not so:
> From lowest place when virtuous things proceed,
> The place is dignified by the doer's deed:
> Where great additions swell's, and virtue none,
> It is a dropsied honour. . . .
>   . . . honours thrive
> When rather from our acts we them derive
> Than our foregoers. The mere word's a slave
> Debosh'd on every tomb, on every grave
> A lying trophy, and as oft is dumb
> Where dust and damn'd oblivion is the tomb
> Of honour'd bones indeed. What should be said?
> If thou canst like this creature as a maid,
> I can create the rest.   (II. iii)

There were indeed many complaints in the Elizabethan and Jacobean period that traditional landowning families were decaying, that the ordered rural society was breaking up and that customary hospitality was in decline. The great majority of such complaints derive from London, the capital city and centre of journalism, beset by the seriously increased numbers of landless men and vagrant sturdy beggars. It was also the centre of expanding manufacturing industries, and hence plagued by new buildings, suburban growth and overcrowding, and furthermore a major port and within easy reach of the southern and eastern ports where sporadic mass demobilizations of soldiers and sailors took place; the latter must have swelled the numbers of petty criminals who found London an excellent place in which to steal, dispose of their goods and evade detection. The contemporary observer must have been prejudiced by these circumstances even if he was not committed to Tudor policies of stratification and the enforcement of social stability, as was the Recorder of London, William Fleetwood, whose memoranda[32] to Burghley about London's thieving vagrants are full of righteous indignation, or John Stow, whose history of the city so often deplores the new building taking place all round its boundaries.

John Stow indeed shows how attractive the theme of dying traditions of hospitality can be, especially in the hands of an old chronicler. In *The Survey of London*[33] we read how in Henry VI's reign

> Richard Nevill, Earl of Warwick, with six hundred men, all in red jackets, embroidered with ragged staves before and behind . . . was lodged in Warwicke lane; in whose house there was oftentimes six oxen eaten at a breakfast, and every tavern was full of his meat; for he that had any acquaintance in that house, might have there so much of sodden and roast meat as he could prick and carry upon a long dagger.

Stow is characteristically at his best with events, like this one, some distance away. There is a perceptibly elegaic note to his final instance of the old order's custom:[34]

> The late Earl of Oxford, father to him that now liveth, hath been noted within these forty years to have ridden into this city, and so to his house by London stone, with eighty gentlemen in a livery of Reading tawny, and chains of gold about their necks, before him, and one hundred tall yeomen, in the like livery, to follow him without chains, but all having his cognisance of the blue boar embroidered on their left shoulder.

It is perhaps a subject more interesting as colourful romance than as objective history. It is true that some great aristocratic houses dwindled in riches and pomp during this period, but it should be remembered that James I and Buckingham gave to the aristocracy a sum equivalent to half the total cost of Elizabeth's war with Spain from 1585-1603[35] while many landowning families did not decline or crumble through the undermining by merchants and city usurers. The origins of landowning families must frequently have been successful merchants, citizens and tradesmen in the reigns of Elizabeth's ancestors no less than in her own. Thus Stokesay Castle, which still stands in Shropshire, was built as a fortified manor house some time between 1240 and 1290 largely to call attention to the improved social status of an enriched successful merchant named Sir Lawrence de Ludlow.[36]

G. R. Elton warns that we ought to beware of imposing on the Tudor period theories of class derived from the sociology of the early nineteenth century, and theories of the rise of new men which have been applied to the fourteenth and sixteenth centuries as well as the seventeenth centuries. The literary critic who applies such unguarded generalizations to complex artistic works is in danger of actual error, like that of J. F. Danby, discussing Edmund's words in *King Lear* I. ii. Edmund declares 'Legitimate Edgar, I must have your land' and Danby (in *Shakespeare's Doctrine of Nature*) comments as follows: 'this society is that of the medieval vision. Its representative is an old king ... The other society is that of nascent capitalism. Its representative is the New Man'. To this we might oppose the comment of Elton[37] that

> at all times men try to better themselves by approximating to a social ideal. Those that succeed (always a minority of those that try) come as new men into established ranks, but in a society as flexible as that of England they generally get established in a generation or two, just in time to bewail in their turn the arrival of others from below. Now the social ideal of Tudor England was the landed gentleman ... if a vaster generalisation still may be hazarded it is this: from the decay of feudalism proper round the year 1300 to the rise of an industrial and urban society round about the year 1850, the social ideal of England was that of the landed gentleman.

The gentry probably refuses to acknowledge itself dead even today, and Evelyn Waugh was forced to admit that his novel *Brideshead Revisited*, written in 1944 to mark the spoliation of those 'ancestral seats which were our chief national artistic achievement', seems rather an over-anticipation. 'The English aristocracy has maintained its identity to a degree that then (1944) seemed impossible,' Waugh did later observe (not without satisfaction) in 1959.[38]

Returning to the Tudor period, it might be noted that there had been rich merchants before Henry VII was crowned. That is to say, enterprising individualists manipulating capital and trade had grown rich for long years before Henry VIII caused the monasteries to be dissolved. Nor, indeed, was the sale of peerages and knighthoods by James I and Charles I an abuse because no previous monarch had rewarded with titles those who gave him money and other pedestrian services of the kind. The sale of honours was an abuse because it was performed too often and for too trivial reasons, not because it mocked chivalric ideals still vigorously, exclusively guarded by valorous gentlemen and knights. In Elizabeth's reign New Men were not new. Capitalism was not nascent. That is hardly the word at the end of the Age of the Fugger.

III

THE APPROACHING
EQUINOX

POLITICS AND CITY COMEDY

Towards the end of Elizabeth's reign, plays at Blackfriars, Paul's, and, increasingly, the Globe, register a note of discontent with public affairs, while the other adult companies at the Red Bull, Swan, Rose and Hope largely continue to evoke an air of cheerful patriotism and national self-satisfaction. It has been surmised that this divergence in attitudes to government and monarchy reflects a progressive split in the political attitudes of the two audiences: the first includes lawyers, members of the Commons, merchants and Inns of Court students, nobility and gentry, the second more predominantly tradesmen, citizens, labourers, carriers, apprentices, servingmen.

The proliferation of satiric literature has often been cited as evidence of the widening split in English society, ultimately to end in civil war and the execution of Charles I. Satiric literature is always concerned with the corruption and mismanagement of affairs – in Jonson's words 'the times deformitie' – and in fact there is continuity between Elizabethan and Jacobean political and social satire. There is also continuity between the two centuries in the realm of social and political conflict, which is in vital respects related to economic history. The period is one of progressive alteration in the balance of power; as, in an hourglass, the sand pours from the upper bowl to the lower, so gradually power drained from the monarch to the Commons, as his income dwindled and as their understanding of the situation grew and their control of finances tightened. The Jacobeans did not know and hardly would have guessed that one day James's successor would die under the axe; but the parliamentary opposition to James directly developed into that opposition which Charles knew and feared. As R. Ashton remarks in *The Crown and the Money Market*, Charles found the economic situation desperate in 1640, and the Commons knew how to wield it as a weapon: 'there is no better index of the weakness of the royal financial position in 1640 than the recourse to the pepper loan, the threat to coin brass money, and – most desperate of all – the calling of Parliament.'[1] Dominating the political scene, as I have indicated, was the progressive redistribution of power from the monarchy to the Commons; and the importance of this is indicated in the warning of Francis Bacon:[2]

> Shepherds of people had need know the calendars of tempests in state; which are commonly greatest when things grow to equality; as natural tempests are greatest about the *Equinoctia*.

The fundamental questions are about the nature of the state: is the state a family, a commonwealth, or is it based on legal contract? If private property is an inalienable right of the individual citizen, can his property be taken from him without his consent? If mercantile laws and foreign policy directly affect citizens, should they not have a right to be consulted through their representatives in Parliament and, if they see fit, to refuse subsidies? Is government more of a science than a divine mystery? Has the monarch two bodies, or one? These issues are focused in the Jacobean constitutional conflict. In the later Tudor period royal authority was growing stronger and the concept of the divine right of kings was being exalted. However, Tudor absolutism did not develop into complete absolutism in the early Jacobean period, although the divine right concept was by no means abandoned. The problem facing James I and Charles I was that the cost of government, which was their responsibility, was rising while the royal income was falling, and at the same time their power did not extend to control of their subjects' private property. Indeed as the Tudor concept of divine right became strong, so simultaneously the growing amount of private property owned by influential subjects strengthened the medieval concept that property was a right belonging to subjects.

The royal aim was therefore to achieve recognition of absolute prerogative in Council and Star Chamber, and legal sanction in common law courts, so that funds could be levied for government without the recourse to the Commons which Elizabeth had been forced to make. It is characteristic of the complexity of the situation that at the same time as the decision in the ship money case or Sir Thomas Fleming's decision in Bate's case (1606) upheld the royal prerogative against subjects' rights over private property, many common law cases were decided in favour of subjects' property rights even against private royal prerogative.[3] It was not simply that there were two clear legal arguments. Even the upholders of royal prerogative at the early stage of 1606, in Bate's case, agreed in the 1610 parliamentary discussion that actual taxes could only be granted by Parliament. There was also the notion that the system where the monarch depended on his subjects' agreeing to grant him funds truly reflected the divinity and justice of God, who had ordained and exalted the king but had also given rights of property to the subjects.[4]

James I and Charles I needed, more urgently than the Tudors, to rely on prerogative institutions to govern the country, because they were unable to carry out their policies smoothly through Parliament as the Tudors had. Of course the Tudor concern to extend and improve local government had demanded the assistance of country magnates who thus expected, and demanded to be, consulted. The Tudor method of government through an admittedly controlled Parliament meant that its members became more active, and that the House of Commons was certain to demand power sooner or later.[5] The growth of Puritanism, emphasizing as it did the importance of the individual, his personal judgement and the rewards attending zealous right conduct, further contributed to a general movement of the subjects away from submissiveness and towards active participation in politics. Thus James I inherited a Parliament which was from the outset less inclined to submit to absolute government.

As the Jacobean age continued, lawyers became the spearhead of the opposition to absolute government. By the 1620s lawyers were well-nigh the most powerful class in the country.[6] They clearly realized the importance of the royal legal victories in Bate's and the ship money case and concentrated on opposing the legal views of royalist judges and counsellors, ignoring the talk about divine right from James himself. In 1628 Wentworth summarized their attitude by observing 'that which passes from White Hall is but a gust . . . but that which is legally done stinges us'.[7]

In the long conflict both sides argued inconsistently, neither defined the crucial point, the 'general welfare'; royalists argued that the king in levying taxes to finance government did so for the 'general welfare', opposition argued that private property must be protected for the 'general welfare'. Royalist judges inconsistently pronounced that the royal prerogative did not come within the competence of the law, but simultaneously pressed for legal decisions confirming that prerogative.[8] Opposition appealed to their position as trustees of the country's good, a merely political argument in a dispute over law and rights, and they used this political argument to encroach on royal prerogative in foreign affairs and to justify new aggressive procedures. Thus on both sides old traditional principles are subjected to what looks suspiciously like sceptical analysis, and then disingenuously used to cover new schemes for political power. Neither side is really concerned with attaining that situation where 'mutual respect and love between king and people maintain a proper balance',[9] both sides are struggling for control of the government, although the opposition never formulated their aim so specifically as that. So in the 1628 Parliament Hoskins declared 'we come not in this assembly but to preserve the liberties of the kingdom',[10] and in critical moments members made such appeals as 'If wee should now retourne into our country with nothing for the good of the common wealth they would say that [we have] bene all this while like children in ketching butterflies' (1610) and 'Wee serve here for thousands of tenn thowsands' (1621).[11] The opposition encroached on royal prerogative in foreign policy, while the very insistence of royalists on the divine right theory 'exposed the glaring contrast between their conception of monarchy and the actual kings, James and Charles, who sat upon the throne.'[12]

The royalists knew that co-operation must exist between ministers and Parliament, and they knew that much of the Tudor success in strengthening and unifying the nation had been done in Council and Star Chamber, and all of it under powerful rulers. Faced with work to do, many could have justified absolutism on practical grounds alone. They saw that the king must maintain his authority over his subjects. It is striking indeed that Francis Bacon's advice to James in 1613 to deal differently with the Commons, to 'put off the person of a merchant and contractor and rest upon the person of a king'[13] exactly anticipates the social theory of Thomas Hobbes – and interestingly relates to Rochester's ridicule of Charles II in *The History of Insipids* as a 'Lewd King':

> But wonder not it should be so, Sirs,
> When Monarchs rank themselves with Grocers.

It is paradoxical that the entrenched attitude of opposition to innovations which characterizes Complaint tradition, and provides city comedy with its criteria, should censure policies and actions of the king and hence align itself with the parliamentary opposition.

Corruption at Court was a fact as well as a traditional preoccupation of satiric art. Stone in *The Crisis of the Aristocracy*[14] notes that heavy debts contracted by the courtiers in the 1590s caused many to resort to corruption to maintain themselves, and thereafter bribery seems to have become an accepted part of Court routine. In the 1620s Stone calculates an unrecorded revenue of the Crown in bribes, fees, favoured rents and gifts of about £500,000 – a vicious burden exacted in an obnoxious and inequitable way. The financial ethics of such serious public men as Salisbury, Cranfield, Strafford, being involved in the grant and fee system of reward for governmental service, differed only in degree from those of the parasites they attacked. The downfall of Francis Bacon in 1621, when a viscount and Lord Chancellor of England, for accepting bribes, is a spectacular instance of this corrupt system at its worst, even though it seems there are few mitigating circumstances in Bacon's case.[15] Consequently, it is difficult to read his solemn essay 'Of Riches' without a certain sense of irony. A document such as *The Secret History of the Reign of James I*, though written in thoroughly conventional Complaint style, is disrespectful of authority and discusses the royal administration with attention to the actions themselves and the king as a man like other men. Though arguing for a return to traditional methods of government and therefore still opposed to innovation, these satirists inevitably aligned themselves with those thinkers who wanted change of another sort, though at this stage (before 1620) no Protestants yet contemplated revolution. In the Jacobean age the drama registers a split in the social fabric and an uneasy dissatisfaction with political affairs; it is characteristic of the confused atmosphere that the satire should attack the king and yet resist change; perhaps it is too much to ask that the dramatists, having articulated the conflict, should not reflect its confused, inconsistent, fragmentary and ambiguous manifestations as they occurred.

Unlike James, Elizabeth I, though never relaxing her hold on Parliament through Burghley, yet knew how to accede to the petitions of her subjects, when there was no alternative, with a good grace. When the outcry against monopolies in 1601 persuaded her to withdraw them she took the opportunity to evoke with brilliant eloquence the ideal of Tudor monarchy in her speech to the Commons:[16]

> Though God hath raised me high, yet this I count the glory of my crown, that I have reigned with your loves ... Though you have had and may have many mightier and wiser princes sitting on this seat, yet you never had nor shall have any that will love you better ... And I pray you, Mr Comptroller, Mr Secretary, and you of

my council, that before the gentlemen depart into their counties you
bring them all to kiss my hand.

James I did not win the hearts of the Commons, and Francis Bacon
might have had James in mind when he wrote his essay 'Of Great
Place' and advised:[17]

> Preserve the right of thy place; but stir not questions of jurisdiction:
> And rather assume thy right, in silence and *de facto*, than voice it
> with claims and challenges. Preserve likewise the rights of inferior
> places; and think it more honour to direct in chief than to be busy in
> all. Embrace and invite helps and advices touching the execution of
> thy place; and do not drive away such as bring thee information, as
> meddlers; but accept of them in good part.

James disobeyed such ground rules, and Notenstein ascribes the
sudden flowering of the opposition in the Commons to precisely this
neglect. In a situation where the new monarch was all too unfavourably
compared with his predecessor, it was unfortunate for him that
economic difficulties and certain abuses should have put the Commons
on the offensive, and that he did not ensure that his wishes were well
represented, numerically, in the lower House. The progressive alienation of the Peers meant that local elections, which he did not trouble to
nurse like the Tudors, were not dominated by a royalist nobility either.
Thus the two Houses quickly grew in numerical opposition, and the
growth of the Whole House Committee progressively annihilated the
effectiveness of royal councillors in the Commons.[18]

James's interest in government was at the outset notoriously
unzealous. Here is what the Venetian ambassador communicated to
the Doge on 10 February 1605:[19]

> I hear the King has written a letter to the Council, in which he tells
> them that having been recently for nearly three weeks in London he
> finds this sedentary life very prejudicial to his health; for in Scotland
> he was used to spend much time in the country and in hard exercise,
> and he finds that repose robs him of his appetite and breeds melan-
> choly and a thousand other ills. He says he is bound to consider his
> health above all things, and so he must tell them that for the future
> he means to come to London but seldom, passing most of his time in
> the country in the chase; and as he will be thus far away from court
> he cannot attend to business, and so he commits all to them...

Many who went to him with petitions and grievances have been told
to go to the Council, for they are fully authorised ... This is the cause
of indescribable ill-humour among the King's subjects.

The king, it was plainly well known, cared not for the Commons. On
the other hand there was sufficient popular interest in parliamentary
business to arouse demand for copies of speeches and the subsequent
introduction of parliamentary newsletters. Beaulieu wrote in February
1610 'the Parliament here doth chiefly now occupy the Minds of our
Court and the Tounges of our Exchange',[20] and the Venetian
ambassador notes in 1605 how affairs were discussed in public:[21]

> *many members openly declare* that as there is no war with Spain, no
> war with Holland, no army on the Scottish border ... they cannot
> understand why the king, who has the revenues of Scotland should
> want money. They add that the people are far more heavily bur-
> dened ... for the king stays so continually and so long in the
> country ... and whenever he goes a-hunting the crops are ruined.

It is only necessary to glance at *The Secret History of the Reign of
James I* to see how scandalous rumours might turn country gentlemen
and nobility over to the opposition. In addition to the scandals of his
Court and his actions once he was crowned, James had begun to alien-
ate the nobility as soon as he set foot in England. On his way south had
he not created forty-six new knights at a go before breakfast at
Belvoir?[22] Did not the displeasure at his indulgence to Scottish nobility
above the English nobility register almost as soon as he arrived in
London?[23]

Personal grievances among the nobility arising from the king's failure to favour their allies or kinsmen at Court were soon aggravated by
the prolific sales of knighthoods (and peerages after 1615). Since the
ordinary resources of the money market were quite inadequate it was
inevitable that the crown should seek special expedients. These fell into
the categories of forced public loans, private loans from rich merchants,
ordinary public loans, the sale of monopolies, favouring of informers as
a cheap instrument of government, and the sale of peerages, baronet-
cies and knighthoods. The impersonal credit system was not yet functioning satisfactorily for government requirements, and these royal
attempts at solvency seriously affected relations with the Stuarts'
subjects. James having debased the dignity of knighthood until it was
hardly worth having, Charles fined large numbers of the gentry the
total of £173,537[24] for spurning it. The price of a baronetcy dropped

from £700 in 1619 to £220 in 1622; even in 1606 Cranfield was able to buy 'the making of six knights' for £373 1s 8d. Finally in 1641 when Charles made 128 baronets, more of them joined the opposition than the royalist side, so base had the honour become. There were earlier instances of the unpopularity of James's sale of honours; the York herald in 1616 tricked the Garter King of Arms into granting a coat of arms to Gregory Brandon the common hangman. C. R. Mayes has remarked that 'the sale of peerages (was) a practice wholly offensive to the landed classes and one which contributed significantly to the growing opposition to the crown'.[25] The broader significance of the prolific references in city comedy to this practice is apparent.

Finally there was the hostile reaction both inside and outside the Court to James's foreign policy, especially towards Spain, and Catholics generally. The notorious Spanish ambassador Gondomar had a subtle and complex relationship with England's king; James accepted a Spanish pension from him as a gesture of good will, though a number of important courtiers seem to have felt that their Spanish pensions obliged them to supply Gondomar with otherwise unobtainable information. The routine payments for military and political intelligence are recorded in Gondomar's accounts:[26]

> M. La Forest and other persons in the French embassy, for valuable news, 4,533 reals; to a servant of Mr Secretary Lake's, for summaries of important dispatches, 3,000 reals; to the person who gave me copies of the treaties of Gravelines from the English archives, 1,200 reals.

What may have been no more than largesse to palace servants came to 4,844 reals. English Catholics would have been a natural and ready source of information to Spain, and Sir William Monson, since 1604 commander of the English Channel fleet, is an instance of an important informant in receipt of a fat Spanish pension from Gondomar. On the other hand Sir John Digby, ambassador to the Spanish Court, had great success in getting copies of all Gondomar's most important and secret dispatches to Madrid from London. Digby broke the codes and kept James supplied with copies in clear. English informants at Court in London kept Gondomar posted as to which of his recent secret dispatches was now being read by James in London as well as by Philip in Madrid. This went on for years, 'to the helpless exasperation and cynical amusement of all concerned', according to Garrett Mattingly in his lively account of the affair.[27]

Gathering intelligence might be routine work for all embassies, but

English Protestant haters of Spain persisted in their suspicion of Spanish intentions, and did not find Gondomar so amusing. Certainly James's decision to appease Spain by ordering the execution of Sir Walter Raleigh in 1618 did not result in any immediate treaty with Spain. It was felt as an English humiliation at the hands of Spaniards, Machiavels and Catholics. Riots broke out in London and the Spanish embassy was sacked. Raleigh's execution, exhibited on the most public of stages, was seen as a tragic consequence of Court corruption, royal spinelessness, and betrayal of the old Elizabethan spirit. Middleton's play of 1621, *A Game at Chess*, explicitly attacking Gondomar, had a tremendous success, and reveals the general hostility to the English Court and its foreign policy very clearly.

Yet the attitudes of the early Stuart monarchs in seeking to impose absolutist government on England are entirely consistent with developments in most continental European monarchies in the seventeenth century.[28] James I knew the Spanish ambassador would sympathize when he complained in 1614 of the behaviour of the members of his House of Commons: 'at their meetings nothing is heard but cries, shouts and confusion. I am surprised that my ancestors should ever have permitted such an institution to come into existence'.[29]

The Jacobean masques, with extravagant scenes, costumes and machines by Inigo Jones, were intended to support James in his ambition to rival continental Courts in magnificent display and magnanimity; it has been said that their continuation by Charles I was no substitute for efficient government. These artistic expressions of absolutist doctrine (however Ben Jonson's ironies might strive to purify and chasten them) were accompanied by a major architectural revolution, for the Banqueting House erected in Whitehall was planned by Inigo Jones to be only a small part of a projected great palace, expressly intended to rival those massive assertions of absolutist principle, the palaces of the Escurial and the Louvre. Had Charles I succeeded in getting the money to build Inigo Jones's Whitehall, London would have gained a palace large enough to fill a great deal of St James's Park, in plan a single rectangular mass, more than double the size of the Escurial. John Summerson coolly observes of this plan that it 'would have been for Louis XIV to excel if he could. Had Charles I lived to build it, the new Whitehall would have been a grave and fitting backcloth for the bloodier revolution which it would most certainly have helped to precipitate'.[30]

In the crowd at the execution of Sir Walter Raleigh stood John Eliot,

John Pym, and Edward Hyde.[31] For such spectators as these, satiric city comedy and Court tragedy in the Jacobean theatres would have been of the greatest immediate interest. The plays affirm traditional common attitudes but they also set them in sharply focused contemporary terms; in this sense both city comedy and Jacobean tragedy are serious expressions of intellectual and spiritual, social and political upheaval in the England of the time, and the prevailing instability of the culture informs the whole artistic design of the plays.

IV

TO STRIP THE
RAGGED FOLLIES
OF THE TIME

The intellectual and social climate of the 1590s was evidently congenial to the spirit of satire, and in very different ways both Donne and Shakespeare had already accomplished much in the satiric mode by 1600. The revelations of satire are often unpleasant and alarming, and they are expressed cruelly. Satire can turn things upside down, finding truths in the undignified, the nonsensical, the squalid, the base. One might instance the first act of Shakespeare's *Julius Caesar* as an exposition informed by a critical, ironic spirit, which spares none of the characters who appear; the stage-image of Caesar's triumphant procession is set in a dense context of commentary by other characters, yet these characters draw attention to each others' bias while speculating about Caesar's hidden motives. Caesar's procession is presented to the audience a second time so that they may gauge how shrewd is the judgement of Brutus and Cassius, and finally Shakespeare concentrates on the satiric voice of Casca, which must have sounded too sour had it been heard before this moment, before the audience had learned what it now knows. Coming when it does, the voice of Casca may indeed be judged the truest and keenest response to the situation. Are not Marullus and Flavius, whom the audience saw minutes earlier, now 'put to silence' at Caesar's order? Casca's flat plain statements strip the events he describes of dignity, authority, excitement, bringing out their mechanically schematic pattern and so implying that they must have been contrived, rehearsed, and then not for performance to discriminating spectators such as himself or Brutus but merely for groundlings, 'tag-rag people', 'rogues':[1]

> I saw Mark Antony offer him a crown – yet 'twas not a crown
> neither, 'twas one of these coronets – and, as I told you, he put it

by once; but for all that, to my thinking, he would fain have had it. Then he offered it to him again; then he put it by again; but to my thinking, he was very loath to lay his fingers off it. And then he offered it the third time; he put it the third time by; and still he refus'd it, the rabblement hooted, and clapp'd their chopt hands, and threw up their sweaty night-caps, and uttered such a deal of stinking breath because Caesar refus'd the crown, that it almost choked Caesar; for he swooned and fell down at it. And for mine own part I durst not laugh, for fear of opening my lips and receiving the bad air.   (I. ii. 236-49)

In Shakespeare's *Troilus and Cressida* the acute and bitter insights of satire are again allowed, though being embodied in Thersites they are qualified by the repellent perversity of his deeply diseased vision, which sees that Ajax 'wears his wit in his belly and his guts in his head' and asks whether if Agamemnon 'had boils full, all over, generally . . . And those boils did run – say so. Did not the general run then? Were not that a botchy core?'

Shakespeare's is a highly personal and original art, accommodating the satiric voice among many other different strands of style, convention, and dramatic tradition, from which organic unity is created in the plays at deep levels of the creative process. Thus the *King Henry IV* plays, or *Julius Caesar*, testify to the truth of Dr Johnson's insight that 'Shakespeare's plays are not in the rigorous and critical sense either tragedies or comedies, but compositions of a distinct kind'.[2] In each play, Shakespeare, exploring a distinct imaginative territory, necessarily evolves a style and mode unique to that particular work. It is important to distinguish the difference from Jonson, who in his early experimental 'humour' plays had strict and formal and self-consciously limited preoccupations, as he sought to evolve a dramatic mode closely equivalent to non-dramatic classical Roman satire. Soon afterwards, in the tragedy *Sejanus*, the powerful potential of his single-mindedness bears fruit, and makes us remember Francis Bacon's remark that we are beholden to Machiavelli and other writers who 'openly and unfeignedly declare or describe what men do, not what they ought to do'.

In the Prologue to the revised version of *Every Man in His Humour*, Jonson implicitly acknowledges and affirms the critical doctrine of Sir Philip Sidney and his memorable mockery of the popular stage. Nashe too had ridiculed popular playwrights, 'a sort of shifting companions, that runne through every arte and thrive by none, to leave the trade of

Noverint whereto they were borne, and busie themselves with the
indevors of Art, that could scarcelie latinise their necke-verse'.[3]
Jonson's humour plays exhibit fidelity to Sidney's precepts for main-
taining scholarly and human decorum in stage comedy, so susceptible
as it is to debasement: 'For what is it to make folks gape at a wretched
beggar, or a beggarly clown; or against law of hospitality, to jest at
strangers, because they speak not English so well as we do? What do we
learn?'[4] The precepts strike one as doctrinaire and chilling to the comic
imagination, when expressed with bald and severe absoluteness, as
here, yet there is much of the exuberance of Nashe in Sidney's prose in
the *Defence*, and his recommended comic persons are familiarly
Jonsonian when he actually lists them; they are exemplary types, but
full of life: 'a busy loving courtier, a heartless threatening Thraso, a
self-wise-seeming school master, an awry-transformed traveller';
these, 'if we saw walk in stage names, which we play naturally, therein
were delightful laughter, and teaching delightfulness'.[5]

The affinity of this programme of didactic comedy with the rise of
verse satire, also modelled on classical Roman traditions, is at once
clear when we turn to the satires of Donne. His fourth satire[6] has a
vividly English setting and its confident use of vernacular tone, rhythm
and vocabulary sets Jonson the best kind of example. The satirist's
sharp eye brings a scene vividly to life in a dramatic situation. The narrative is expertly shot, cut and edited, mixing close-up detail with panoramic and tracking shots in a sustained rhythm as we witness a series
of small dramatic episodes in city and Court. The poet adopts the
persona of satiric observer, pestered with an absurd, gossipy companion. As he makes his approach we at first make out only impressions in
long-shot:

> Towards me did runne
> A thing more strange, then on Niles slime, the Sunne
> E'r bred; or all which into Noahs Arke came;
> A thing, which would have pos'd Adam to name;
> Stranger then seaven Antiquaries studies,
> Then Africks Monsters, Guianaes rarities.   (17-22)

Close up, his clothes tell an observant eye a familiar shabby story: his

> cloths were strange, though coarse; and black, though bare;
> Sleevelesse his jerkin was, and it had beene
> Velvet, but 'twas now (so much ground was seene)

Become Tufftaffatie; and our children shall
See it plaine Rashe awhile, then nought at all.   (30-4)

The reader is enlisted as a sympathetic audience to the narrator's 'asides':

> Then, as if he would have sold
> His tongue, he prais'd it, and such wonders told
> That I was faine to say, If you 'had liv'd, Sir,
> Time enough to have beene Interpreter
> To Babells bricklayers, sure the Tower had stood.   (61-5)

The annoyingly persistent gossip serves Donne's purpose by being in himself exemplary of the time's deformity. He poses (as Sir Politick Would-Be is to pose in Jonson's *Volpone* in 1605) as a subtle politician:

> More than ten Hollensheads, or Halls, or Stowes,
> Of triviall houshold trash he knowes; He knowes
> When the Queene frown'd, or smil'd, and he knowes what
> A subtle States-man may gather of that;   (97-100)

as he talks on he ranges over many abuses and evils:

> He names a price for every office paid;   (121)

and pretends to know

> Who loves whores, who boyes, and who goats.   (128)

He departs with money politely extorted from the satirist, who is left with a bitterly working imagination and surveys the town:

> 'Tis ten a clock and past; All whom the Mues,
> Baloune, Tennis, Dyet, or the stewes,
> Had all the morning held, now the second
> Time made ready, that day, in flocks, are found
> In the Presence, and I (God pardon mee.)
> As fresh, and sweet their Apparrels be, as bee
> The fields they sold to buy them; For a King
> Those hose are, cry the flatterers; and bring
> Them next weeke to the Theatre to sell;
> Wants reach all states; Me seemes they doe as well
> At stage, as court; All are players; who e'r lookes
> (For themselves dare not goe) o'r Cheapside books,
> Shall find their wardrops Inventory.   (175-87)

The satirist's disgust is further sharpened by the entrance of Court
ladies and a refined dandy, both satisfyingly offended in their turn by
the rough intrusion of bold Glorius, whose coarse violence is enacted in
Donne's poetry. The series of short syntactic and rhythmic units gives
disjointed, abrupt movement, the hard consonants and monosyllables
jostling and colliding; it is rough and careless:

> Whose cloak his spurres teare; whom he spits on
> He cares not, his ill words doe no harme
> To him; he rusheth in, as if arme, arme,
> He meant to crie; And though his face be as ill
> As theirs which in old hangings whip Christ, still
> He strives to look worse,   (222-7)

The satirist gratefully escapes through the Great Chamber which, he
notes, is hung with ironically appropriate pictures of the seven deadly
sins, and the poem ends.

In satire Donne's persona has a distinct effect on the response of his
readers; it invites and directs the reader's self-conscious detachment,
his astringent, intelligent glee or disgust rather than any sympathetic
identification with characters, scenes or experiences presented through
the persona's narrative. When Ben Jonson set out to write critical
comedy he inevitably became involved in establishing a new relationship between the play and the audience corresponding to that
between satiric poetry of the Horatian kind and its readers.

It happens that the clearest illustration of the process by which the
satiric form began to find expression on the stage in the late 1590s is a
play by George Chapman, *An Humorous Day's Mirth*, of 1597. This
play is slight in content and weak in comic imagination, but it does give
dramatic articulation to foolish characters as in a verse satire by offering
a survey of types of folly rather than by relying on a causally connected
plot. The revival of elements from the Tudor Interlude and Estates
Morality is clear and materially important at this point:[7]

> *Colinet* The sky hangs full of humour, and I think we shall
>   have rain.
> *Lemot* Why, rain is fair weather when the ground is dry and barren,
>   especially when it rains humour, for then do men, like hot
>   sparrows and pigeons, open all their wings ready to receive them.
> *Colinet* Why, then, we may chance to have a fair day, for we shall
>   spend it with so humorous acquaintance as rains nothing but
>   humour all their lifetime.

Lemot True, Colinet, over which will I sit like an old king in an old-fashion play, having his wife, his council, his children, and his fool about him, to whom he will sit, and point very learnedly, as followeth:
'My council grave, and you, my noble peers,
My tender wife, and you, my children dear,
And thou, my fool – '
Colinet Not meaning me, sir, I hope!
Lemot No, sir: but thus will I sit, as it were, and point out all my humorous companions. (ii. 3-21)

Lemot's function is also to effect the isolation of a character, from his stage companions and from the audience's sympathy. Such characters are to be viewed analytically, we are to see them with the satirist's critical eye, and Lemot's commentary on the action from which he is detached invites a similar detached attitude from the audience. For example in one sequence the audience watches Lemot and Florilla meet Labervele, whom they have both planned to gull. But Labervele privately takes the audience into his confidence to assure them that Florilla is faithful to him alone. The audience is involved in a three-cornered pattern of deceit; it must conceal its glee at Labervele's egotistic absurdity which allows him to be gulled. However the effect is not only to isolate Labervele and ridicule him, but to expose the motives and conduct of Lemot and Florilla. The audience's participation is not sympathetic:

Labervele I long to see the signs that she will make [*Aside*]
Florilla [*Aside* to *Lemot*] I told my husband I would make
these signs:
If I resisted, first, hold up my finger,
As if I said 'i'faith, sir, you are gone',
But it shall say, 'i'faith, sir, we are one'.
Labervele [*Aside*] Now she triumphs, and points to heaven,
I warrant you! (vi. 82-8)

So, in a subsequent sequence,[8] Lemot produces a witty, epigrammatic description of a character, who then speaks, provoking Lemot to criticize the speech in an aside to other detached observers. Lemot tells these observers that he will demonstrate another aspect of the character's folly; he does so absolutely as he predicted, and observers on stage applaud this entertainment elicited from the gull.[8] The

sequence (vii. 50-216) in which Lavel enters 'with a picture, a pair of
large hose, a codpiece, and a sword' intended to provoke Dowsecer's
humours ('To put him by the sight of them in mind of their brave states
that use them') clearly illustrates the rudimentary basis of comedy in
Chapman's play.

Here then is the verse satire of Donne, in form at least, transferred to
the stage where the medieval and Tudor conventions of didactic drama
could be readily adapted to its basic needs. Chapman's experiment is
poor stuff, perhaps; but it has relevance to Jonson's search for a
dramatic form in which 'to strip the ragged follies of the time'. For the
sequences in Chapman's play may be distinguished from popular
Elizabethan drama by their lack of relation to a narrative or main plot.

Jonson's first significant success as a playwright came the next year,
1598, when his comedy *Every Man in His Humour* was performed at
the Globe. In the same year and on the same stage Shakespeare's *King
Henry IV* also appeared: a panoramic survey of the nation's social
classes, in the historical process yet also in some ways timelessly
representative. The low-life scenes in London, dominated by Falstaff,
set new standards of convincing, detailed depiction of familiar
contemporary low life. Jonson's comedy, by comparison, presents a
much restricted range of social types, observes the unities of time and
place, excludes history, and underlines his strict concern for classical
decorum by setting the play in one city in Italy, not all over England.
This helps to reinforce the impression that abstract principles, literary
and dramatic, were uppermost in his mind at this early stage. The links
with *King Henry IV* – the prodigal son motif, the braggart type, scenes
of low life – are actually very superficial, even in the revised version of
Every Man in His Humour which Jonson wrote in his maturity and
transferred to a densely detailed London setting.

Every Man in His Humour is constructed on the plan of classical
Roman comedy, in which, typically, a well-bred young man becomes
involved with courtesans, pimps and parasites, aided by his witty
servant who approves of his enterprise. The young man's father comes
looking for him in the city but is duped by the servant, and after various
witty schemes a resolution comes from the intervention of some divine
or human authority. Such a comic schema allows a dramatist to choose
whether to emphasize a cynical or moralizing view of the story;
moreover, there is scope for expansion of the narrative to include a
variety of urban types and episodes, such as those improvised by the
commedia dell' arte.

With Sidney in mind, Jonson took care to adapt this pagan story to Elizabethan propriety, and reserved most of the Italian exuberance for the subjective fantasies rather than the actual behaviour of his characters.[9] His adaptation is best understood by working backwards from that moment at the end when the intervening figure of Justice, in the person of Dr Clement, awards emblematic punishment to Bobadilla the braggart and Matheo the poetaster. Bobadilla is to stand public ridicule, dressed in fool's motley with a rod at his girdle, and Matheo is to wear sackcloth – the ashes will come from his poems, which Clement sets alight as he gives his verdict. This corrective emblem affirms society's humane values in manners, arms and arts, and the play as a whole may now yield up its schematic design to us: it exhibits the wide variety of ways in which people betray and distort the meaning of education, poetry, love and social hierarchy. The action's setting in the city emphasizes how these values are peculiarly at risk in the unstable, crowded, busily competitive urban world of strangers – of surface impressions, like financial deals, involving credit – be it in Florence or in London. Since the characters are grouped in relation to these themes, the dynamic of the play is essentially in the critical exhibition of these pretensions, and so the familiar Roman comic story-line serves mainly a mechanical function of frame. Self-sufficient episodes serve to exemplify ideas, and only secondarily do they generate a causal plot.

The individual episodes formally acknowledge that the world of *Every Man in His Humour* is fragmented, not organically unified. The corrective conclusion lacks inner imaginative conviction, and the real power of Jonson's creative art goes into characters each of whom is convinced of his own centrality. Although Jonson's comic design provides the audience with a superior viewpoint from which they can, theoretically, exercise discriminating judgement as they witness the collisions in which characters challenge one another's rival solipsistic delusions, it is difficult in practice to accept that the play's prescriptions of normality, of balance and restraint, can be applicable to characters so wholly committed to these perfected delusory self-images. The sequence in which the poetaster goes to visit the braggart in Act I. iii may be taken as an instance.

Matheo knocks at a door which is opened by a humble householder, a city water-carrier called Cob. It is very early, just past six in the morning. Matheo condescends to Cob, but then has to endure Cob's mockery on the subject of lineage, for Cob claims to be descended from the first red herring 'that was eaten in *Adam, & Eve's* kitchin'.

(The savour of this ironic jest, as we are to learn a few minutes later, is that Cob knows Matheo's father to be a local fishmonger.) When Cob tells Matheo that the 'gentleman' he seeks is Cob's guest, Matheo suffers further discomfiture, intensified by the blunt account Cob gives of Bobadilla's drunk and disorderly state the previous night (he refused to go to bed and now lies stretched on a bench with two cushions under his head and his cloak wrapped about him). Matheo, compulsive in his ambition, remains undaunted by these revelations. So, sublimely unconscious of the fact that 6.30 a.m. is not a fashionable hour for polite visits, he has Cob's wife announce his arrival to Bobadilla. Cob, meanwhile, ruminates on Matheo's absurd pretensions: a son of an honest man and a good fishmonger, to read 'these same abhominable, vile (a poxe on them, I cannot abide them) rascally verses, *Poetrie*, *poetrie*'. Yet Cob's aggressive philistinism in one direction is matched by a self-assertive social pretension in another, for he is absurdly vain about having learned to swear like Bobadilla ('by the life of Pharaoh') and naively envious of the gallant's style of taking tobacco. Is this, one wonders, why he has allowed Bobadilla to evade payment of his bills, which are now as high as forty shillings?

Jonson now shows us Bobadilla in all his undignified intimate squalor, waking up badly hung-over, dishevelled, a basin for emergencies beside him, in desperate need of a restorative cup of small beer. It is, he finds, too late to prevent the embarrassing visit of the unidentified 'gentleman' now announced by Tib. The imminent entrance threatens total humiliation and loss of face; but of course (as the audience will happily anticipate) Matheo for his part will be so perfectly agog at the privilege of such a meeting that he will impose his fantastic wish-fulfilling vision on the reality before him. He had at first scornfully dismissed Cob's house as a 'base, obscure place', before learning that Bobadilla was staying there. Now, he contrives a choice compliment on it as a 'very neat, and private' lodging (as he waits in vain for Tib to bring a stool, there being nowhere to sit down). Bobadilla, struggling to make himself presentable, gratefully takes up the point, condescending to confide that a man of his popularity must take unusual measures to protect himself from crowds of exhausting idle visitors, naturally preferring a few 'peculiar and choice spirits, to whom I am extraordinarily engag'd, as your selfe, or so'. He indulges Matheo by noticing the book he ostentatiously carries and Matheo at once begins declaiming play-scraps, as a predictable prelude to interminable recitation of his own verses. Bobadilla is certainly not going to stand much of that, and so challenges Matheo's performance with one of his own. He begins to get dressed in choicely fashionable garb – a reverse strip-tease which, climaxing in the pulling on of boots, switches Matheo's mind from one obsession, poetry, to another, the gentleman's art of fencing. It is difficult by this stage of the scene for the audience to be sure how far Bobadilla is consciously manipulating Matheo, for we can see that certainly several of the braggart's own fantastic pretensions have been triggered. Bobadilla produces a vigorous verbal flourish intended to dispose of the pretensions to swordsmanship of Matheo's acquaintance Giuliano (in his absence, of course): 'he ha's not so much as a good word in his bellie; all iron, iron'; but then Bobadilla is badly shaken to hear that Giuliano used the word 'bastinado', for this is a most dangerous thrust at his own exclusive copyright to exotic modish terminology. It must be answered, and with a display of the full repertory of the postures and jargon of duelling. Bobadilla will of course leave the actual fighting to Matheo, and he conducts his fencing lesson not with steel swords but with wooden *bedstaffs*. These ludicrous props perfectly focus the audience's attention on the absurd gap between the noble science of defence, the idea of duelling, and this grotesque pair. Bobadilla's instruction is graphic: 'twine your bodie more about . . . Hollow your bodie more sir, thus: now stand fast on your left leg, note your distance, keep your due proportion of time: oh you disorder your point most vilely.' (I. iii.199, 201-3) When it comes to the point of Matheo actually looking likely to make a thrust, even with a mere bedstaff, the braggart hastily cries off, pretending to become bored, and seizes as an excuse on Matheo's use of the unfashionable term 'veny' instead of '*stoccado*'. This must of course make any further fencing practice unthinkable.

Bobadilla is certainly a coward, but he is also probably feeling the worse for wear – Tib has not, we notice, yet brought the small beer he ordered. A little condescension, he guesses, should earn him a free breakfast from the humbled Matheo, so he assures the gull he will even teach him the art of deflecting a pistol bullet with the point of his rapier (though in all modesty he cannot guarantee the method will work against hailshot). Such refinements are best considered, however, in a gentlemanly environment, and he suggests to Matheo a visit to 'some priuate place where you are acquainted, some tauerne or so'. The air of relaxation, the considerate emphasis on finding somewhere a gentleman like Matheo will feel at his ease, is perfectly fabricated. Bobadilla, though fighting against his hangover and the slave to his pretensions, shows to what lengths a Jonsonian character will go when driven by the conviction that things can be arranged for his primary benefit and by the will to impose his manic view of himself upon a discrepant external reality that keeps insistently intruding.

The sharply focused detail of such an episode's narrative serves to stress the obstinate reality of this external communal world and its imperatives. The location of the scene at 6 a.m. is an instance. Cob as a water-carrier must perform his task very early. Today he is late, for he has spent half the night trying to deal with the drunken braggart, who has no proper work to get up for, and now Cob finds himself answering questions from Matheo, who instead of working for his fishmonger father is driven out at daybreak by his ambition to be acknowledged a poet and a gentleman. Cob's wife says little; she fails to bring Bobadilla his beer or Matheo a stool; does she bring a bedstaff only because she hopes that Bobadilla will actually make his own bed for once? This narrative's detailed texture serves at every point to reflect the main abstract themes. Indeed so completely are these themes embodied in the characters' distorted psychology and their colliding schemes of personal self-assertion as they struggle with the obstinate facts of their surroundings, that the spectacle of folly acquires, it may be felt, an unexpected but convincing authority as a mirror of the world. The ideas of conversion, correction and transformation embodied in the play's conclusion seem to take too superficial and mechanical a view of the nature of aberration; the tension between communal and personal needs and values is a permanent source of instability, however accommodated by the lenient mood of comedy in this play.

Jonson's genius, given licence by the critical design and the emphatic conclusion of the judgement scene which provides a disciplined frame, is freed to generate a fascinating peopled world of nonsense that challenges any complacent conventional assumptions about what is normal. In *Every Man in His Humour* it is the very temperateness of the critical comedy (as recommended by Sidney) that permits so much invention; yet it appears that Jonson concluded that the audience needed a more aggressive and assertively abrupt redirection of their expectations. His next play, *Every Man out of His Humour*, consequently expresses a much more determined public didactic purpose, and it makes structural innovations to which it calls explicit attention in a spirit of severity associated with the contemporary fashion in non-dramatic satire.

Every Man out of His Humour begins with an Induction. On to the
stage erupts the Presenter, Asper, followed by two gentlemen,
Cordatus and Mitis, who are anxious lest his outspoken views get him
into trouble. After several long satiric declamatory speeches Asper
notices the audience for the first time, salutes them politely, but assures
them he will not flatter them, desiring only their true judgement. He
has plenty to say about bad habits among audiences as well as playwrights, and defies that popular audience taste so well understood by
Jonson's character Antonio Balladino in *The Case Is Altered*, who, as
pageant poet to the city, boasts that he would not change his style as a
writer if they paid him twenty pounds a play. Balladino scorns the taste
of gentlemen, what he likes is a good strong plot:

> Why looke you sir, I write so plaine, and keep that old *Decorum*,
> that you must of necessitie like it: mary you shall havé some now
> (as for example, in plaies) that will have every day new trickes,
> and write you nothing but humours: indeede this pleases the
> Gentlemen: but the common sort they care not for't, they know
> not what to make on't, they looke for good matter, they, and are
> not edified with such toyes.   (I. ii. 58-65)

So far as Jonson's Asper is concerned, if the audience do not appreciate
his play it is they who are guilty – of mere envy. The range of subjects
which come under Asper's verbal lash, and the insistently rough tone
and diction, indicate that he has read the Elizabethan satiric poets, but
Jonson's provision of two moderate companions helps distance our
attitude to his 'right *Furor Poeticus*'; at last Asper goes off to prepare to
act the part of a satiric-melancholic called Macilente. The formal and
theoretical innovations of *Every Man out of His Humour* are consequently explained to us by the more moderate companions, Cordatus
and Mitis. We learn that the combination of satire and comedy is to be
'somewhat like *Vetus Comoedia*' – and Old Comedy, according to
Horace, was the source of satire, since that was where Lucilius took his
model. Cordatus recalls how many innovations were introduced into
both form and style of comedy by classical practitioners; Aristophanes
having perfected a mode of exuberant dramatic abuse of contemporary
social and political folly, there were fresh innovations from Menander,
from Plautus – and so why not from Ben Jonson? The precedent holds
good in terms of Renaissance critical theory and is developed eloquently
in Jonson's *Discoveries* where classical authors are recommended as
'Guides, not Commanders', for 'to all the observations of the *Ancients*

we have our own experience: which if wee wil use, and apply, wee have better meanes to pronounce'. The verb 'to English' is thus revealed in its full significance, and 'to translate' appears a somewhat servile and passive activity. The setting of the play is 'the Fortunate Island', an equivocal recognition of the law of unity of place; here too a break is formally announced with the Roman convention followed in *Every Man in His Humour*. Before the Induction ends we get a further oblique view of Asper by Carlo Buffone; this is to illustrate Buffone's humour as a public, scurrilous and profane jester, yet it is so entertaining, gossipy and casual in its dismissal of literary theory and rules that it disarms, and then, indeed, it strikes through to a shrewd insight when it affirms rebellion and nonsense as integral elements in Jonson's art. It is an Aristophanic moment when we learn how Asper/Jonson will toss off four or five glasses of wine in quick succession and 'looke vilanously when he has done, like a one-headed CERBERUS (he do's not hear me I hope) And then (when his belly is well ballac't, and his brain rigg'd a little) he sailes away withall, as though he would worke wonders when he comes home' (*Induction*, 340-5).

Now the action gets under way in Asper's play as Macilente expresses his humour, envy: the active, destructive expression of melancholy caused by disappointed ambition for 'that place in the world's account, which he thinks his merit capable of'. His first soliloquy in this vein is at once followed by critical commentary from the model spectators, Cordatus and Mitis, whom Jonson has permanently installed on stage as a means of continuously qualifying our engagement with events throughout Asper's play, so that in effect the drama consists in the dialogue between Cordatus-Mitis and the Asper play. The spectator's experience is to develop his response, first judging and savouring Macilente's exposure of folly and crime, then stepping back, so to speak, to match his own estimation of Asper's unfolding play against the judgement provided by the intrusive running commentary of Cordatus and Mitis. Jonson presents a commentary as an integral part of the dramatic experience.

Given this strong theatrical emphasis on self-conscious theorizing, not enough imaginative interest is invested in the persons of Cordatus and Mitis, who are mere ciphers. It may not be unfair to compare them to the noble audience at the Tragedy of Pyramus and Thisbe in *A Midsummer Night's Dream*, for that Shakespearian instance suggests the potential of a play within a play for exploration of the formal, technical, aesthetic and psychological elements of the dramatic experience. Here in *Every Man out of His Humour* Jonson is prepared only to assert on the stage the special harsh tone, bitter flavour, strict formal regime, and insistent critical attitude of the new mode of dramatic satire. Had Buffone been allowed to sit with Cordatus, might a more searching discourse have resulted? As it is, the authority of satire is protected from the real challenge of folly. Jonson's programme inhibits him from exploring the more profound and sometimes dark moral implications which he has already touched on in *Every Man in His Humour*. It is difficult to see the seed of Volpone in Macilente because, precisely when Macilente begins to become interesting, he threatens the overall design and Jonson shuts him off. Thus when he has fed upon the beauties of Fallace's person and discourse he bursts out in painfully contorted passion:

> Would to heauen
> (In wreake of my misfortunes) I were turn'd
> To some faire water-*Nymph*, that (set vpon
> The deepest whirle-pit of the rau'nous seas,)
> My adamantine eyes might head-long hale
> This iron world to me, and drowne it all. (II. iv. 161-6)

This verse disturbingly enacts the condition of self-consuming, accelerating, malicious envy, inducing a sexually confused vertigo, dominated by surreal and fearful imagery. Yet, formally speaking, this is only an appropriate envious reaction to the completed exemplary scene of Deliro and Fallace; the next self-sufficient exemplary scene is to begin, so Macilente's outburst is curbed, while Cordatus and Mitis coolly – indeed almost in boredom – point out the entrance of Fungoso apparelled like Fastidious Brisk, and in a moment or two Macilente is to be found expostulating with apparent conviction that it is an intolerable state of affairs when fools have satin suits.

The survey of folly in *Every Man out of His Humour* traverses a variety of types (as the epigrammatic character-sketches prefaced to the published text advertise), yet the self-sufficient episodes, though intended to stress the generic and abstract nature of the satire, have the effect of isolating the characters from social processes, by contrast with *Every Man in His Humour* or mature city comedies. The sense of aimlessness in the play's central scene, set in the middle aisle of St Paul's (III. i), is very deliberate, as the commentators on stage are made to stress; for rather than make the comedy out of intrigue plots and causal narrative stories, Jonson's aim is to make it as Cicero recommends, *imitatio vitae*, *speculum consuetudinis*, *imago veritatis*. This aim was to be successfully achieved only when the setting itself fulfils a symbolic unifying function, as in *Bartholomew Fair*.

The course set in the so-called Comical Satyres, *Every Man out of His Humour*, *Cynthia's Revels*, and *Poetaster*, is to put the whole comic substance in a critical perspective and so to insist that the audience adopt a self-conscious stance of alert, informed, critical observation. The revolutionary fervour of the enterprise accepts the risk of chilling the comedy and reducing its imaginative and intellectual complexity.

In *Cynthia's Revels* Jonson contrives an exemplary action, conceived to present an ideal poet in a play somewhat sharply dedicated 'to the speciall fountaine of manners: the Court' and bold enough to remind the Court to

> render mens figures truly, and teach them no lesse to hate their deformities, then to loue their formes: For, to grace, there should come reuerence; and no man can call that louely, which is not also venerable. It is not pould'ring, perfuming, and euery day smelling of the taylor, that conuerteth to a beautiful obiect; but a mind, shining through any sute, which needes no false light, either of riches, or honors to helpe it.

The foolish types in *Cynthia's Revels* are too mechanical, the employment of mythical elements in a simple allegorical scheme is not complicated by that local detailed inventiveness in character and motive which is so potent a feature of Jonson's art at its best. In short, there is no drama because there is no true quarrel. The social and moral seriousness of the theme, Court manners and society, is self-evident, and the dangers of self-love, of obsessive self-assertion, have strong dramatic potential; but there is a merely schematic significance in the action. It presents fatuous water-flies idiotically obsessed with trivia, none of them alive enough to present any serious threat to the principles exemplified in the didactic scheme, nor alive enough to complicate the informing ideas. It may be significant, given these features, that this is Jonson's first play for the boy actors at Blackfriars. Crites, as poet-judge and inventor of a masque in which fools are cast as the virtue they most lack, concludes the revels in judgement. He surveys them with cold satisfaction, but the play makes his tone seem disproportionately violent:

> there's not one of these, who are vnpain'd,
> Or by themselves vnpunished: for vice
> Is like a furie to the vicious minde,
> And turnes delight it selfe to punishment.   (V. xi. 130-3)

These lines anticipate the dark world of *Sejanus* or *Volpone*, and propose a more profound yet still affirmative moral scheme for corrective, satiric comedy. In *Poetaster*, Jonson's second Blackfriars play, the character of Ovid offers a centre for this kind of graver comic experience, connected thematically with a series of exemplary humourous episodes, arranged in the manner of a graduated spectrum which is to be familiar in mature Jonsonian comedy (for instance, the apt and exact punishment of gulls and rogues in *The Alchemist*, from Dapper to Tribulation Wholesome to Epicure Mammon). In accordance with this scheme Ovid's banishment takes place in advance of the boisterous Aristophanic indignities visited on Crispinus.

Poetaster's setting in Augustan Rome, by contrast with *Every Man out of His Humour* and *Cynthia's Revels*, provides Jonson with a more secure and substantial urban base for the episodic narrative form. The lower social orders, the poetasters and citizen Albius and his wife, fit into place equally well in Augustan Rome or Elizabethan London. There is much liveliness (reminiscent of *Every Man in His Humour*) in these low comic portraits, and their rebellious folly, philistinism, social pretension, and obtuseness are sympathetically indulged by Jonson. Demetrius is a dimwit, but his dismissal of Horace is wonderfully conceived from within; dullness is alive here:

> Alas, sir, HORACE! hee is a meere spunge; nothing but humours, and observation; he goes up and downe sucking from every societie, and when hee comes home, squeazes himselfe drie againe. I know him, I.   (IV. iii. 104-7)

It is in releasing his creative energies in such characters that Jonson reaches his full stature as a poet and dramatist; we may recall W. B. Yeats's remark 'that all happiness depends on the energy to assume the mask of some other self; that all joyous or creative life is a re-birth as something not oneself'.

Though Jonson ensures that Horace has the last word over the braggart Captain Tucca, we may also remember the Captain's distorted and fragmented image of the poet:

Hang him fustie *satyre*, he smells all goate; hee carries a ram, under his arme-holes, the slaue.
A sharpe thornie-tooth'd *satyricall* rascall, flie him; hee carries hey in his horne: he will sooner lose his best friend, then his least iest. What he once drops vpon paper, against a man, lives eternally to vpbraid him in the mouth of euery slaue tankerd-bearer, or waterman.

(III. iv. 367-8, IV. iii. 109-13)

Tucca's wild aggression frequently modulates into self-congratulation or changes direction to gain the favour of whoever happens to be present at the time. It is a splendid moment in the concluding judgement scene when Tucca assumes equal authority with Caesar, Virgil and Horace in condemning Crispinus and Demetrius: 'Thou twang'st right, little HORACE; they be indeed a couple of chap-falne curres. Come, we of the bench, let's rise to the *urne*, and condemne 'hem, quickly' (V. iii. 340-2). Tucca is punished by being forced to wear a pair of vizards, Janus-like, to emblemize his duplicity, and then a purge is ministered to Crispinus to make him vomit up all the barbarous, raw and crude words which distort his speech and make his verses grotesque. This is an emblematic affirmation of pure values in language, and hence in feeling and manners, central Jonsonian concerns; but at the same time it is wonderfully preposterous and grotesque farce. The episode brings into focus a central Jonsonian comic paradox. The aberrations of a dunce like Crispinus are indispensable to Jonson's art, for they sharpen, enliven, and extend the comic analysis. They result in a more inclusive, intelligent and magnanimous comic form, authentically Jacobean yet in imaginative touch with Aristophanes:

> *Crispinus* O, no: ô—ô—ô—ô.
> *Horace* Force your selfe then, a little with your finger.
> *Crispinus* O—ô—*prorumped*.
> *Tibullus Prorumped*? What a noise it made! as if his spirit would haue prorumpt with it.
> *Crispinus* O—ô—ô.
> *Virgil* Helpe him: it stickes strangely, what euer it is.
> *Crispinus* O—*clutcht*.
> *Horace* Now it's come: *clutcht*.
> *Caesar Clutcht*? It's well, that's come up! It had but a narrow passage.

Crispinus O—
Virgil Againe, hold him: hold his head there.
Crispinus *Snarling gusts—quaking custard.*
Horace How now, CRISPINUS?
Crispinus O—*obstupefact*.   (V. iii. 510-27).

In his Comical Satyres Jonson sought to reconcile the wide-ranging
preoccupations and discursive manner of verse satire with the art of
dramatic comedy. In these plays the embodiment of the poet as
acknowledged guardian and tutor of the commonwealth's ideals, in
personal, social and artistic action, often appears too puritanically
austere and immaturely inflexible. The formal, theoretical and imaginative struggle fought by Jonson in composing the Comical Satyres
nevertheless helps to provide the basis for his rapid, confident acceleration within three or four years into mastery, not only as a dramatist
but also as a poet, a maker of Court masques, and a literary theorist. In
the history of city comedy the special significance of Comical Satyre is
two-fold; as propaganda, it gives assertive prominence to the need for
self-conscious critical awareness in the audience and to the primacy of
critically impelled general ideas as informing dramatic experience,
while as theatre, it provides through its loose form in which self-
sufficient scenes are suspended (by montage, not linear narrative) a new
flexible mode for the expression of ideas and attitudes to which
inherited Elizabethan genres of comedy were either formally inhospitable or ideologically hostile.

V

MARSTON
AND THE COURT

FOLLY AND CORRUPTION

'What is the robbing of a bank compared to the founding of a bank?'
(BRECHT)

As the fashion for critical comedy spreads in the early Jacobean period, city comedy dramatists turn their attention to devising strong frame plots which in themselves could give critical expression to social and cultural attitudes and energies. Thus in 1605 Jonson writes *Volpone*, Marston *The Dutch Courtezan*, Middleton *Michaelmas Term*. As the genre matures the emphasis in a city comedy may fall on individual episodes, related by juxtaposition and contrast to some focal idea rather than to a causal narrative story-line; or it may fall on the symbolic and exemplary significance of the main plot itself; or it may combine a symbolic plot and individually exemplary episodes; but there is always an overriding concern with leading ideas, with the critical significance of what is shown.

Jonson's aims in the Comical Satyres may be seen more sharply in their context by contrast with two dramatists who have been identified as targets of Jonson's satiric mockery in *Poetaster*: one, Thomas Dekker, being caricatured as Demetrius, the other, John Marston, as Crispinus. Both wrote for the rival company of boy actors who played at Paul's. Dekker's comedy *Satiromastix*, in part a reply to *Poetaster*, reveals him to be a conventional Popular playwright who has only the most superficial grasp of the theory and form of Comical Satyre, whereas the young Marston, already the author of non-dramatic satiric poetry and a member of the intellectually self-conscious literary circles in the Inns of Court, is at once responsive to the formal and ideological possibilities of the new comic form.

Dekker's *Satiromastix* is constructed on wholly conventional Popular lines, and only the most cursory and superficial glance could suppose it to be a satiric comedy. Its main plot, in verse dialogue, deals with a love test and its romantically happy outcome in a tragi-comic climax: we learn that the heroine, supposedly dead, had really only taken a potion, like Shakespeare's Juliet. The satiric matter in the play is expressed in a sub-plot where the Horace from Jonson's *Poetaster* is mocked. Most of this sub-plot lacks the verbal style and satiric technique of Jonson and is reminiscent of Shakespearean models – *King Henry IV* and *Romeo and Juliet*. Dekker reproduces Jonson's Captain Tucca, but he too vacillates between his defined Jonsonian original and that less coherent braggart of Shakespeare's, Ancient Pistol. The dependence of Dekker on Shakespeare may be partly commercial calculation, but it is also expressive of more ingrained habits. Typically, Dekker uses a sturdy narrative main plot and sub-plot, stereotype characters designed to please well-established audience tastes, and comic dialogue derivatively focused on catch-phrases rather than on verbal fantasy and psychological collision. Dekker in *Satiromastix* borrows the most obvious tricks from Jonson but produces only a veneer; the effect is conventionalized low comedy, as when Horace is made to exhibit his humour of envious, aggressive, personal spite:[1] 'dam me if I bring not's humor ath stage – scurvy lymping tongu'd captaine, poor greasie buffe Jerkin, hang him'(I. ii. 132-4). If indeed the Horace-Tucca sub-plot was added as an afterthought to a romantic main plot already on the stocks, that would perfectly exemplify the kind of crude ramshackle business of play-making which Jonson persistently attacked in his critical pronouncements and his dramatic practice in Comical Satyre. Were we to suppose that Dekker's intention in *Satiromastix* was deliberately to flaunt his journeyman's wares in Jonson's face, to infuriate him, we might be able to approve his scheme; but for that to be an acceptable reading of the play it would be necessary to establish the presence of an informing irony of tone and manner. This is in fact very evidently absent. *Satiromastix* is not *Eastward Ho*. Jonson/Horace is rebuked in Act IV. iii of *Satiromastix* in the following terms:

> th'ast entred Actions of assault and battery, against a companie
> of honourable and worshipfull Fathers of the law . . . thy
> sputtering chappes yelpe, that Arrogance, and Impudence, and
> Ignoraunce, are the essential parts of a Courtier . . . thou cryest
> ptrooh at worshipfull Cittizens, and cal'st them Flat-caps,

cuckolds, and banckrupts, and modest and vertuous wives
punckes and cockatrices.   (IV. iii. 184-6, 189-90, 194-6)

Here is only staid disapproval of Jonson's satiric anti-establishment
stance and of his disrespect for worthy cockneys. The appeal is to a
sentimental, pompous, stereotyped response, to patriotic and parochial
identity in the audience. Dekker strives for a tone and stance of
manliness and sincerity, but the effect is ludicrous, as of a bit-part in a
Jonsonian comedy.[2]

We can see from the sub-plot that Dekker has some talent for
straightforward situation comedy and for slapstick. There is some real
response to the theatrical vitality of Jonson's comic characters (if
imitation is the sincerest form of flattery) but Dekker's explicit gesture
of genial reconciliation to the supposedly diseased figure of Horace/
Jonson could only have struck Jonson as the height of impudent
complacency. Indeed Jonson's worst apprehensions about the incor-
rigibility of dunces must have been confirmed when Dekker's two supposedly wholesome poets, Crispinus and Demetrius, offer Horace/
Jonson their pity:

Crispinus We come like your Phisitions, to purge
    Your sicke and daungerous minde of her disease.
Demetrius In troth we doe, out of our loves we come,
    And not revenge   (I. ii. 247-50)

By contrast with Dekker, the significance of Marston's response to
the theory and practice of Jonson in the Comical Satyres is complex.
Marston had the distinction of being early singled out for notoriety as a
satiric poet, and probably in the same year that his poems were burned,
in 1599, his first signed play, *Antonio and Mellida*, appeared at Paul's,
performed by boy actors. It shows an eager and studious responsiveness
to Jonson both in its Induction and in the use of exemplary episodes to
display Court folly and affectation – and here we can recognize material
from Marston's own non-dramatic satires blended with elements from
Every Man out of His Humour and *Cynthia's Revels*. At the same
time, *Antonio and Mellida* is not a single-minded Jonsonian Comical
Satyre on the theme of Court folly. Marston's design allows for the
inclusion of a wide and disparate range of theatrical styles and areas of
experience; these are articulated by contrast and juxtaposition rather
than plot-dynamic. Furthermore, the action of the play is given an

added dimension by the sequel, *Antonio's Revenge*, which has a consciously parallel structure. Being written in a sombre key, it casts a retrospective shadow over the action of the first play.

In spirit, *Antonio and Mellida* strives towards the condition of Jacobean tragi-comedy, towards *The Malcontent* and *Measure for Measure*. In *Antonio and Mellida* Marston utilizes romantic elements (the flight of hero and heroine from the Court into a pastoral landscape is probably borrowed from Sidney's *Arcadia*) but he makes no attempt to integrate them; on the contrary, he allows them to establish their own distinct and intense atmosphere and structure of feeling. For example, in Act III the exiled Antonio calls upon an attendant boy to sing a song of grief to match his own at Mellida's absence, while, unknown to him, Mellida herself, disguised as a page, stands by concealed and listening. As the song ends she steps forth, encourages Antonio to reach a paroxysm of grief and then delicately guides him towards their ecstatic recognition scene, which then takes place. A fantastic, exotic and artificial dramatic style is designed to achieve this moment, its bizarre quality exalted by the shift into Italian dialogue, each line ending in the beloved's name. This moment once achieved, Marston follows it promptly with a sceptical and detached critical comment from a Lylyian page, who considers this curious use of Italian for dialogue: 'if I should sit in judgement, 'tis an error easier to be pardoned by the auditors' than excused by the author's'.[3]

To Marston, the meaning of the recognition scene can only inhere in the moment of its theatrical performance – its musical element helps focus our awareness of this essential truth – so that once the moment is past it can only be sustained through an imaginative act of memory; while the performance itself, no longer able to sustain it, presents a contrasting mood evoked in reaction. The separated elements of the play are each allowed their own claim on the attention of the audience. The critical comedy of those episodes illustrating Court affectation and folly are allowably light in their absurd effects, but the design of the play as a whole also associates them with darker kinds of deformity, psychological isolation, ambition and corrupt government. Feliche, a character who invites us in the Induction to accept him as a contented Stoic, free of envy yet alert to others' faults, wishes to be acknowledged as responding judiciously, not intemperately, as he observes the Court in Act II. i. There Rossaline, a Court lady, complains of the stink of somebody's socks then disdainfully fends off a fool, Balurdo; when he tells how he wears crimson satin at 'eleven shillings, thirteen pence, three pence halfpenny a yard' he only makes Rossaline spit in sheer disgust. Feliche's reaction is very similar, for he cries

> O that the stomach of this queasy age
> Digests or brooks such raw unseasoned gobs
> And vomits not them forth! O slavish sots!   (II. i. 87-9)

When Feliche ends this outburst the two fools Balurdo and Forobosco continue to exhibit their Jonsonian-type humours, and Feliche acts the satiric Presenter:

> *Balurdo* ...my leg is not altogether unpropitiously shap'd. There's a word: 'unpropitiously'. I think I shall speak 'unpropitiously' as well as any courtier in Italy.
> *Forobosco* So help me your sweet bounty, you have the most graceful presence, applausive elocuty, amazing volubility, polish'd adornation, delicious affability—
> *Feliche* Whop! Fut, how he tickles yon trout under the gills! You shall see him take him by and by with groping flattery.
> *Forobosco* —that ever ravish'd the ear of wonder. By your sweet self...I'll do you as much right in all kind offices—
> *Feliche* —of a kind parasite.
> *Forobosco* —as any of my mean fortunes shall be able to.
> *Balurdo* As I am a true Christian now, thou hast won the spurs.
> *Feliche* —for flattery.
> O how I hate that same Egyptian louse,
> A rotten maggot that lives by stinking filth
> Of tainted spirits. Vengeance to such dogs
> That sprout by gnawing senseless carrion!
>   (II. i. 101-9, 115-24)

Yet if we do unironically and seriously accept Feliche's moral commentary, we must suppress for the moment our memory of the Induction: there the actor playing Alberto (in the play which has yet to begin) castigates the character of Balurdo, and his speech is applauded by the actor who is to play Forobosco. Alberto's eloquence creates strong feelings, but then the pose is cast negligently aside:

> *Alberto* Ha, ha; one whose foppish nature might seem to create only for wise men's recreation, and like a juiceless bark, to preserve the sap of more strenuous spirits. A servile hound that

loves the scent of forerunning fashion; like an empty hollow
vault still giving an echo to wit, greedily champing what any
other well-valued judgement had beforehand chew'd.

Forobosco Ha, ha, ha; tolerably good; good, faith, sweet wag.

Alberto Umph; why 'tolerably good; good, faith, sweet wag'? Go,
go; you flatter me.

Forobosco Right; I but dispose my speech to the habit of my part.

(*Induction*, 33-43)

When we recall the discrepancy in appearance and voice between the
youthful boy actors and the adult characters they impersonate, it is
clear that for the orginal audiences at Paul's a certain element of
detachment and awareness of stylization must have been constituent
parts of the imaginative experience of watching the play; and Marston
here goes out of his way to stress the self-consciously artificial status of
his dramatic fiction. In the play itself abrupt transitions of mood and
style sustain the self-consciousness of the audience, so that extravagant
emotional behaviour or gross affectation in speech will sometimes
prompt a detached analysis of technique from a spectator who was,
moments before, engrossed by the play. Again, in *What You Will*
Francisco, whom we have already witnessed rehearsing his impersonation of another character, Albano, subsequently meets him face to
face. Albano suffers from an acute tendency to stutter when under
stress; here is part of Francisco's rehearsal for the impersonation:[4]

Francisco Where is the strumpet? where's the hot vain'd *French?*
Lives not *Albano?* Hath *Celia* so forgot
Albano's love, that she must forthwith wed,
A runne-about, a skipping *French-man* —

Jacomo Now you must grow in heate and stut.

Francisco An odde phantasma! a beggar! a Sir! a who who who
what you will! a straggling go go go gunds, f f f f fut —

Andrea Passing like him, passing like him. (III. i)

The audience can judge the performance for themselves, for in a
moment the 'real' Albano enters and delivers a straight version of
Francisco's parody lament on inconstancy; there is a strength of feeling
in Albano's speech which is disturbing in this equivocal context:

the soul of man is rotten
Even to the core; no sound affection.

> Our love is hollow-vaulted, stands on proppes
> Of circumstance, profit or ambitious hopes.
> The other tissue Gowne or Chaine of pearle
> Makes my coy minx to nussell twixt the breastes
> Of her lull'd husband, tother Carkanet
> Deflowres that Ladies bed.   (III. i)

The audience's response is ludicrously dislocated when Albano's passionate declaration dissolves a moment later into irresistibly comic stuttering. Everyone in Venice (the play's setting) has heard that an impostor is pretending to be Albano (who is rumoured to have been drowned) in order to block his wife's remarriage to a poor French knight. When the real Albano turns up, nobody will believe he is not the impostor. Affinities with Shakespeare's *Comedy of Errors* and *Twelfth Night* are apparent, and no doubt intended to attract the Inns of Court and royal Court taste which approved those two comedies. Yet at the end of the play the readiness with which Albano succumbs to complacent Venetian social norms as soon as his identity is acknowledged has its specially Marstonian ironies; this un-Shakespearean reconciliation has been felt to confirm the dominance of 'seeming', of epicurean values, relentless festivity, and the suppression of dissent.[5]

In his next play, *The Malcontent*, a study of Court life, Marston adopts a sharply satiric style and explores a deeper and more intensely polarized social dialectic. The play is a tragi-comedy, a form made necessary by the scale of crime and vice to be accommodated within a comic resolution. It seems likely that it was written and performed in the year of James I's accession, 1603, even though the theatres were closed because of plague for most of that year.[6] Three other satiric Court comedies also first appeared at this time, utilizing the same plot motif of the disguised duke: Marston's own *The Fawn*, Middleton's *The Phoenix*, Shakespeare's *Measure for Measure*. In these plays ironic stress is placed on the gap between theory and practice which confronts a ruler. When, either by choice or by usurpation, the ruler is excluded from his rightful position, his association with his subjects on relatively equal terms gives insight into the miseries of oppression or of laxity and the resilience of vice and crime and instinct. The subject's view yields truths which compete with those truths seen from the ruler's throne.

The arrival of the new monarch James I and the establishment of his Court gave fresh topicality to the subject of Court corruption, which

Marston had already treated in his *Antonio* plays; and there was a
subsidiary topicality in reflecting the new monarch's well-known
interest in the philosophy of government. More dangerously topical,
and reflecting the bitter gossip which spread like wildfire in the first
months of the new king's rule, was the emphasis Marston gives in *The
Malcontent* to the dangers of flattery, susceptibility to favourites,
luxurious display, irresponsible distribution of honours, and unre-
strained ambition for place and rewards.

In the dedicatory epistle Marston protests his innocence of any
personal or topical allusions, local or foreign, on the grounds that there
is no real Duke of Genoa. That this is a routine defence of satire
will be readily acknowledged; yet a similar protestation from Hamlet
about *The Murder of Gonzago* – that, being the image of an action
done in Vienna, there is no offence in it – deliberately intensifies the
suspicions and anxieties of the Danish Claudius. Furthermore the
printing history of the first three editions of *The Malcontent* supports
the assumption that the play had a notorious reputation at Blackfriars,
where topical comment was a speciality, and the fact that the King's
Men took the trouble to steal the play and perform it at the Globe
testifies, perhaps, to its current scandalous impact as well as to its
inherent dramatic quality.

The Malcontent is important as an early Jacobean response to Court
life, for although its debts to Jonson's Comical Satyres in the satiric
presentation of Court manners are obvious, it achieves a fresh penetration through the use of a frame-plot which is itself symbolic and
exemplary. The deposed lawful duke, Altofront, is at the same time
Malevole, a satiric malcontent. Malevole/Altofront is a dramatic
metaphor for the imaginative art of the satiric poet, encouraging vice
and folly in order to exhibit their true nature and contrive their
exposure and correction, yet gravely preoccupied by the relation
between stoical distrust of the world and epicurean commitment to
appetite. Altofront/Malevole has a dramatist's intuitive understanding
of the vices which breed in the Court, and he can enter imaginatively
into the criminal mentality so as deftly to deflect its menace into self-
parody, as when Mendoza invites him to carry out a murder in Act
III. iii:

> *Mendoza* Let's grasp; I do like thee infinitely; wilt enact one thing
> for me?
> *Malevole* Shall I get by it?   *Mendoza gives him his purse.*

Command me; I am thy slave beyond death and hell.
Mendoza Murder the Duke!
Malevole My heart's wish, my soul's desire, my fantasy's dream,
    my blood's longing, the only height of my hopes! How, O God,
    how? O, how my united spirits throng together! So strengthen
    my resolve.
Mendoza The Duke is now a-hunting.
Malevole Excellent, admirable, as the devil would have it! Lend me,
    lend me, rapier, pistol, cross-bow – so, so, I'll do it.
Mendoza Then we agree.
Malevole As Lent and fishmongers.   (III. iii. 70-83)

In the first act Malevole vigorously performs the role of bitter railer,
in the manner of Shakespeare's Thersites, his attitude of general
hostility keeping a distance between himself and the corrupt
courtiers. These early scenes provide the audience with a satiric
exposition of the play's characters and a self-conscious performance
(from Malevole/Altofront) of the conventional stage role of
malcontent: asked by Pietro, the usurper, whence he comes,
Malevole replies 'From the public place of much dissimulation, the
church' (there he talked, he says, with a usurer). Soon he switches to
the attack by greeting members of the group: 'And how does my
little Ferrard? Ah, ye lecherous animal! my little ferret, he goes
sucking up and down the palace into every hen's nest, like a weasel'
(I. iii. 21-4); and 'how does my old muck-hill overspread with fresh
snow? thou half a man, half a goat, all a beast. How does thy young
wife, old huddle?' (I. iii. 35-8). Malevole avoids the kick aimed at
him and continues his tirade of unwelcome truths, carefully pitched
in the malcontented vein so that his source of information, and his
insight, will be taken as perverse fantasy, which, however
disconcertingly accurate, may be safely disregarded in public. The
audience will be amused by the reactions Malevole elicits from the
courtiers; then, after he has had a splendid session exciting Pietro's
extravagant jealousy and shame at becoming a cuckold, Malevole in
private sheds his mask and shifts his role to that of Altofront, the
grave philosopher-ruler. He confides in his trusted companion Celso
that he lost his dukedom for want of those old instruments of state,
'Dissemblance and Suspect':

> My throne stood like a point in midst of a circle,
> To all of equal nearness, bore with none,
> Reigned all alike, so slept in fearless virtue,
> Suspectless, too suspectless   (I. iii. 11-14)

This abstract theory is at once followed by a short episode illustrating
how influence and ambition determine conduct and attitudes in a
decadent Court. Bilioso appears, having learned of Malevole's sudden
rise in ducal favour. The dialogue sensitively exhibits his compulsive
wriggling, fawning manoeuvres to discover what favour Malevole has
won and how he won it: 'His grace presents you by me a chain, as his
grateful remembrance for—I am ignorant for what;—marry, ye may
impart—yet howsoever—come—dear friend—dost know my son?'
(I. iv. 61 – 4). Each pause marks a calculation, to decide whether a
further card must be played. Ground is only conceded under pressure.
Bilioso probably does not expect such deliberate resistance and it
disconcerts him, having been used to despise Malevole, but in any case
he never pays until he must. Faced with Malevole's resistance, he
calculates that it must derive from the effects of some as yet unrevealed
excess of ducal favouritism. In this rising star, Malevole, he cannot
therefore afford *not* to invest, but he takes care to offer his son's sweet
mistress before he feels forced to offer the most valuable bribe, his own
young wife. Malevole reduces Bilioso to complete humiliation, then
gives him a parting insult, comparing him to a pigeon-house full of
stink. Bilioso takes this obsequiously, as he must, and fawns his way
out. To Bilioso such arrogance only confirms Malevole's rise to favour.

   The exposition is clear in its satiric-didactic intent, and no less clear
is the function of the frame plot in allowing the development of loose
exemplary episodes which survey the diverse manifestations of Court
corruption, some frivolous and farcical, some darkly serious and
painful. As the exposition in Act I suggests, the scheme of the play as a
whole places great stress on attitudes to sex as a guide to the moral and
social depravity and psychological motivation of satirized characters.
The most ostentatious figure of sexual libertinism is the bawd
Maquerelle; her function frees her from the obsession which partially
blinds most of the Court and she can be resiliently candid as a heartless
observer of this society:

> some must be fools, and some must be lords; some must be knaves,
> and some must be officers; some must be beggars, some must be

knights; some must be cuckolds, and some must be citizens. As for
example, I have two court-dogs, the most fawning curs . . . Now that
dog which I favour I feed; and he's so ravenous that what I give he
never chaws it, gulps it down whole without any relish of what he
has, but with a greedy expectation of what he shall have.

(V. ii. 44-55)

Malevole's reaction to this speech must be tautly ironic, under the
circumstances, for he is about to test the fidelity of his (that is,
Altofront's) own wife, Maria, by tempting her to forsake her lost
husband in favour of Mendoza. Malevole gives Maquerelle and the fool
Passarello a toast to Altofront, then works the conversation round to
the point of asking the bawd whether the late Duke Altofront's wife
Maria will succumb to Pietro's attempted seduction of her. Maquerelle
flippantly pretends to suppose it a matter of astrological timing, then of
giving rich presents, but she warns Malevole that Maria is, sad to say, a
cold creature; we are reminded of Pompey in *Measure for Measure*
when Maquerelle complains that Maria's chastity 'had almost brought
bed-pressing out of fashion': for all her candour, she can achieve no
more than a reductive and ultimately cynical view of human feeling and
human nature. Yet such a condition is the necessary antidote to the
sexual hysteria which prevails elsewhere in the Genoese Court, and it is
by way of Maquerelle that the audience is led to witness Maria's stoical
fortitude and ideal fidelity to her lost husband Altofront. Here the
intimate experience of Malevole/Altofront, first in sexual doubt and
then in affirmed marital fidelity, is set in counterpoint to the irrational
jealousies and degrading sexual animality which prevail elsewhere in
the diseased Court of the usurper. Malevole knows how to activate the
ever-susceptible eroticism and uncontrolled, anarchic epicureanism of
that society, which he evokes in a strikingly seductive image of
Jacobean Court festivity:

When in an Italian lascivious palace, a lady guardianless,
Left to the push of all allurement,
The strongest incitements to immodesty –
To have her bound, incensed with wanton sweets,
Her veins filled high with heating delicates,
Soft rest, sweet music, amorous masquers, lascivious banquets,
sin itself gilt o'er, strong fantasy tricking up strange delights,
presenting it dressed pleasingly to sense, sense leading it unto the
soul, confirmed with potent example, impudent custom, enticed

by that great bawd Opportunity; thus being prepared, clap to her easy ear youth in good clothes, well-shaped, rich, fair-spoken, promising-noble, ardent, blood-full, witty, flattering —

(III. ii. 34-46)

Malevole's is a performance worthy of any spectator's applause; only as it accelerates (so taking Bilioso, Malevole's victim, deep into its imaginative vision of erotic anarchy) do we become progressively alert to its meditated rhetorical design and Malevole's gradual emotional detachment, which identifies Bilioso with an emotion now deliberately extended to breaking-point and seen as absurd. The sheer speed and precision of his calculation, whatever surprises Malevole encounters, seem to indicate that the playwright is deliberately straining our belief in the action's literal probability. A metaphysical truth is sought by paradox here, for at such moments the play's narrative is conceded to be merely a fiction, naturalistically speaking, so that a spiritual affirm-ation can be expressed. One might cite, as an instance, Malevole's discovery that the body of Fernese, though covered in blood, still has life in it:

Fernese O!
Malevole Proclamations! more proclamations!
Fernese O! a surgeon!
Malevole Hark! lust cries for a surgeon.
    What news from Limbo?
    How does the grand cuckold, Lucifer?
Fernese O, help, help! and save me!
Malevole Thy shame more than thy wounds do grieve me far ...
    Now 'gins close plots to work; the scene grows full,
    And craves his eyes who hath a solid skull.

(II. v. 140-6, 160-1)

Malevole's exuberant, instantaneous reaction to signs of life in Fernese seems to express both an instant grasp of how to incorporate the information into his plans and a witty recognition that, if he saw it played upon the stage, he would condemn this turn in the plot as an improbable fiction.

The dramatic style sustains this persistent larger-than-life mode, so that the modulations of subtle and broad parodic treatment keep a soph-isticated audience on their toes, critically engaged, absorbed yet self-conscious, aware of literary and dramatic allusion (to *The Odyssey* and *Hamlet*, especially) as an important element in the significance of what is shown. In this perspective the final masque makes self-consciously explicit and literal the metaphoric dominance of masks in the preceding action and dialogue. A Court of a usurper surrounded by flatterers is a mere travesty, aptly exposed, unmasked by confronting it with the emblem of duplicity and seeming; only through his mask as Malevole can Altofront experience degradation as homeopathic cure and recover his true, integrated self, at once human being and ruler of Genoa.[7] The ceremonies of Court life, reflected in Court masque theatre, provide the especially heightened order through which exposure, correction and restoration can be safely and authoritatively achieved. This symbolic moral reordering is made emphatically by art.

Yet a question remains; for if the concluding Court masque stresses the emblematic moral ordering achieved by the play's art, it also qualifies the nature of the reconciliation Marston offers. The play presents political realities with closely-focused analytic attention, and its depiction of the instability and weakness of individuals in political and private life is equally ruthless in its candour and its pessimism. The conventions of Comical Satyre allow for the confrontation of the individual characters with moral truth and the consequent hope of spiritual renewal in them; the larger-scale world of political affairs in *The Malcontent*, however, is not transformed by an equivalent process, but by an external and unseen agency,[8] the Duke of Florence, and an inexplicably resurgent populace. At the political level Providence seems to be dangerously susceptible to devaluation from a mysterious supernatural presence to an artistic convention. In effect, certainly, the imaginatively significant terms of the play's affirmation are strictly personal and ideal, focused on the transcendent Renaissance metaphysical conceit of the world as a stage, life a play, and man no more than a poor player. In the political world stability cannot be bred.

The year 1604 (probably)[9] saw the appearance of another Court play by Marston, *The Fawn*; but here he chooses not to pursue the darkly serious political themes but concentrates instead on the texture of Court society in a generally high-spirited comic atmosphere calculated to appeal to the Inns of Court element in the Coterie audience at Blackfriars. Furthermore, the fashionable manners and witty dialogue of this satiric comedy do nothing to discourage expectations of scandalous topical comment, and a pointed emphasis could be given to such traits of Gonzago's as his self-admiring wisdom, his self-conscious display of rhetorical skill, his susceptibility to flattery, his wishing to be thought a philosopher and poet, and to be addressed as 'royally wise and wisely royal'.[10] Furthermore, the contrast with the visiting, disguised Duke Hercules, who seeks revenge on Court flatterers and achieves rapid favour in his own role of Court flatterer, makes a sufficiently pointed satiric comment on life at the real Court of King James as reported by contemporary observers. One of Marston's particular successes in *The Fawn* is in fact the depiction of gossip and rumour at work in a Court and the constant anxious awareness of spies and informers covertly at work; this gives full substantiation to Duke Hercules's attitude:[11]

> I think a prince
> Whose tender sufferance never felt a gust
> Of bolder breathings, but still liv'd gently fann'd
> With the soft gales of his own flatterers' lips,
> Shall never know his own complexion.
>
> (I. ii. 306-10)

This speech follows his first experience of Urbino's Court, where courtiers have maliciously distorted his son Tiberio's account of his absent father. When the courtiers notice Faunus, the newcomer, overhearing them, their reaction is alarm: 'Now the jail deliver me, an intelligencer! Be good to me ye cloisters of bondage. Of whence art thou?' There must have been added point to this for the original audience at Blackfriars, for it was known to contain its proportion of intelligencers (scornfully addressed directly, at times, by the dramatists in Prologues and Epilogues, and occasionally reacting actively enough for plays to be officially censored – as happened with *Philotas*, *Eastward Ho*, *The Dutch Courtezan* and *The Isle of Gulls*).

The air of sophistication in this Court society is to a great extent created by the dialogue, lightly mercurial in direction, very quick to react to any flicker of the unusual in the passing scene, each speaker feline in his intuitive sense of altering emotional attitudes. Marston, always an accomplished artist in integrating all the resources of theatre, makes deft use of costume, properties, ceremony and social manners to create fully realized images of life without subduing the satiric and critical point. The following episode illustrates the exactly observed world of malice, self-assertion, and neurotic ambivalence in manner. Intelligence and ambition shrivel in the confines of the Court's claustrophobia, its galleries of exaggerated poses and unserious rituals which are nevertheless very real corridors of power and wealth, always tense:

Enter Hercules *freshly suited.*

Nymphadoro Behold that thing of most fortunate, most prosperous
  impudence, Don Faunus himself.
Herod Blessed and long lasting be thy carnation ribbon, O man of
  more than wit, much more than virtue, of fortune! Faunus, wilt
  eat any of a young spring sallet?
Hercules Where did the herbs grow, my gallant, where did they
  grow?
Hercules No, I'll none. I'll eat no city herbs, no city roots, for here
  in the city a man shall have his excrements in his teeth again
  within four and twenty hours. I love no city sallets. Hast any
  canary?
Nymphadoro How the poor snake wriggles with this sudden
  warmth.   Herod *drinks*.
Herod Here, Faunus, a health as deep as a female.
Hercules 'Fore Jove, we must be more endear'd.   (II. i. 27-42)

As in *The Malcontent*, disordered sexuality is a prominent feature of
this society, moving between the poles of Herod's lustful cuckolding of
his own brother and Don Zuccone's frantic jealousy over a chaste wife.
At the centre of the play is an exuberant, good-natured and healthy
youthful tale of bawdy, borrowed from Boccaccio, in which Gonzago's
daughter tricks him into conveying messages to her lover Tiberio. The
wise philosopher-ruler is thus shown unintentionally giving detailed
instructions to the young suitor about how he should reach his daughter's bedchamber. Whether or not Gonzago is intermittently identified
with King James, an audience including many young gentlemen from
the Inns of Court could be expected to respond enthusiastically when
Hercules as the disguised father willingly helps his son reach
Dulcimel's bedchamber and gives his blessing as a priest marries the
pair. The joke is on Gonzago for so readily and persistently trying to
deter Tiberio's suit. In Gonzago we recognize a shadowy anticipation
of Justice Overdo in Jonson's *Bartholomew Fair*, although the
emphasis in Marston's comedy is balanced so that we need feel little
real concern on behalf of Dulcimel, faced with an unsympathetic father.

  As the Jacobean age proceeds, Court corruption and political tyr-
anny cease to be treated in comedy and become increasingly the
province of satiric tragedy and tragi-comic romance. Meanwhile in a
parallel development, critical comedy concentrates on the city as a

setting, depicting the tensions between commercial and social pressures and moral values, between human needs and the conditions of life for men in crowded cities in pursuit of commercial power, wealth and fashion.

The comedies are set increasingly frequently in London itself. A comparable rise in London's self-consciousness is to be noticed in pageantry in the same period. The Court masque increasingly absorbs those traditions of pageantry focused on the monarch and withdraws them from public and civic shows; at the same time the city of London develops, in the Lord Mayor's Show, an increasingly elaborate and lavish display to celebrate the capital's chief citizen.[12] Denied occasions for royal entries and progress pageants, London turns to its own Lord Mayor as a focus for communal pride and self-assurance. In the following chapters we will be concerned with the main body of plays in the genre, set in the city and concerned with courtiers only occasionally. The political comment and significance of these plays is not narrowly focused on monarch and Court; but precisely for that reason they have their own political aspect.

VI

MONEY MAKES
THE WORLD GO AROUND

THE CITY SATIRIZED

By about 1605 the genre becomes established with such plays as
Jonson's *Volpone*, Marston's *Dutch Courtezan* and Middleton's
Michaelmas Term. It is at that point that repertory hack-writers
begin to try to cash in on the new fashion for city comedy, and their
derivative work provokes the parody *Eastward Ho*. Although the
precise dates of Middleton's early comedies have not been conclusively
established,[1] my present concern is to trace the formal and thematic
evolution of this first phase of comedies satirizing city life, and in these
terms Middleton's *The Phoenix* presents the simplest form and the
clearest evidence of imitation of early Jonson and Marston and so
demands to be placed first. The comedies *A Mad World My Masters*
and *Your Five Gallants* exhibit certain distinctive qualities of
Middleton's comic art in relatively simple terms, and once these
features have been established it will be possible to recognize the family
resemblances, and the individuality, of single plays by Jonson, by
Marston, and by Middleton himself.

Middleton's comedy *The Phoenix* utilizes a disguised-duke frame-
plot: Phoenix, son of the ageing Duke of Ferrara, goes in disguise into
his own city and there witnesses a variety of folly and vice, on which he
offers, as Presenter, shrewd comment; major intrigues are brought to
succcessful fruition in a concluding judgement scene. The satiric tenor
of the play is sustained throughout, and indeed the affinities with
Marston are unmistakable, yet at the same time some episodes are
assertively derivative of Jonsonian Comical Satyre, showing that
Middleton is conscious of a fashion to be followed and of an audience
alert for the tell-tale allusions. What is distinctively Middletonian,
straight away, is the tight co-ordination of the elements of a scene, for

his is an art which does not delight in the loose construction of Comical
Satyre with its scenes 'in suspension'. A sharp clarity of language, an
ironic wit shaping the dialogue, an economy of scenic design based on
critical ideas, a capacity to evolve ingeniously interwoven, complex
multiple plots, are qualities which go to sustain the excellence of
Middleton's art.

The disguised-duke frame-plot provides an overall political context
in which moral and social values are united, but the interwoven intrigues exhibit directly how corruption in the law or at Court has repercussions on individual lives. For example Fidelio, the trusted confidant
of Phoenix, meets a crooked lawyer, Tangle, who boasts of his new
client the Captain who is arranging to divorce and sell his wife. Fidelio
soon recognizes that this Captain must be his own father-in-law. In due
course, disguised, both Fidelio and Phoenix learn from Proditor, the
nobleman who intends to buy the Captain's wife, that he plots the
Duke's murder and intends Phoenix to be blamed for it. By outwitting
both the Captain and Proditor, therefore, Fidelio and Phoenix each
succeed in protecting a parent from a grave danger while at the same
time affirming general morally didactic lessons. Middleton's dramatic
design itself embodies satiric-didactic ideas: plots themselves are
exempla. At the same time, Comical Satyre's influence is apparent in
the series of gravely uncompromising verse speeches asserting moral
principles in anticipation of, or in reaction to, episodes in which a whole
graduated range of follies and vices is displayed. As Phoenix moves in
disguise through the city he witnesses or becomes an agent in a series of
exemplary episodes satirizing a criminal justice, lawyers, a cynical
captain who hates marriage, an adulterous citizen's wife, a profligate
knight, courtiers and nobility. Phoenix in his disguise as a young
prodigal ('some filthy farmer's son', as the Captain contemptuously
explains, 'he's a gull')[2] elicits a further line of conventional satiric
comment, and the dialogue generally is studded with the satiric
commonplaces which are so popular a feature of city comedy – as for
instance when the groom at the inn justifies the policy of allowing
known criminals as lodgers: 'if we should not lodge knaves, I wonder
how we should be able to live honestly: are there honest men enough,
think you, in a term-time to fill all the inns in the town?' Later, Tangle
the lawyer explains that the noble science of defence is obsolete:

> Sword and Buckler was called *a good conscience*, but that
> weapon's left long ago: that was too manly a fight, too sound a

weapon for these our days. 'Slid, we are scarce able to lift up a
buckler now, our arms are so bound to the pox; one good bang
upon a buckler would make most of our gentlemen fly a' pieces:
'tis not for these linty times: our lawyers are good rapier and
dagger men; they'll quickly despatch your – money.   (II. iii)

More succinctly, Justice Falso and the Knight exchange civilities:

Falso ...I cry ye mercy, sir; I call you a gentleman still; I forget
you're but a knight; you must pardon me, sir.
Knight For your worship's kindness – worship! I cry you mercy,
sir; I call you worshipfull still; I forget you're but a justice.

(II. iii)

The broad farcical atmosphere associated with the Coney-Catching
pamphlets prevails in the fast-moving episodes involving Justice
Falso's men, who are part-time highwaymen. In Act III. i good ironic
situation comedy is made from their suddenly bursting into Falso's
house, still wearing their disguises, with their pursuers at their heels
making hue and cry: Falso, not recognizing them, fears they have come
to rob *him*. They have to take off their false beards before he will be
reassured that they are his own servants, and the irony of this does not
escape them – indeed they remind him, with mild rebuke, that the
wages he pays them are so low that they have to do a few robberies to
make up: ''tis for your worship's credit to have money in our purse'.
Falso is prompted to some nostalgic reminiscences of his own youthful
exploits as a highway robber ('twas e'en venery to me, i'faith, the
pleasantest course of life') though now, as a Justice, he comforts
himself with the reflection that

a' my troth, I think I am a greater thief now, and in no danger. I
can take my ease, sit in my chair, look in your faces now, and rob
you; make you bring your money by authority, put off your hat,
and thank me for robbing of you.   (III. i)

The cool effrontery of this attitude is typical of the Middletonian villain,
yet this heavy rogue has vigorous appetites and considerable comic
attraction, even when (perhaps especially when) Falso seems set on
persuading his niece to commit incest with him. Then, indeed,
Middleton seems to be deliberately and ironically stressing the routine,
conventional nature of the niece's plight – her dead father by his will
has left her in his brother Falso's power – and the emphatically

boisterous style in which the Falso episodes are written seems designed
to complicate any stock response to the moral issues raised. Instead, we
are to savour the sharp ironic wit (as a quick London audience at Paul's
should) as when Falso is told of his brother's death and the terms of the
will:

> *Furtivo* ...made your worship his full and whole executor,
> bequeathing his daughter, and with her all his wealth, only to
> your disposition.
> *Falso* Did he make such a godly end, sayest thou? (I. vi)

Middleton often makes a sharp and neat effect by weighting a word with
ironic resonance, as he does with 'godly' here, or with the groom's
'honestly' in the dialogue quoted earlier. A more extended instance of
the sharply pointed quality of Middleton's dramatic dialogue is the
scene in which the Captain conducts the sale of his wife to the corrupt
courtier Proditor, in the presence of Phoenix and Fidelio, both disguised. Fidelio, supposedly a scrivener, reads the contract while the
Captain counts his money. The didactic point is plainly and sternly
pointed up by Phoenix in an aside:

> *Fidelio* [*reading the contract*] In and to Madonna Castiza, my most
> virtuous, modest, loving, and obedient wife —
> *Captain* By my troth, my lord, and so she is. —
> [*counting the money*] Three, four, five, six, seven.
> *Phoenix* [*aside*] The more slave he that says it, and not sees it.
> *Fidelio* Together with all and singular those admirable qualities
> with which her noble breast is furnished.
> *Captain* Well said, scrivener; hast put 'em all in? —
> You shall hear now, my lord.
> *Fidelio* In primis, the beauties of her mind, chastity, temperance,
> and, above all, patience —
> *Captain* You have bought a jewel, i'faith, my lord. —
> [*counting the money*] Nine and thirty, forty. (II. ii)

The Captain keeps up polite salesman's encouragement, as if he were
in a Cheapside shop, but he is preoccupied with counting the money
accurately and cannot concentrate on sounding convincing. In any case
his mood is complex, for though he is glad to get rid of Castiza he hates
having to kow-tow to Proditor, remarking bitterly in Act I. iii that 'We
must not be uncourteous to a lord . . . His presence is an honour: if he
lie with our wives, 'tis for our credit; we shall be the better trusted; 'tis

a sign we shall live i' th'world'. Later, after the wife sale is completed, Phoenix and Fidelio unmask and subject the Captain to violent punishment and abuse, seizing the money and giving it to Castiza, despite her readiness to be merciful. It is a true perception of Middleton's irony that the Captain remains totally indifferent to Castiza despite her attitude; if he must, he will formally beg, but only on his own hard mercenary terms, and then with barely concealed hatred, for he wishes not so much for pardon as for some of the money, promising to 'pray for you – and wish you hanged [*aside*] – as any man breathing'.

The humiliation of the Captain is confidently achieved by Phoenix and Fidelio here, but in the sequences satirizing the lawyers, deviousness proves to be its own punishment, and the climax of the discomfiture of lawyer Tangle (interminably carrying on his own suits with money gained through ill counsel to other litigants) comes in a farcical fashion as his downfall is exultantly announced by his suitors:

> *1 Suitor* A judgement, a judgement!
> *Tangle* What, what, what?
> *1 Suitor* Overthrown, overthrown, overthrown!
> *Tangle* Ha? – ah, ah! –
> *2 Suitor* News, news, news!
> *Tangle* The devil, the devil, the devil!
> *2 Suitor* Twice Tangle's overthrown, twice Tangle's overthrown!
>
> (IV, i)

There is Marstonian Comical Satyre's cruelty in this punishing reversal, for Tangle's obsessive humour, thus lanced, releases the compressed madness in a grotesque prophecy, shadowed by pain: 'May my bones revenge my quarrel! A *capias cominus?* here, here, here, here; quickly dip your quills in my blood, off with my skin'. These shadows are to lengthen and darken in *Michaelmas Term*, but here the speed of farce keeps them dancing. In the final purgation sequence in Act V there is close imitation of Jonson's *Poetaster* as Tangle is made to spew up legal jargon, assisted by the medicinal powers of Quieto (himself once driven mad by going to law, so he says):

> *Quieto* ... Now burst out,
>   Thou filthy stream of trouble, spite, and doubt!
> *Tangle* O, an extent, a proclamation, a summons, a recognisance, a
>   tachment, and injunction! a writ, a seizure, a writ of 'praisement, an absolution, a *quietus est!*

Quieto You're quieter, I hope, by so much dregs.   (V. i)

In another part of the city Middleton presents a polished sub-plot involving the knight and the citizen's wife; the dexterity of Middleton's management of an episode in this plot is characteristic of his mature excellence. The action begins with Phoenix accidentally jarring the doorbell of the jeweller's house. The maid mistakes him for the knight, lover of the jeweller's wife. Phoenix is pushed inside the house by the maid (it is dark) and he wittily adapts to the situation:

> *Phoenix* Fair room, villainous face, and worse woman! I ha' learnt something by a glimpse a' th' candle. [*aside*]   (IV. ii)

The wife now delivers a homily to Phoenix in which conventional sexual roles are reversed. Her adulterous affair is carried on as a business arrangement in which she calls her lover 'Pleasure' and the knight in return calls her 'Revenue'. She has just stolen a hundred and fifty angels from her husband to pay her lover and this she impatiently hands over to Phoenix, mistaking him for the knight as did her maid. At the same time she complains to him (evidently not for the first time) that a knight's dissolute, profligate ways are very expensive for her:

> How do you think I am able to maintain you? Though I be a jeweller's wife, jewels are like women, they rise and fall . . . What need you ride with a footman before you? . . . Why, there's Metreza Auriola keeps her love with half the cost that I am at:
>   (IV. ii)

The matter-of-fact tone of this dialogue perfectly conveys Middleton's irony. A tradesman's wife actually expects her kept lover to behave like an industrious apprentice and practice thrift, though he is plainly a typical gallant! Furthermore, he is to learn that fluctuations in trade adversely affect the balance of payments! As in *The Comedy of Errors* the immediate situation of mistaken identity makes sober commercial transactions appear absurd – they certainly sound quite absurd to Phoenix, who has a large sum of money pressed upon him, by a woman he has never seen before in his life, while at the same time he is forced to listen to a stern lecture on the virtues of thrift. The comedy is developed by the next twist of the plot, as the maid coldly repulses the real knight on his arrival a little later; he tells her to inform her mistress that 'her Pleasure's here' and she retorts with snobbish contempt: 'Her pleasure? My mistress scorns to be without her pleasure at this time of night. Is she so void of friends, think you?' (IV. iii) The cool prosaic style makes a distinctively new mood, and a variety of source materials is given unity.

So, in *The Phoenix*, Middleton's purposefully firm mode of scenic design and his skill in weaving intrigue plots is able to adapt material from Coney-Catching pamphlets and *commedia dell' arte* convention, while the survey of a range of socially representative types derives from Estates Morality convention[3] and Comical Satyre. The result is a directly and consistently exemplary comedy.

In *A Mad World My Masters* Middleton's remarkable gift for intrigue plotting is exuberantly released, and it is important to emphasize the high-spirited vigour and fast-moving caricature style of the farce, since the ground plan of the plot has a perfectly serious, if highly conventional, satiric point. The main plot concerns Follywit's schemes to get hold of his grandfather's money , while in a parallel sub-plot a gentleman schemes to seduce a citizen's wife. In the conclusion Follywit winds up (through an ironic reversal) married to his grandfather's whore, and the parallel sub-plot character, Penitent Brothel, has a terrifying encounter with a succubus and ends his relationship with the citizen's wife, Mistress Harebrain. The succubus episode provides an opportunity for somewhat gothic, melodramatic farce, as the terrified adulterer is clapped on the shoulder by the strict arrest of the succubus and thinks himself, for an instant, at Elsinore, crying out 'Shield me, you ministers of faith and grace!' The amorously impatient succubus chides him for his limp response, then begins a kind of burlesque magical invocation in rhyme, and dances round him:

> Where's thy courage, youth, and vigour!
> Love's best pleas'd when't's seiz'd with rigour;
> Seize me then with veins most cheerful,
> Women love no flesh that's fearful.   (IV. v)

Middleton could have presented the episode as full burlesque impersonation (like the Queen of Faery episode in *The Alchemist*) but he clearly felt the aesthetic balance of the farce as a whole, no less than the satiric ground-base of the action, required this sin to be cruelly punished; and possibly *The Merry Wives of Windsor* suggested the theatrical viability of this kind of ridicule of lechery.

The building up of sequences of multiple deception involving the puritanical and jealous citizen Harebrain produces dialogue with sharper and more serious ironic effect. The whore presents herself to

Harebrain as the virtuous daughter of a virtuous matron, and Harebrain, taken in, allows her to be his wife's sole companion. He compliments the whore on her mother's virtuous carriage 'in court, city, and country', and the whore coolly replies 'Sh' as always carried it well in those places, sir; – [*Aside*] witness three bastards a-piece'. This virtuous mother we have already overheard discussing business with her daughter; times being hard, she has already sold her daughter's maidenhead fifteen times to make up a dowry for her future marriage. Harebrain urges the whore to give his wife pious instruction (he himself has replaced her copy of *Venus and Adonis* with a devotional work called *Resolution*), yet when the whore tells him that his wife resists instruction, obstinately holding to the strict opinion that every sin is damned, the tradesman makes heavy weather of his half-humourous rejoinder (for he is preoccupied with that stereotype citizen's obsession, lechery and cuckoldry); what? every sin damned?

> There's a diabolical opinion indeed! then you may think that usury were damned; you're a fine merchant, i'faith! or bribery; you know the law well! or sloth; would some of the clergy heard you, i'faith; or pride; you come at court! or gluttony; you're not worthy to dine at an alderman's table! (I. ii)

Later on the whore distracts Harebrain's attention by performing, out of sight in the next room, an imaginary conversation between herself and his wife, while Mistress Harebrain is in reality committing adultery. Delighted at the pious tone of this overheard conversation, Harebrain later recommends his wife to repeat the visit, and she drily replies 'Be not so fierce, your will shall be obey'd' (III. ii). This succinct ironic dialogue expresses considerable emotional and psychological complexity – the curt and cold responses are the product of a brisk, undeceived, but also incipiently bleak view of life, and a kind of hard mirthlessness can be felt when the whore's mother remarks to Follywit, when he tells her of his plan to marry her daughter (his own grandfather's whore, did he but know it): 'I know your grandsire well; she knows him better'; or again, a moment later in this exchange:

> *Follywit* He keeps a quean at this present.
> *Mother* Fie!
> *Follywit* Do not tell my wife on't.
> *Mother* That were needless i'faith. (IV. v)

The irony of situation is the basis for the taut effects of this dialogue, perhaps Middleton's best and most original achievement in this play, and the sequences involving the whore and Mistress Harebrain are strikingly successful in their technique for expressing subtleties and acerbities through plain prose dialogue.

In the main plot Follywit's three successful and ingenious schemes to outwit Sir Bounteous his grandfather are all highly entertaining and exploit a wide range of theatrical resources, climaxing in Act V. ii with a performance of a comedy, *The Slip*, during which several valuables are borrowed (as props) from Sir Bounteous, whereupon the entire company of actors vanish. Unhappily for them they are caught by a constable and brought back, whereupon Follywit contrives to incorporate the constable into the show: each time the constable tries to explain that he has arrested the actors they improvise dialogue to sustain the illusion that he is only another actor. The Justice's chain which Follywit has stolen from Sir Bounteous gives credence to this *lazzo*, and after tying and gagging the constable, much to the amusement of Sir Bounteous, the actors vanish in earnest. The diverse strands of plot come together neatly in Act V. Thus Follywit's triumphant final theft from his grandfather while performing *The Slip* secures him an illicit wedding present, and the feast is intended to serve, without Bounteous knowing, as Follywit's wedding breakfast – likewise free. Unfortunately the stolen watch in Follywit's pocket rings its bell and the theft is discovered; Follywit's bride, the whore, remarks to her mother, *sotto voce*, 'Oh destiny! have I married a thief, mother?' then when Follywit announces his marriage he learns in his turn that the supposed gentlewoman was in fact his grandfather's whore. The exact precision of this ironic symmetry is so witty that any darker personal or moral repercussions must remain implicit.

On the largest scale in *A Mad World My Masters*, the main plot and sub-plot present an ironic equation of sex and money. Sir Bounteous, the well-bred gentleman, keeps open house, though he is too old to make love any more (according to the whore), and he denies Follywit his inheritance; whereas Harebrain is a mean skinflint city tradesman who treats his wife like a piece of property and even thinks of her being seduced in terms of somebody robbing his house, yet he himself is the unwitting agent in arranging his wife's sexual freedom and his own cuckolding.

Middleton's *Your Five Gallants* is ostentatiously conventional in conception, for its characters derive clearly from the Interlude tradition and there is some of the naive and adolescent energy of the older style in

Middleton's play. The five young protagonists are placed in a series of exemplary situations, and there are *lazzi* deriving from Italian popular comedy. The Italian air in the ingenious and fast-moving trickery is reinforced by the solid, traditional, Northern, moral preoccupations of dramatic satire. The clarity with which the components of city comedy declare themselves in this play is remarkable.

Fitzgrave has the role of Presenter, and early on (I. ii) resolves:

> cunningly I'll wind myself
> Into their bosoms. I've bethought a shape,
> Some credulous scholar, easily infected
> With fashion, time and humour . . .
>   I'll see
> Whether their lives from touch of blame sit free.

Soon, in the brothel, he offers commentary on the action:

> None that shall see their cunning will believe it.   (II. i)

He discovers that he has been robbed, and informs the audience in an aside; thus isolating himself from the other characters, he waits behind when they depart and tells us:

> My pocket pick'd? this was no brothelhouse!
> A music school? damnation has fine shapes:
> . . . I will find these secret mischiefs out.   (II. ii)

Later in Act III. iv he plots his progress for our better understanding:

> I have found three of your gallants

and by Act IV. v he is able to announce:

> The broker-gallant and the cheating-gallant:
> Now I have found 'em all.

Meanwhile he has enjoyed Pursenet's pale imitation of Falstaff lying about the Gadshill robbery and soon afterwards suffers Goldstone's foppish humour (recalling *Every Man out of His Humour*).[4] Fitzgrave administers punishment to the vices, and though the over-schematic device of the concluding masque seems laboured, the fact that the gallants are made to admit their sins and suffer correction in a ritualistic manner sufficiently recalls Jonsonian Comical Satyre. Fitzgrave's glee in his role of punisher is notable:

'Twas I fram'd your device, do you see? 'twas I:
The whole assembly has took notice of it.
That you are a gallant cheater,
So much the pawning of my cloak contains; [*to Goldstone*]
You a base thief, think of Coombe Park; [*to Pursenet*]...

(V. ii)

The satiric aims of Middleton are more sharply and seriously realized
here than in *A Mad World My Masters*. There are several confessions
made by characters which give the flavour of moral tract familiar from
Coney-Catching pamphlets. Primero the bawd gallant confesses
proudly that

Many over-cheated gulls have fatted
Me with the bottom of their patrimonies,
E'en to the last sop, gaped while I fed 'em,
Who now live by that art that first undid 'em.   (I. i)

More elaborately and memorably Pursenet the pocket gallant reflects
on the ironically regular, orderly, commercial-style pattern of criminal
civil war:

Does my boy pick and I steal to enrich myself, to keep her, to maintain him? why, this is the right sequence of the world. A lord
maintains her, she maintains a knight, he maintains a whore, she
maintains a captain. So in like manner the pocket keeps my boy,
he keeps me, I keep her, she keeps him; it runs like quicksilver
from one to another.   (III. ii)

A chain of pearl, too, runs like quicksilver from one to another. It
appears in successive trickery sequences, acting as a kind of *leitmotiv*.
Its recurrence suggests to the audience the underlying repetitive,
mechanical nature of seemingly varied criminal schemes.

One remarkable and influential convention in city comedy shaped by
Middleton is the lyrical outburst of the villain of the piece, full of
eloquent high-spirited vitality yet presented with implicit irony. In the
present play the broker gallant rhapsodizes:

Here's a diamond that sometimes graced the finger of a
countess; here sits a ruby that ne'er lins blushing for the party
that pawned it; here a sapphire. O providence and fortune!

(I. i)

This recalls Falso in *The Phoenix*:

> I have been a youth myself: I ha' seen the day I could have told money out of other men's purses, – mass, so I can do now, – ... I remember now betimes in a morning, I would have peeped through the green boughs, and have had the party presently, and then to ride away finely in fear: twas e'en venery to me, i'faith, the pleasantest course of life!   (III. i)

and looks forward to Quomodo's vision of his ill-gotten gains in *Michaelmas Term*:

> O that sweet, neat, comely, proper, delicate parcel of land! like a fine gentlewoman i' th' waist, not so great as pretty, pretty; the trees in summer whistling, the silver waters by the banks harmoniously gliding... Thus we that seldom get lands honestly, must leave our heirs to inherit our knavery: (II. iii)

and beyond that to Old Hoard in *A Trick to Catch the Old One*:

> What a sweet blessing hast thou, master Hoard, above a multitude! wilt thou never be thankful? ... not only a wife large in possessions, but spacious in content; she's rich, she's young, she's fair, she's wise: (IV. iv)

Middleton has no actual sympathy for these characters: they are objectively represented, hard, vigorous, intelligent, farcical yet grim. Materialists fascinated Middleton, and his persistent satire of them often involves serious ambivalence, as in *A Chaste Maid in Cheapside*. If the ironic designs of his plots have been seen by some critics as Calvinistic in the determined purpose with which they show vice to be ultimately its own punishment, nevertheless it is precisely in the judgement scenes that we often find Middleton's ambivalent attitude most disconcerting, for orthodox righteousness seems to take little account of the actual texture of experience as the main body of the dramatic action has exhibited it. Fixed formulae of the law or conventional morality seem less and less acceptable even when made to coincide with the artistic conventions of comic form. In many of the great comedies of the age, by dramatists of widely differing style, moral and legal orthodoxy is seriously challenged. Towards the end of the seventeenth century Molière's *Dom Juan* was recognized (rightly) by the orthodox as an offensively ironic work, yet in 1518 Machiavelli's *Mandragola* showed a young man scheming to seduce a virtuous young wife by manipulating a number of people, including her own mother and her holy confessor, who finally overwhelm her resistance. The wife finds that the only remaining certainty she has to go on is the evidence of her senses. Her lover gives her pleasure, which at least is something positive and new, and so she works out a formula – is it sublimely pious? profoundly cynical? admirably, boldly honest? – which seems to answer to the truth of her experience. She tells her lover:[5]

> Since your guile, my husband's folly, the simple-mindedness of my mother, and the wickedness of my father-confessor have led me to do what I should never have done of my own free will, I must judge it to be Heaven that willed it so, and I cannot find it in myself to refuse what Heaven wishes me to accept.

And so the play simply ends, and everyone lives happily ever after. The riddling quality of this conclusion is enriched by the excitingly free play of the dramatist's intelligence, and his nerve in sustaining a matter-of-fact tone in his insistently anarchic treatment of conventional taboos.

In *The Dutch Courtezan* Marston is careful to stress his interest in ironic inspection of orthodoxy and convention, and he takes much trouble to gather a thoroughly conventional set of city comedy characters and a double plot reminiscent of Middletonian comedy and of *Measure for Measure*. Its chief features are the exposure and correction of ill humours in a gallant, Malheureux, and a Puritan tradesman, Mulligrub the vintner. Both of these characters are brought through complex intrigues to the very point of execution, when at last conversion overtakes them; their physicians, themselves perhaps purged by the gratuitous cruelty they have shown to their victims, impose a rigidly festive interpretation on the events, and while the shock of the double revelation still reverberates the comedy ends.

From the opening moments of the play Marston's characters discourse freely and at length about their attitudes to trade, law, the city, domestic life, sex, marriage, property, and the human body itself; indeed the discussions about prostitution in the first two scenes present it for our attention as inseparable from the idea of city life, since it graphically associates capitalist exploitation with disease, hypocrisy, degradation and crime on the one hand, and with amusement, easy profits, and frank instinctive imperatives on the other. There is insistence, in these discussions about prostitution, that business is

business, life in London is hard, that a puritanical obsession with sexual
vice only helps obscure the equally harsh facts of other kinds of trade;
Cockledemoy is not merely sophistical when he says[6]

> no trade or vocation profiteth, but by the losse and displeasure of
> another, as the Marchant thrives not but by the licentiousnes of
> giddie, and unsetled youth: the Lawyer, but by the vexation of
> his client, the Phisition, but by the maladies of his patient, onely
> my smoothe gumbde Bawd lives by others pleasure, and onely
> growes rich by others rising. O mercifull gaine, O righteous in-
> come.
>
> (I. ii. 41-7)

Freevill is broadminded if callous. He points out that survival must
come first:

> A poore decayed mechanicall mans wife, her husband is layd up,
> may not she lawfully be layd downe, when her husbands onely
> rising, is by his wifes falling? A Captaines wife wants meanes,
> her Commander lyes in open field abroad, may not she lye in
> civile armes at home? A waighting Gentlewoman that had wont
> to take say to her Lady, miscaries, or so: the Court misfortune
> throwes her downe, may not the Citie curtesie take her up? Doe
> you know no Alderman would pitie such a womans case?
>
> (I. i. 102-10)

This ironic view of prostitution as a model for all forms of city
enterprise is developed in the sub-plot's depiction of the city vintner's
wife, conniving at her husband's dishonest business and hypocritical,
like him, in her use of Puritan jargon while being a snob, sexually loose,
and, if someone else is paying, a glutton; Marston makes her much less
sympathetic than Shakespeare's Mistress Quickly, though she would
be quite at home in a Middleton comedy or as a neighbour to the goldsmith's wife in *Eastward Ho*. Here she takes delivery of a goblet from
Lionel:

> ile remember your master an honest man, he knew me before I
> was maryed, an honest man hee is, and a crafty, hee comes
> forward in the world well, I warrant him, and his wife is a proper
> woman that she is, well, she has ben as proper a woman as any in
> Cheape, she paints now, and yet she keeps her husbands old
> Customers to him still. Introth a fine fac'd wife, in a wainscot

carved seat, is a worthy ornament to a Tradesman shop, and an
atractive I warrant, her husband shall finde it in the custome of
his ware, Ile assure him, God bee with you good youth, I
acknowledge the receit. *Exit Lionell*. I acknowledge all the receit
sure, tis very well spoken, I acknowledge the receit, thus tis to
have good education and to bee brought up in a Taverne. I doe
keepe as gallant and as good companie, though I say it, as any she
in *London*, Squiers, Gentlemen, and Knightes diet at my table,
and I doe lend some of them money and full many fine men goe
upon my score, . . . nay, though my husband be a Citizen and's
caps made of wooll, yet I ha wit, and can see my good assoone as
another, for I have all the thankes. My silly husband, alasse, hee
knowes nothing of it, tis I that beare, tis I that must beare a braine
for all.   (III. iii. 4-19, 22-6)

The range of characters is designed to present a wide spectrum of
attitudes, for against Mistress Mulligrub we can set, for comparison,
the sweet idealized piety of Freevill's betrothed, Beatrice, the intensely
possessive and cruel Dutch courtesan Franceschina, and the bright,
disconcertingly candid young Crispinella, who objects to the custom
that obliges her to be kissed by gentlemen as a mark of gentle manners,
however physically repulsive the gentlemen may be – 'though his un-
cleane goose turd greene teeth ha the palsy' – and whose realistic assertion that marriage is often without virtue, as virtue is more often
without marriage, is consistent with her determination to speak what
she thinks in honest freeness, so making it 'her necessity to thinke
what is good' (III. i. 38-9).

Precisely the opposite condition afflicts the young gallant
Malheureux, who at first dogmatically condemns prostitution. This he
does with such unprovoked intensity that we must recognize him to be
unhealthily, unstably immature, like Angelo in *Measure for Measure*.
His friend Freevill's interest in sexual matters is not entirely straightforward, either; he covertly mocks Malheureux for the anxious pressure of his puritanism, tempting him with the offer of Franceschina's
favours: 'dost thou not somewhat excuse my sometimes incontinency
with her enforcive beauties? Speake.' Later, the anguished Malheureux finds that Franceschina will only accept him as a lover if he murders
Freevill, and after some tortured indecision Malheureux brings himself
to confess this to his friend. Freevill, with an apparently equal demonstration of friendship, devises a scheme whereby Malheureux can enjoy

Franceschina: Freevill is to make himself scarce so that Malheureux can plausibly claim to have murdered him. If Malheureux should be in danger of suffering for the crime, a rendezvous is arranged so that Freevill can reappear to disprove the allegation. Yet in fact Freevill intends to terrify Malheureux out of his obsession with the whore. He avoids the rendezvous and follows events – including Franceschina's vindictive exultation at his own supposed death – by adopting a disguise. Freevill's feigned death and his disguised observation of reactions to it is a plot motif which recurs in *Volpone* and *Michaelmas Term*, and here in *The Dutch Courtezan* it is connected also with *Measure for Measure* in that Freevill's character, relationships and motives uneasily combine aspects of the roles of both Lucio and the Duke – Lucio's morally equivocal wit, his sexual licence, his treachery and sadism, and the Duke's devious and intricate machinations to effect moral and spiritual homeopathic cures. Freevill seems content to accept that, as he puts it, 'No love's without some lust'; as for his motives in prosecuting the feigned-death plot, he dismisses doubt in these terms:

> But is this vertue in me? No, not pure,
> Nothing extreamly best with us endures,
> No use in simple purities, the elementes
> Are mixt for use   (IV. ii. 41-4)

and asserts that, simply, the end justifies the means.

Yet involved in those means is Franceschina, who loves Freevill, even though her passions are ungovernable. To Freevill it is enough that she is a prostitute, and foreign; how ludicrous for her to suppose that human feelings, rather than commercial relations, could ever connect her to him! He dismisses her claim to be treated as a woman, indeed he does not even bother to tell her that he is getting married, merely noting with amusement in Act II. i that Franceschina must by now have heard about that and 'no question sweares, Gods Sacrament, ten Towsand Divells'. In fact Marston stresses that Franceschina's sufferings are painful, though she remains grotesque in speech and continues as the focus of uneasy melodrama rather than seriously sustained experience. Freevill's culpability in callously manipulating her is explicit, yet her vicious contempt for Beatrice, whom she mocks for grieving at Freevill's reported death, prevents us from fully sympathizing with Franceschina either. Finally, Marston seems to be deliberately inviting us to remember the Duke in *Measure for Measure* when we are shown Freevill, in disguise, observing and overhearing wicked schemes so that he may frustrate them in a suitably sensational *coup de théâtre* by unmasking himself the moment before Malheureux is executed. Yet Marston makes no effort to press the allegorical possibilities of the role, leaving the Freevill-Malheureux plot singularly secular — a problem comedy in which moral pragmatism and a sceptical irony prevail, as if the prosaic realities of modern London life, and the endemic frustrations it imposes on the public and private self, must gravely qualify the affirmative possibilities of tragi-comedy, leaving it disturbingly close to farce. In *Volpone* and *Michaelmas Term* the prevailing mode is cruel farce, utilizing a tightly designed plot, a fast-paced action and sardonic style; the dialogue persistently succeeds in the uncommon mode of black comedy. Volpone's Venice, like Barabas's Malta and Quomodo's London (in *Michaelmas Term*) is a society devoted to commerce, mercantile capitalism, and ruthlessly unprincipled competition. Nothing is grown in this version of a society exclusively devoted to trade and composed of warehouses, vaults and granaries, docks, banks, merchants' palaces, prisons, and, now and then, a church. The self-governing political system of Renaissance Venice furnished an apt and ironic analogy to the mercantile government of the city of London, with its guilds, companies, lord mayor and officials, so that as well as displaying his cosmopolitanism Jonson is making pointed satire (like Marlowe's) on the English when he emphasizes so carefully the exact location of *Volpone* in Venice.[7] In *Michaelmas Term*, on the other hand, Middleton is explicit about the immediately contemporary image of London presented in the play, and makes no bones about the significance of the Morality pattern imposed on the action.

In his villainous merchant Quomodo he presents the commercial Machiavel, conventional to city comedy, whom we have met before in Marlowe's merchant of Malta, Barabas:

> give me the man
> Who out of recreation culls advantage,
> Dives into seasons, never walks but thinks,
> Ne rides but plots: (I. ii)

while in *Volpone* Mosca delivers the most memorable hubristic soliloquy in city comedy about the skill of the trickster and the joys of witty duplicity:

> But your fine, elegant rascall, that can rise,

And stoope (almost together) like an arrow;
Shoot through the aire, as nimbly as a starre;
Turne short, as doth a swallow; and be here,
And there, and here, and yonder, all at once;
Present to any humour, all occasion;
And change a visor, swifter, then a thought!
This is the creature, had the art borne with him;

(III. i. 23-30)

There is much opportunity for discursive critical comment on current manifestations of social disorder and conspicuous consumption; the traditional topics of non-dramatic satire and complaint are given fresh eloquent expression, as when a one-time prodigal in *Michaelmas Term* contemplates London anew:

Woe worth th'infected cause that makes me visit
This man-devouring city! where I spent
My unshapen youth, to be my ages curse,
And surfeited away my name and state
In swinish riots, (II. ii)

and in *Volpone* villain and servant share, in private, the joke of parodying moral concern; their taste, we are to learn, is for refining on their pleasures, going only for the finest 'sting':

Volpone   I turne no moneys, in the publike banke;
    Nor vsure private—
Mosca   No, sir, nor deuoure
    Soft prodigalls. You shall ha' some will swallow
    A melting heire, as glibly, as your *Dutch*
    Will pills of butter, and ne're purge for't;
    Teare forth the fathers of poore families
    Out of their beds, and coffin them, aliue,
    In some kind, clasping prison, (I. i. 39-46)

In *Volpone* the plot is so conceived that Volpone and Mosca can torment their victims with elaborate and exquisitely wrought devices. The early sequence in which Corbaccio visits Volpone is full of admirably sharp ironies; Mosca persuades him he is Volpone's heir, and that Volpone is mortally sick at last:

Mosca   A freezing numnesse stiffens all his ioynts,
    And makes the colour of his flesh like lead.
Corbaccio 'Tis good. (I. iv. 43-4)

This black comedy is doubled by the fact that the audience knows that Volpone is fully awake and listening to Corbaccio, that he is delighting in Mosca's device, while there is metaphoric truth in Mosca's grotesque portrait of his master. The ambiguity of Mosca's motives in viciously ridiculing his patron emerge in the next sequence with Corvino when, unsuspicious of Mosca, Volpone comments on the Corbaccio *exemplum*, himself returning the savage ridicule:

> *Volpone*   Nay, here was one,
> Is now gone home, that wishes to liue longer!
> Feeles not his gout, nor palsie, faines himselfe
> Yonger, by scores of yeeres, flatters his age,
> With confident belying it,   (I. iv. 151-5)

In the next sequence Mosca encourages Corvino to express all the hate in his bowels, and both yell insults at the supposedly deaf and dying Volpone:

> *Mosca*   Those filthy eyes of yours, that flow with slime,
> Like two frog-pits; and those same hanging cheeks,
> Couer'd with hide, in stead of skin: (nay, helpe, sir)
> That looke like frozen dish-clouts, set on end.
> *Corvino*   Or, like an old smok'd wall, on which the raine
> Ran downe in streakes.
> *Mosca*   Excellent, sir, speake out;
>   (I. v. 57-62)

Volpone compliments Mosca, on Corvino's exit, tells him:

> Thou hast today out-gone thy selfe.

Looking over the gold and jewellery he has been brought, and recalling the deceptions practiced by Mosca, he declares:

> Why, this is better then rob churches, yet;
> Or fat, by eating (once a mon'th) a man.   (I. v. 91-2)

Jonson presents a sub-plot in a lighter comic vein involving a fatuous, gossipy couple, Sir Politique and Lady Would-Be: Sir Politique has, he says, not come abroad to pursue

> That idle, antique, stale, grey-headed proiect
> Of knowing mens minds, and manners, with VLYSSES:
>   (II. i. 9-10)

Instead his mind is full of catalogues of absurd, trivial or obstinately perverse distortions of ideas from politics, scientific experiment, capital investment in industry, astrology, portents. He has heard that a professional clown was a spy and received intelligence

> (For all parts of the world) in cabages;
> And those dispens'd, againe, to' Ambassadors,
> In oranges, musk melons   (II. i. 70-2)

and the demonstration of his fatuously trivial mind is clear and harsh; here Peregrine reads from Politique's diary:

> I went, and bought two tooth-pickes, whereof one
> I burst, immediatly, in a discourse
> With a *dutch* merchant, 'bout *ragion del stato* ...
> I cheapen'd sprats: and at *St MARKES*, I vrin'd.
> 'Faith, these are politique notes!   (IV. i. 139-41, 144-5)

In the Would-Bes we recognize two potentially ideal tormentors for Morose in Jonson's *Epicoene*, not to be written for another six years. Volpone's suffering of Lady Would-Be's chatter has a Horatian satiric precedent and offers the welcome spectacle of Volpone bested; Sir Pol's humiliation under his politic tortoise-shell is good Comical Satyre and a rumbustious Aristophanic piece of stage business.

Yet when Volpone moves in for the seduction of Celia, the deep centre of the play's imaginative power is made apparent. The increasingly offensive, voyeuristic perversity of Volpone's temptations provoke Celia to increasingly chill, prudish over-reaction; and Volpone depraves and corrupts our response as an audience, for we enjoy his extravagant attack on Celia and find ourselves applauding, urging him on to more and more daring and sadistically shocking extremes. We become enlisted with Mosca as fascinated commenders of his audacity, which gives Volpone so much sadistic pleasure that the seduction of Celia ceases to be of paramount importance; it is the contemplation of his own fantastic imaginings which absorbs his erotic energies. The comic drive itself becomes inverted as the play becomes a festive exhibition of the energies of death.

In the trial scene in *Volpone* the decisive argument is based on contriving a situation where the flat truth has the effect of a lie. Volpone, feigning sickness, is brought in on a couch to the court; Voltore presents him to the court wholly accurately and truthfully, and he is acquitted:

> See here, graue fathers, here's the rauisher,
> The rider on mens wiues, the great impostor,
> The grand voluptuary! do you not think,
> These limbes should affect *venery?* . . .
> Perhaps, he doth dissemble?   (IV. vi. 23-6, 29)

The intelligence and the intensity of savagery in Volpone sufficiently dominate the play to necessitate an error of judgement by Mosca to bring about his fall. Mosca does not realize that rather than be outwitted and ridiculed, Volpone by nature would prefer to destroy everything he can, along with himself; for he has what Hobbes defined as 'a perpetual and restless desire for power after power that ceaseth only in death'. The suspicion that Volpone is unlucky to fall is not without justification.

Michaelmas Term, though like *Volpone* having a powerful villain who is the Presenter and sardonic commentator on some of the main episodes, works more through implication than Jonson's play; though it seems clear that Quomodo's creation owes something to Volpone. The darker, violent atmosphere of London in *Michaelmas Term* seems also to derive from the impact made on Middleton by *Volpone*, yet it is an individual creation. Middleton's usurer has common blood with Volpone, but he lacks his fantastic imagination and his intelligence; he lacks, too, a parasite with the sublime art of Mosca.

   Michaelmas Term has for a main plot an exemplary prodigal fable. The young innocent abroad is conventional and Middleton clearly indicates the kind of play we can expect in the opening scene, when the conventional situation itself is perfunctorily sketched and it is the urgent activity in the language, the compression of statement, which urges us that the play will be alive. Soon enough Quomodo appears, with his two parasites; his vitality and his greed surge in the dialogue, full of active verbs:

> *Quomodo* . . . I have seen what I desire.
> *Shortyard* A woman?
> *Quomodo* Pooh, a woman! yet beneath her,
>   That which she often treads on, yet commands her;
>   Land, fair neat land.
> *Shortyard* What is the mark you shoot at?
> *Quomodo* Why, the fairest to cleave the heir in twain,
>   I mean his title; to murder his estate,

Stifle his right in some detested prison:
There are means and ways enow to hook in gentry,
Besides our deadly enmity, which thus stands,
They're busy 'bout our wives, we 'bout their lands.   (I. i)

A moment later Quomodo scents his prey (the animal imagery of
Volpone is discreetly acknowledged in these Middletonian metaphors
of hunting and fishing):

I have inquired his haunt—stay,—hah!
ay that 'tis, that's he, that's he!...
Observe, take surely note of him . . . Keep foot by foot with him,
out-dare his expenses, flatter, dice and brothel to him . . . drink
drunk with him, creep into bed to him, kiss him, and undo him,
my sweet spirit.   (I. i)

Quomodo has recognized Easy among other gallants chatting, in this
opening scene, in the middle aisle of Paul's. The play has other
sequences of typical city life, with gallants gambling and courting
prostitutes. Easy, the landowning prodigal, is matched against Lethe,
cynically dedicated to rising at Court and to making a financial killing
by marriage. Lethe's christian name, Andrew, his suppressed real
surname, Gruel, and his enquiry of the other gallants 'Are you not
knights yet?' are the basis of the plausible conjecture that he is
intended as a caricature of a typical Scotsman on the make in King
James's new monarchy. Lethe is appalled to recognize his own mother
approaching him, for he had thought her safely at home: 'Does she
come up to shame me, to betray my birth, and cast soil on my new
suit?' His mother however does not recognize him, taking him in his
smart clothes for a gentleman and therefore no son of hers. Middleton
makes a hard Hogarthian point about Lethe's heartless ambition; he
does not reveal his identity to his mother, but accepts her as a servant:

Mother   I'll wait upon your worship.
Lethe   Two pole off at least.
Mother   I am a clean old woman an't like your worship.
Lethe   It goes not by cleanness here good woman; if you were fouler,
so you were braver, you might come nearer.   (I. i)

Yet there is a final chilling twist; the mother too has her social and
sexual ambition: 'there's no woman so old but she may learn, and as an
old lady delights in a young page or monkey, so there are young

courtiers will be hungry upon an old woman.' (I. i) The *exemplum* is juxtaposed to one involving a Country Wench, a familiar stereotype of innocence who, likewise, is easily persuaded by Hellgill's seductive rehetoric:

> *Hellgill* thou art fair and fresh;
> the gilded flies will light upon thy flesh. (I. ii)

The art of Middleton in this play is at its best in the sequences where Quomodo and his assistants weave their web about Easy. Here the urbanity, the teamwork and polished technique by which Easy is persuaded into borrowing from Quomodo bring the play into the plane of high comedy; Quomodo, affecting ignorance of Easy's identity, and Shortyard (his assistant) the reassuring friend to Easy, admirably cast the net:

> *Shortyard* Must the second party, that enters into bond only for
> fashion's sake, needs be a citizen? what say you to this
> gentleman for one? [*pointing to EASY*]
> *Quomodo* Alas, sir! you know he's a mere stranger to me: . . . he
> may inn here to-night, and ride away tomorrow: . . .
> *Easy* I hope you will not disparage me so: 'tis well known I have
> three hundred pound a-year in Essex . . .
> *Quomodo* Well, master Blastfield, because I will not disgrace the
> gentleman, I'm content (II. iii)

Middleton here brilliantly breaks the mood for a moment, giving a sudden insight into the strain under which the deceivers are working:

> *Easy* No sir, now you would, you shall not.
> *Quomodo* Cuds me, I'm undone! he's gone again. [*aside*]
> *Shortyard* The net's broke. (II. iii)

But the second episode is successful, these schemers are full of inventiveness, they recover straight away, and Easy is won over by the invitation to ridicule Quomodo – an opportunity which his parasites, like Mosca, take delightedly. Here the mock ridicule is, however, a prelude to the real ridiculing of Quomodo in Act V, for Middleton takes more revenge on his villain than did Jonson on Volpone:

> *Shortyard* Master Easy, mark my words: if it stood not upon the
> eternal loss of thy credit against supper —
> *Easy* Mass, that's true.

Shortyard The pawning of thy horse for his own victuals —
Easy Right, i'faith.
Shortyard And thy utter dissolution amongst gentlemen for ever —
Easy Pox on't!
Shortyard Quomodo should hang, rot, stink —
Quomodo Sweet boy, i'faith! [*aside*]
Shortyard Drop, damn.
Quomodo Excellent Shortyard! [*aside*]
Easy I forgot all this . . . How does master Quomodo? is the bond
     ready?   (II. iii)

Here the style is Middleton's, though the inspiration seems clearly to
have been *Volpone*. Indeed, the final trick by which Quomodo is
outwitted, the signed document cancelling Easy's debts, is used in
precisely the same way as Volpone's signed will giving all to Mosca.
And so, in the end, Everyman successfully evades the snares of the
devil, though it is the devil who has vigour, intelligence, awareness, a
lustful enjoyment in his gains and the manipulation of circumstances,
in accordance with Nick Machiavel's methods; for Quomodo, like
Volpone, like Barabas, as Machiavel notes,[8]

     smiles to see how full his bags are cramb'd;
  Which mony was not got without my meanes.

VII

CONVENTIONAL PLAYS
1604–7

> In the study of art no less than in the study of man, the mysteries of success are frequently best revealed through an investigation of failures. Only a pathology of representation will give us some insight into mechanisms which enabled the masters to handle this instrument with such assurance.
> (E. H. GOMBRICH)

The form and style of the genre attains a certain maturity between 1604 and 1606, as we have seen in the discussion of *The Dutch Courtezan*, *Volpone* and *Michaelmas Term*. It is a sign of the growing maturity, and also of the popular success of the plays, that in these years a number of lesser repertory playwrights and 'dressers of plays' produced hurried imitations and adaptations of the new genre, working with their cruder methods of conventional play-making. These playwrights made no innovations, they adapted the most striking and novel elements in the work of talented writers but did not generate fresh life: their imitation was that of 'a Creature, that swallowes, what it takes in, crude, raw, or indigested'.[1] Yet the fact that such writers were attracted to the genre at all suggests that it might not have been as unpopular and financially unrewarding as Professor Harbage claimed in *Shakespeare and the Rival Traditions*.[2]

In this chapter I shall be concerned with a selection of conventional plays which sought to please the audience for city comedy in the Coterie theatres. In these plays it is notable that weakness is due to the playwright's failure to understand that satire is dialectical: it always presents the audience with an argument. Too often these conventional plays offer a simple comedy of love or deception, and flavour this form, not that of the genre, with city comedy features. Yet to examine such

plays shows how a conventional playwright went to work in writing for
the genre's enthusiasts, what elements he though it best to emphasize,
what struck him as typical. It should be easy to gauge the influence of
the three major dramatists on their imitators, and to show which
conventions were vital.

The collaboration of Dekker and Webster in 1604, which produced
Westward Ho and its successor *Northward Ho*, directly provoked the
three parodists who based the main action of *Eastward Ho* on the
farcical river journey by London types. *Westward Ho* and *Northward
Ho*³ were perhaps understandably provoking to Jonson, whose sharply
visualized epigrammatic descriptions and satiric set pieces on absurd
'humorous' characters are faithfully reproduced as soon as the play has
begun in order to reassure the audience that it is the real thing, true city
comedy. Here in *Westward Ho* Justiniano presents us with a cuckold
in a manner reminiscent of Jonson's Musco:

> His cloak shrouding his face, as if he were a Neopolitan that had
> lost his beard in Aprill, and if he walk through the street, or any
> other narrow road (as tis rare to meete a Cuckold) hee duckes at
> the penthouses, like an Antient that dares not flourish at the
> oath taking of the *Pretor*, for feare of the signe-posts?
>
> (I. i. 156-61)

Unfortunately, Dekker's intelligence does not manifest itself and give
point and meaning to the scene described: there is *no* satiric point, in fact.

It might be illuminating to begin with a short consideration of plot
and articulation in the two plays. In *Westward Ho* Justiniano believes
himself cuckolded and determines to watch his friends being deceived
in like manner; there is a superficial similarity to the disguised-duke
plot, and Justiniano seems at first likely to be the play's Presenter and
Vice in one:

> I resolve to take some shape upon me, and to live disguised heere
> in the Citty; they say for one Cuckolde to knowe that his friend is
> in the like head-ake, and to give him counsell, is as if there were
> two partners ... Have amongst you Citty dames? You that are
> indeede the fittest, and most proper persons for a Comedy,
>
> (I. i. 220-3, 225-6)

In fact, however, Justiniano is only occasionally a detached commentator, and then his comments are brief and perfunctory, and

designed to get a laugh at all costs; so he persuades the wives to take a
boat from Blackfriars, and remarks: 'O the quick apprehension of
women, the'ile groape out a mans meaning presently'(III. iii. 95-6).
When trying to persuade the wives to meet some young men at a wine
house, he urges them on:

> why, even now, at holding up of this finger, and before the
> turning downe of this, some are murdring, some lying with their
> maides, some picking of pockets, some cutting purses, . . . some
> wives are Cuckolding some Husbands.   (II. i. 186-90)

Justiniano does contrive trickery episodes, but they are not *exempla*
and they develop a straightforward 'story' which is not organized to
make a strong didactic point. The play moves forward in a literal-
minded style. In one scene we see Justiniano persuading the wives to go
to a wine house. In a subsequent scene they arrive there, and decide to
go somewhere else. The play ends, in fact, when all the characters
arrive at the same place together for the first time.

Here too the Popular affiliation of the dramatists with the self-
indulgent taste of the citizenry is apparent. The wives who have readily
agreed to meet the gallants at Brentford lock the door and keep them
out when they actually get there, for citizen virtue, as in *The Merry
Wives of Windsor*, is proof against corruption, though the hot jealousy
of the citizen husbands is doused in ridicule as they arrive to catch their
wives out, and they in turn are ridiculed with evidence of their own
visits to prostitutes.[4] Here there is no parallel with *The Merry Wives*,
but, disappointingly, the satiric criticism of petty hypocrisy and
vulgarity is superficial and the play's deeper dynamic expresses a
coarse, complacent and complaisant air of communal self-congratulation.

The play has a straightforward Popular comic action – a strong
emphasis on what happens. Soliloquy is used to inform the audience of
a character's proposed line of action:

> Wel my husband is gon to arrest *Monopoly*. I have dealt with a
> Sargeant privatly, to intreate him, pretending that he is my
> Aunts Son, by this meanes shal I see my young gallant that in
> this has plaid his part.   (III. i. 38-41)

It is candidly utilitarian in spirit, however difficult to follow. There are
two sequences in rather poor blank verse dealing with an attempt at
seduction and an exposure and correction of this sinfulness. The

Popular sensationalism is evident in the use of the corpse which only seems dead and rises once the reversal is effected. It seems as though the playwrights felt that a play wholly in prose, with no lofty main plot upholding the high style of love comedy, was too great a departure for them; hence the somewhat weak rhetoric of the penitent villain, vowing platonic love:

> Mine owne shame strikes me dumb: henceforth the booke
> Ile read shall be thy mind, and not thy looke.   (IV. ii. 165-6)

Justiniano rounds the play off in a mood of cheerful inconsequence: 'all is but a merriment, all but a May-game' (V. iv. 278).

Northward Ho similarly has an action involving a journey from London for the purpose of seduction and adultery, and there is a formal blank verse episode in which the virtuous wife rejects the suit of a corrupt lecher in Popular romantic comedy style. Once again the merchant who suspects himself of being a cuckold – his name here is Maybery – contrives various trickery episodes to gull those who would deceive him, and once again the method of articulation, like the plot, is Popular in its concern with mere mechanical causation:

> *Maybery* . . . hee railes upon her, wills me to take her in the Act . . . hee's pulling on his bootes, and will ride along with us; lets muster as many as wee can.
>
> *Bellamont* It wilbe excellent sport, to see him and his owne wife meete in *Ware*, wilt not?   (IV. i. 268-74)

The play is superior to its predecessor in its symmetry of design, the surer control and the ingenuity of the *lazzi* and the firmer direction of dialogue. There is a notable superiority in the opening scene of *Northward Ho*. Here is no longwinded elaboration of motive and situation; instead two men are, as it were, interrupted in the middle of a conversation and what we need to know is conveyed in implication. The action is directly under way, and soon the two set to work arousing the suspicions of Maybery about his wife. The curt suddenness of the exchange seems strikingly life-like:

> *Greenshield* In the passage of our loves . . . she bestowed upon me this ringe which she protested was her husbands gift.
>
> *Maybery* The poesie, the poesie – O my heart, that ring good infaith?
>
> *Greenshield* Not many nights comming to her and being familiar with her –

Maybery Kissing and so forth.
Greenshield I sir.
Maybery And talking to her feelingly.
Greenshield Pox on't, I lay with her.
Maybery Good infaith, you are of a good complexion.
Greenshield Lying with her as I say: and rising some-what early
     from her in the morning, I lost this ring in her bed.
Maybery In my wives bed.   (I. i. 88-103)

The weight of this is carried by implication, a fact acknowledged by the
two men who note that Maybery has given no outward sign of emotion,
and so resolve to 'with-draw, and give him leave to rave a little'. This
economy of effect, this sureness and control reminiscent of Middleton,
is to be observed when Doll wrings fifty pounds out of Allom by
pretence at passionate anger:

Doll Oh I shal burst, if I cut not my lace: I'me so vext! my father
     hee's ridde to Court one way . . . one of his men (like a roague as
     he is) is rid another . . . and here was a scrivener but even now . . .
Allum How much is the bond?
Chartley O rare little villaine.
Doll My father could take up, upon the barenesse of his word five
     hundred pound . . .
Allum What is the debt?
Doll But hee scornes to bee — and I scorne to bee —
Allum Pree thee sweete Mistris *Dorothy* vex not, how much is it?
                         (II. i. 135-7, 140, 143-9)

Similarly direct and purposeful is the scene where Maybery tests out
Greenshield's story (II. ii. 35-58) and the gulling of Greenshield in
Act III. ii has the firmly shaped form of an *exemplum*. These scattered
signs of the influence of Middleton relate the play directly to his early
comedy, but the play remains largely similar to *Westward Ho* in its
simple causal plot and articulation derived largely from the journeying
of the characters from one street to another. Both plays articulate
complex plots and the audience is directed simply to the intrigue and
the cleverness with which it is worked out, though of course neither
play has an intrigue of sufficient intelligence or witty design to reward
the audience's closest attention.

    The conventional playwright tends to *flavour* his plot with the
genre's style of dialogue, references, and settings; these he regards as

the plainest distinctive elements of the genre. John Day's Induction to
The Isle of Gulls clearly sets out this approach:[5]

> ist any thing Criticall? Are Lawyers fees, and Cittizens wives laid
> open in it: I love to heare vice anotomised, & abuse let blood in
> the maister vaine, is there any great mans life characterd
> int? . . . and there be not Wormewood water and Copperes int, Ile
> not like it.

In *Northward Ho* and *Westward Ho*, heeding the demands of this
imaginary city comedy spectator, the playwrights have flavoured their
plot with satiric set pieces, with many metaphors and similes drawn
from stock themes of the satirists; there are typical London types
presented as, of course, scurrilous and prone to thieving, deception and
adultery. Great attention is paid at the *beginning* of the play to catching
the style of bitter, Marstonian satiric prose, to the emphasis on the city
and the fact that the characters are citizens, and to the detailed setting of
the scenes in specific streets and taverns of London as in the Coney-
Catching pamphlets. It is indicative that so little of the method of satiric
comedy is understood by Dekker and Webster that their trickery
episodes suggest imitation of Jest Books. Setting Coney-Catching
episodes in specific parts of London was similarly intended to give
sensational interest to otherwise very commonplace material. Both in
the insistence on the 'city' setting and on the geography of London we
may see a similar purpose to that of the pamphleteers.

Hence, in *Westward Ho*, there is an insistent use of the prefix 'city':
we find 'Citizens wives', 'City Mercers and goldsmiths', 'City bawds',
'a good Citty wit', 'high wit from the City', 'O the pollicy of women,
and Tradesmen', 'Jealousie hath undone many a Cittizen', 'Citty
dames . . . proper persons for a comedy', 'you have few Cittizens speake
well of their wives behind their backs'. In *Northward Ho* similarly 'our
young sonnes and heires in the Citty', 'custome of the Citty', 'Cittizens Proverbe', 'you do many devises for Cittizens wives: I care not
greatly because I have a Citty Laundresse already, if I get a Citty Poet
too', 'neare a Gentleman of them all shall gull a Citizen' – such references frequently have no other function than to insist that the play is set
in the city of London.

The playwrights adopt the same technique with names of streets and
areas of London; hence the conventional references to proceeding up
Holborn towards Tyburn, 'the Brokers in long lane' (*Northward Ho*)
'the middle Ile in *Pawles*' (*Westward Ho*), and other references to

Bucklersbury, the Exchange, Bedlam, Fleet Street, the Counter, St Martins, the Stillyard, Blackwall, Limehouse, Brentford, Ham, Bridewell, Shoreditch, Woodstreet, Ludgate, Grays Inn, Westminster, Croyden, Charing Cross, Putney, Queenhithe, Lambeth, Coalharbour, Pudding Lane, Cheapside, Wapping, Moorfields, Highgate Hill, Cuckoldshaven, Enfield, Ware, Bishopsgate, Guildhall, Lumbard Street, St Clements; though most of these occur in both plays, it is nevertheless an impressive list, and a technique which the writers of *Eastward Ho* took note of when they came to compose their parody.

A characteristic feature of these two plays is the reliance on well-established stereotype characterization in a tradition quite different from that of Marston or Middleton. A whore in *Northward Ho* does not remind us of Franceschina so much as of Doll Tearsheet:

> the rotten toothd rascall, will for six pence fetch any whore to his maisters customers: and is every one that swims in a Taffatie gowne Lettis for your lippes? uds life, this is rare, that Gentlewomen and Drawers, must suck at one Spiggot: . . . I'me as melancholy now as Fleet-streete in a long vacation.
>
> (I. ii. 43-6, 51)

Nor is it wholly surprising that the Captain whose 'humour' is roaring recalls Fluellen of Shakespeare's *Henry V*, while the Dutchman Hans van Belch is treated with the good humour that Hans the shoemaker receives in that Popular comedy set in London four years earlier, the *Shoemakers' Holiday*. Certainly the many references to satiric themes and the jests about sex have their effect in creating an atmosphere similar to that in a city comedy; and since this was perhaps the aim of the collaborators, it may be inappropriate to dwell long on the more serious weaknesses of the two plays.

The two relevant plays by Day reveal further evidence of this indecorous mixing of styles and character types, for Day, like Dekker, was by training a Popular repertory playwright. Day had a marked allegiance to those early Shakespearean comedies which had been published, his habitual method of dramatic composition was Popular, and in composing his Coterie work he flavoured his plays with intensive imitation of the satiric and bitter passages in three successful or notorious comedies which had most recently appeared: *Westward Ho*, *Northward Ho*, and the later *Eastward Ho*. Though many of these echoes are from the last and the best written of the three plays, and the most plainly satiric – indeed its political satire led to the prosecution of the authors – even that play, *Eastward Ho* is dense with satiric references which had become conventional to the genre by late 1604. Dekker and Webster helped to make such references characteristic by constantly reiterating them in carelessly uninventive form; in every scene of these three plays John Day could have found satiric 'flavouring' for his own work.

There is probably another major source for Day's city comedies, though its influence in Jacobean drama is so widespread that it can perhaps be assumed automatically: it is Shakespeare's *Henry IV* and – to some extent – *Henry V*. What is striking about those plays in relation to city comedy is the close accuracy with which they rendered the London scenes of low life, the trickery episodes presented by the disguised Prince Hal and his servant Poins, and the strong feeling for the London locality. The episodes in which Hal tricks Falstaff and talks with low-life characters, and the episode in which Falstaff tricks Mistress Quickly into allowing him to continue living off her, find echoes in the tavern and bawdy-house episodes in *Westward Ho* and *Northward Ho*. Such figures as Pistol and Fluellen persist in the imagination of repertory playwrights, not only Dekker but typically Day and the author of the conventional Middletonian comedy *The Puritan Widow*, with its Corporal Oath and Captain Idle. In *The Isle of Gulls* those jests which do not derive from Coterie comedy are in the style of Shakespearean comedies which had been published – *Love's Labour's Lost* and *A Midsummer Night's Dream*, for example – and, inevitably, *Henry IV* and *The Merry Wives of Windsor*.

Day is able to imitate Popular romantic comedy because his Coterie work is still in its form and articulation regular, causally plotted drama with a romantic main plot and low-life sub-plot; though it has satiric *exempla* too. In *Law Tricks* Day certainly does his best to embitter the action with elements of Italianate evil and corruption; indeed he contrives to include poisoning, attempted adultery, seduction for financial profit, disguises and dissolute prodigality in a plot which already has a disguised-duke outline, with the duke Fernese observing all and judging at the end. The distinction to be made between Day's handling of the disguised-duke plot and Marston's is the lack of conviction, of intensity, in Day's articulation of evil characters; Lurdo may be ostensibly a Machiavel and a Malcontent, but he seems to be engaged rather in a charade than a real attempt at seduction of Emilia, who in any case is playing a game with him:[6]

> *Emilia* Ile in your presence sit uppon his knee,
> Exchanging kisses; If you speake to me
> Ile pout in scorn . . .
> *Lurdo* Square to my humour fit.
> *Emilia*   I was a Beggar borne . . .
> Traded in lust and gainefull brothelrie.
> *Lurdo* The fitter for my turne.   (III. i)

The couplets divided among the two bantering characters emphasize Day's lack of serious purpose and feeling for the satiric mode.

Law Tricks, like *The Isle of Gulls*, follows the pattern established by Dekker and Webster of heavy satiric flavouring at the *beginning* of the play. Hence the exchange between the cynical Malcontent Lurdo and Polymetes:

> *Lurdo* Prince, be a Lawyer.
> *Polymetes* Of all Land-monsters some that beare that name
> Might well be sparde, whose vultur Avarice
> Devoures men living: they of all the rest
> Deale most with Angells and yet prove least blest.   (I. i)

Soon Lurdo is explaining how a brace or two of dead wives enrich a skilful widower, and his Italian deviousness in plotting arouses the ironic admiration of Emilia:

> *Lurdo*   A private doore
> a secret vault and twentie odde tricks more . . .
> *Emilia* My Lord, your Law-plot's most judiciall.   (II. i)

The equivalent cynical courtier-malcontent in *The Isle of Gulls* is Dametas, and before his appearance the audience is provided with several epigrammatic descriptions of him which proclaim their derivation to be partly from city comedy but as much, perhaps, from Lyly:

> *Hippolita* Why your quotidian, *Dametas* the Court surfet, hee that
> dwells in your eye, like a disease in your blood . . .
> *Violetta* Fie upon him, he becomes the great chamber worse then a
> Gentleman-usher with wry legges.
> *Hippolita* He is the most mishapen sute of gentility that ever the
> Court wore.   (Sig A4ʳ)

It is clear that this dialogue is influenced by Comical Satyre's ridicule of mannerisms; but the two princesses Violetta and Hippolita have a different parentage, from early Shakespearean comedy:

Violetta	By the faith a me, well led,
Lisander	Would I might lead you.
Violetta	Whither?
Lisander	To my bed.
Violetta	I am sure you would not?
Lisander	By this aire I would.
Violetta	I hope you would not hurt me, and you should.
Lisander	I'de love you sweet.
Violetta	Sowre, so I heard you say.
Lisander	Accept it then.
Violetta	Of what acquaintance pray? (Sig E1ʳ and E1ᵛ)

Day's taste for delicate gaiety is shown in his frequent use of such words as 'game' and 'comedy', and 'sceane of mirth': *The Isle of Gulls* has plenty of satiric dialogue, but the plot itself subdues the violent or savage elements which we are led to expect from the early exchanges:

> I tell thee knave I could hang thee by my pattent, if it were granted once, Ile tell thee how it runnes, It allowes mee 24 knaves, 6 Knights, 10 fooles, 13 fellons, and 14 traytors by the yeere, take em howe, why, when, and where I please …
> such Court-spyders, that weave their webbes of flatterie in the eares of greatnesse, if they can once entangle them in their quaint trecherie, they poysen em   (Sig B2ʳ, B2ᵛ)

In the latter part of the play a second Machiavel is introduced to keep the satiric allusive interest of this Coterie comedy alive; the Machiavel explains his conventional lineage: 'My great Graundfather was a Rat-catcher, my Grandsier a Hangman, my Father a Promooter, and my selfe an Informer' (Sig E4ᵛ). This derives from *Westward Ho* III, ii. 5-10; when he describes his criminal activities, he echoes *Your Five Gallants* III. ii and *Eastward Ho* II. ii. 11-16; when Manasses brings in the two messengers who describe the abuses and discontent in the kingdom since the duke has abandoned it, the passages which most plainly refer to contemporary Jacobean discontents and James's habitual impatience with government (when it conflicted with country sports) have actually been lifted almost verbatim from Sidney's *Arcadia*. In this sense we can say that *The Isle of Gulls* is a genuine, if sporadic, contemporary political satire, although even here the satire consists largely in allusions, not in the *dramatisation* of the satiric-didactic view of the playwright. Thus the duke seems to have no

interesting or even general personal similarity to James I, Dametas is a
merely conventional dramatic figure, the rival princes even if dressed as
English and Scots still offer little witty criticism of either. They are in
fact conventionalized figures based on the young nobles in *Love's
Labour's Lost*, and act out elements in the plot of Sidney's *Arcadia*. As
the conclusion of *The Isle of Gulls* shows, the play is of an Italianate
form and it ends when all the trickery episodes are complete, the last
episode involving the winning of the two princesses by one pair of
princes with the blessing of the duke (or king, as the speech prefixes call
him once or twice in the 1606 quarto).

Since *The Isle of Gulls* was designed by Day partly to 'cash in' on the
notoriety gained by the Blackfriars comedy of the preceding year,
Eastward Ho, he made sure that the vital element – satire of James I,
his court and his new knights – should be prominent. Hence
Dametas's remark, in retort to the captain's claim to the rank of
gentleman: 'Why so I hope are wee sir, and of the best and last edition,
of the Dukes owne making' (Sig B2^r). Hence, too, the frequent and
often unnecessary references to 'policy' and the corruption of the
Court. This is the technique once more of flavouring a straightforward
play with fashionable matter. In *Law Tricks* Day is aiming at the
Middletonian kind of city comedy with its extensive and accurate
setting among lawyers, merchants and financiers with much turning
on the decision in court and the signing of mortgages, bonds, and so
forth. In *Law Tricks* therefore we find many references to law and legal
terms, though the plot of the play contains no legal matter whatsoever.
There are numerous uses of 'law' as a prefix with little gain in
meaning:

Lurdo A secret vault and twentie odde tricks more . . .
Emilia My Lord your Law-plot's most judicial   (p. 29)

Win She intends to make a Gull of the Prince
    (And an absolute Goose of you).
Lurdo Still good in Law: ile fetch him ore of all,
    Get all, pursse all,   (p. 36)

Lurdo   Neither the Law nor I
    Know any reason why Horatio—
    But mum, Law-tricks!   (p. 18)

Similarly, Day uses legal terms either gratuitously or incorrectly:

> Ile have a trick
> By way of Habeas Corpus to remove
> This talking Gossip   (p. 46)

> I made thee and the rest away by a bill of Conveyance at his back
> (p. 66)

> But *nuda veritate*, in bare truth,
> And *bona fide*, without circumstance,
> *Splendente sole*, the bare sun nere saw
> A wench more capable of wit and law.   (p. 78)

In both plays he reveals his allegiance to the Elizabethan popular theatre; the low prose invective, like the low-life characters, could well be found in his own *Blind Beggar of Betnal Green* (1600?) or in one of Dekker's Popular comedies.

If Day's *The Isle of Gulls* only truly resembles a city comedy in those places – of which there are many – where it imitates *Westward Ho*, *Eastward Ho*, *The Dutch Courtezan*, *Your Five Gallants*, *Volpone*, *Every Man in His Humour* and the rest, yet it did bring down the wrath of the authorities, who committed sundry of the actors to Bridewell because of its political satire. Thus, obliquely, Day earns his place among the playwrights in the genre.

Barry's *Ram Alley* is in some respects the most successful of the conventional plays; this may be because it faithfully imitates Middletonian comedy. The main plot has certain recognizable similarities to *A Mad World My Masters* and *A Trick to Catch the Old One*, and there are certain echoes in the dialogue, for example in the gleeful soliloquy of the lawyer Throat which recalls those of Quomodo or Old Hoard:[7]

> My fate looks big! Methinks I see already
> Nineteen gold chains, seventeen great beards, and ten
> Reverend bald heads, proclaim my way before me.
> My coach shall now go prancing through Cheapside . . .
> I now in pomp will ride, for 'tis most fit,
> He should have state, that riseth by his wit.   (III.i)

Again, when early on we are given a satiric character sketch of Throat, the firm syntax of the verse and the economy of statement proclaim the stylistic influence of Middleton:

> Thus: in Ram Alley lies a fellow, by name
> Throat: one that professeth law, but indeed
> Has neither law nor conscience; a fellow
> That never saw the bar, but when his life
> Was call'd in question for a cosenage.
> The rogue is rich; to him go you,　　　　　　　　(I. i)

The purposeful dialogue directs our attention to the plotting, which is complex but also witty, and provides some excellent surprise *peripeteiea* and disguise deceptions in the Middletonian manner. When Oliver appears to wed his widow and William ridicules him, the dialogue recalls Middleton with some precision and the form is that of a Comical Satyre sequence:

> *Oliver*　Good morrow, bride, fresh as the month of May,
> 　　I come to kiss thee on thy wedding day.
> *William*　Saving your tale sir . . .
> 　　The truth is, I have laid my knife aboard.
> 　　The widow, sir, is wedded.
> *Oliver*　Ha!
> *William*　Bedded.
> *Oliver*　Ha!　　　　　　　　(V. i)

Throat the lawyer, like Old Hoard the miser in *A Trick to Catch the Old One*, marries a whore under the impression she is respectable and rich; Throat's ridiculous entry of the house he believes he owns in Act IV is admirable situation comedy emerging wittily out of the main deception plot, while such sequences as that in which the whore twists her way out of the clutches of a sergeant are given densely local colour and technical accuracy in the manner of Middleton, and distinctly not the mode of Shakespeare's Pompey or Mistress Quickly:

> *Sergeant*　　I have an action
> 　　At suit of Mistress Smell-smock, your quondam bawd:
> 　　The sum is eight good pound for six weeks' board,
> 　　And five weeks' loan for a red taffeta gown,
> 　　Bound with a silver lace.
> *Whore*　I do protest,
> 　　By all the honesty 'twixt thee and me,
> 　　I got her in that gown in six weeks' space
> 　　Four pound, and fourteen pence given by a clerk
> 　　Of an inn-of-chancery that night I came
> 　　Out of her house;　　　　　　　　(IV. i)

The fast-moving and well-controlled plotting and the sinewy economy of the dialogue suggest that Barry imitated Middleton – the play was probably written after *A Trick to Catch the Old One*, with which it seems to have the closest similarity – but of course it lacks the assurance, the clarity and order of Middleton's dramatic articulation and its dialogue is without the vigour, the subtlety or the variety of its model. There is the constant use of conventional satiric allusions as in the work of Dekker and Webster or Day, and the obtrusive flattery of the Inns of Court students and their prowess with the ladies. The characters are not given full vigorous independence, even Boutcher the chief trickster and Throat the villain lack such individuality as would free them from their Middletonian parents. But the play has formal characteristics of the genre.

There is another significant source for the play – Jonson's *Volpone*. The first appearance of Throat is when he emerges from his study, in which there are books and money bags on the table. He then delivers a rhapsody to gold and its source in legal affairs which is obviously based on Volpone's hymn to gold in Act I of that play; the rhythm of the opening lines is unmistakably similar:

> Chaste Phoebe, *splende*; there's that left yet,
> Next to my book, *claro micante auro*.
> Ay, *that's the soul of law*; that's it, that's it
> For which the buckram bag must trudge all weathers.

Ram Alley has certain formal characteristics of city comedy. The disguised and detached commentator and satirist appears in the person of Constantia, who offers didactic comment at the conclusion of a scene early on: 'Pandarism! why, 'tis grown a liberal science' (I. i). In a later sequence, possibly echoing the scene in *Volpone* where Volpone is abused for 'Those filthy eyes of yours, that flow with slime' (I. v), William abuses his father to Taffeta, whom he desires; his father is in hiding and overhears everything. The father then explodes with rage, rushes out and abuses William in his turn. A sequence in which the bragging captain is ridiculed is actually crueller and more deliberate than the beating of Pistol with the leek in *Henry V*; were it not for Barry's obvious debt to Shakespeare's play-scrap mouther in creating Captain Face, we might be led to compare it with the exposure of Tucca's cowardice in *Poetaster* IV. vii. It is a sign of Barry's derivative method that he should choose the easiest and most obvious model of a stage braggart to lash in the manner of Jonson or Marston, just as he chooses the most hackneyed of all tragedies, the *Spanish Tragedy*, to parody in the manner of early Marston, derisively but unimaginatively and unwittily.

Barry's play contains elements chosen from the best plays in city comedy; they are well integrated into his firm and intelligent plot, and the atmosphere is successfully flavoured with the stock allusions and jests from city comedy and has effective sequences set in prison, in the suburbs, in the lawyer's house. The London scene is frequently referred to by naming particular streets and areas, as in *Westward Ho*, *Northward Ho* and, for that matter, as in Middleton's city comedy. Barry seems to have modelled his play on the latest and freshest of Middleton's plays performed at the rival Paul's Boys' Theatre, and in this he shows his efficiency as a conventional repertory writer, always ready to adapt to the latest successful fashion. His play is for the most part too lighthearted, like Day's; the episodes lack the serious implications and the satiric purpose of Jonson or Middleton, but in those where he has imitated the *form* of the satiric sequence characteristic of city comedy, his achievement is higher than that of Dekker and Webster, Day, or such less relevant writers as Armin, Field, or Machin. The moral of this is obvious. Form is paramount, and shapes style.

I have chosen to deal only with the more interesting conventional plays here in order to attempt to show the characteristics of these plays, to indicate how they were made and what the conventional writers thought most remarkable and successful in the genre. It may also reveal something of the quality of the best plays in the genre if we set beside them the work of writers whom Jonson dismissed as 'rogues'. Yet it is an indication of the sustaining richness reposing in the genre's conventions that Barry's wholly undistinguished conventional play should be so manifestly actable and effective. Here we may note an analogy with the history of the Coney-Catching pamphlet, another 'kind' in which wholly conventional methods of composition produced lively, firm and enduringly attractive popular literature. Barry's play is effective because he so fully grasped and used the conventions, not at all because he was more *original* than Day or Dekker.

Now that the study of the first phase of city comedy is complete, it may be worthwhile to review the question of the relationship of the genre to the Jacobean background. I have been concerned to stress the formal and conventional elements in the realism of the plays and to demonstrate that the important plays constitute intelligent moral criticism of society. Political satire in Marston is not remarkable for providing a historian with otherwise unobtainable information about the workings of government; rather the imaginative force of the plays repeatedly stresses what is felt with an acute immediacy, whatever precedent satiric tradition might contain – the Court in the years from 1599 to 1605 in Marston's plays is a place of conspicuous expenditure, favouritism, treachery, moral decadence and ruthless ambition, and its ruler is ineffectual. By comparison the fact that the plays contain many known (and perhaps many undetected) allusions to actual contemporary personalities seems of lesser importance. Coterie satiric plays with their audiences containing Inns of Court students, lawyers, young gentry and nobility are themselves an interesting ephemeral feature of the first decade of the Jacobean age, but their fashionable scandalous impersonations of prominent people cannot be described as criticism of political affairs in the sense that we can give that description to Jonson's *Sejanus* or Shakespeare's *Julius Caesar*. Jonson normally moves away from a specific fact or personality to a general idea and a symbolic fiction, as his literary and dramatic theory tirelessly recommended. It is ultimately pointless to attempt to identify an individual as his satiric target in his creation of Volpone, who embodies avarice and perversity in a grand dramatic caricature, and Volpone probably has more in common with Marlowe's Barabas than with any historical person. The clear dramatic lineage of usurers in city comedy at once affirms the historical interest in the type while reducing the significance of any conjectural portraits of real London merchants in the plays. The original audience at Jonson's *Bartholomew Fair* might properly have been reminded of King James from time to time when listening to Justice Overdo,[8] and this would have been a legitimate part of the enjoyment; but the play as a whole subsumes such witty, intermittent allusiveness into a grand abstract design which constitutes a dialectical account of society. At that level city comedy makes its most valuable comment on Jacobean politics.

In Jonson and Middleton, who utilize the conventions of Roman comedy, specific contemporary details of law and business are chosen to complicate and resolve plots, but it is the Roman convention itself, in offering an ironic analogy of Jacobean society, which must strike us as significant. The anarchic, acquisitive society of the city is insistently depicted in terms of poverty and crime, and the extraordinary, hypocritical attitudes of authority are as insistently debunked in the plays. Pompey in *Measure for Measure* speaks for many city comedy characters when he reacts to the admonitions of Escalus: 'I thank your worship for your good counsel; but I shall follow it as the flesh and fortune shall better determine.' (II. ii. 240-1). The damage done by uncontrolled extortionate usury, the anxieties of debt, foreclosure and risky investment, which furnish intrigue plots for the plays, are linked to the miseries induced by the law relating to wards and inheritance, so giving a selective emphasis to issues in Jacobean society which, modern historians agree, have wider historical importance. The sharper and bolder the dramatic art of the playwright, the more cogent is his satiric, critical diagnosis. By contrast a non-satiric chronicle play like Heywood's *If You Know Not Me You Know Nobody* (Part II) may give a laboriously detailed account of the building of the Royal Exchange in London, depicting the historical character Sir Thomas Gresham and taking much trouble to include authentic detail for its own sake, but its attentiveness to authenticity in external details of fact is rendered ineffectual because of the complete failure to grasp social and political principles and implications. The portrait of Gresham is a piece of banal mercantile hagiography, as when he reacts to the news that an investment of sixty thousand pounds is lost by *dancing his care away*. It is a kind of paradox that the more a playwright stylizes character and setting to accord with the requirements of the satiric-didactic schema, so stressing underlying patterns in the seemingly contingent circumstances of everyday city life, the more closely he is likely to engage contemporary issues.

We have seen how the plays are set more and more frequently in London itself: a crowded, confusing maze of streets, business houses and brothels, law courts, prisons and inns. These settings are evidently meant to interest an audience for whom they are familiar in daily life. The distinctive emphasis on London may reflect the city's growing self-consciousness, and we might recall that the rise of the London 'season' has been traced to this period,[9] while the city continued to grow as a social centre for the gentry, many of whom sent their sons to the Inns of Court (if not Oxford or Cambridge) to acquire some general education and social poise rather than academic or professional qualifications. The playwrights of city comedy were clearly aware of these students and ex-students as an element in their audience (the playwrights themselves had close connections with the Inss of Court) and it might be argued that these circumstances *explain away* city comedy's increasing interest in dishonest and ruthless money-lenders and lawyers, in a city which is itself presented as largely corrupt and hostile, governed by impersonal (and inhuman) laws of chance and the money market.

Clearly there is some force in the argument that it became rather the fashion to scourge the vices of the city. However, such an explanation takes insufficient account of the playwrights' increasingly ambivalent attitude towards the skilful, ruthless materialist who knows how to manipulate capital and the technicalities of the law – and in this sense, of course, Jonson's *Volpone* certainly is a significant comment on the Jacobean background. In the plays the growth of emphasis on the capitalist and lawyer in the city is accompanied by an increasing ambivalence of attitude towards their methods and appetites. In both respects we may consider that city comedy is a significant reflection of developments in the political and economic life of the age, and certainly may be related to profound sources of conflict and change in early seventeenth-century England.

As for the city of London itself, it is obviously a most significant subject for study in the plays, where the reactions of characters to its size and complexity have, at times, a strikingly modern ring. We saw in the more conventional plays of 1604-7 how deficient art diluted the atmosphere created in such plays as *The Dutch Courtezan* or *Michaelmas Term*, so that the London setting of *Westward Ho* was not much more convincing than that in a Coney-Catching pamphlet by Greene, and it might be noted that precisely this point is made by the three intelligent collaborative authors of the splendid parody *Eastward Ho*, who emphasize the crudity of their targets by ironic iteration of hoary clichés in plot and character and also moral-didactic comment. Here for example the prodigal-gallant Quicksilver discourses with mistress Synnedefie:

> *Quicksilver* … Ile to the Court, another manner of place for maintenance I hope then the silly Cittie … I shall bee a Marchaunt forsooth: trust my estate in a wooden Troughe as hee does? What are these Shippes, but Tennis Balles for the windes to play withall? Tost from one waue to another; Nowe vnderline; Nowe ouer the house; Sometimes Bricke-wal'd against a Rocke, so that the guttes flye out again; Sometimes strooke vnder the wide Hazzard, and farewell Mast(er) Marchant.
>
> *Synnedefie* Well *Francke*, well; the Seas you say are vncertaine: But hee that sayles in your Court Seas, shall find 'hem tenne times

> fuller of hazzard . . . hee that rises hardly, stands firmely: but hee
> that rises with ease, alas, falles as easily.
>
> *Quicksilver* A pox on you, who taught you this morallitie?
>
> (II. ii. 57-9, 61-71, 88-92)

Inflated burlesque of the details of city life is further displayed in the
whole series of conventional situations and parodies of attempts at local
colour. The burlesque incorporates some true satiric comment:

> *Touchstone* Yes, Maister Deputy: I had a small venture with them
> in the voyage, a Thing, cald *a Sonne in Lawe*, or so. Officers, you
> may let 'hem stand . . . One of 'hem was my prentise, M(aister)
> *Quicksilver*, here, and when he had 2. yeare to serue, kept his
> whore, & his hunting Nag, would play his 100. pound at
> *Gresco*, or *Primero* . . . he was a Gentleman, and I a poore
> *Cheapeside* Groome. The remedie was, we must part. Since
> when he hath had the gift of gathering vp some small parcels of
> mine, to the value of 500. pound disperst among my customers,
> to furnish this his *Virginian* venture; wherein this knight was
> the chiefe, Sir *Flash*:   (IV. ii. 223-5, 227-30, 234-9)

In this passage an ironic relationship is established between the vaunted
exploits of voyagers (Drake is earlier saluted by Sir Petronell Flash in Act
III. iii) and the debased, contemptible and un-heroic background of
money-lenders, investors and contacts in the city. Such contemporary
satire in *Eastward Ho* is certainly shrewd, but it should be noticed that it is
expressed through an ironic burlesque of dramatic 'realism', through a
deliberate self-conscious parody of conventional city comedy 'London'
characters and settings. By calling attention to their parody of crude
dramatic realism Jonson, Chapman and Marston direct us to the real
satiric concerns – both literary and social – which underlie the whole
play, and reveal perhaps unexpectedly sophisticated possibilities in critical realism. We are given not literal accuracy of reporting but intelligent
dialectic.

 In the main course of city comedy up to *The Devil Is an Ass* of 1616
the city background is of importance for its continuous contribution to
the dramatic atmosphere. There is often an imaginatively creative
interplay between the dramatic action and the urban settings. In
Marston we first see how the city background can intensify and mirror
the bewilderment and suffering of his characters, and in subsequent
plays the London backgrounds seem often to reflect, ironically, the
intricacies and unpredictable (though constant) hazards of the city,
which is at once familiar yet hostile and impersonal.

VIII

MIDDLETON
AND JONSON

'Hang art, madam, and trust to nature for dissembling'
(CONGREVE, *The Old Bachelor* III. i)

Michaelmas Term, I have argued, marks an advance in Middleton's art; in that play the dark and savage potential of the action expresses itself with a power more usually found in satiric tragedy. *Michaelmas Term* may be seen to echo the influential *Volpone* of Jonson, and the influence of Marston, too, in dramatizing violence, iniquity and disease in familiar urban locations is equally apparent. The conventional elements are organized into a powerful dramatic whole by the psychological penetration which informs the character drawing and the pointed thematic imagery. The intensity with which *Michaelmas Term* is written, the urgency with which the action is articulated, testify to the inspiration Middleton found in the genre city comedy at this point of its early maturity.

Comedy with elaborate, fast-moving and complex intrigue deriving from Italian convention demands a decorum in which characterization is slight: Shakespeare himself obeyed this decorum when he wrote *The Taming of the Shrew*. Middleton, however, modifies what he takes from the Italian tradition. In *Michaelmas Term* and the later *A Trick to Catch the Old One* the fast-moving complex Italianate intrigue recurs, but the subtler motivation of character and the sharper insight which informs the writing produces a more satisfying drama – the characteristic elements are re-ordered.

It will be recalled that there is a sequence in *Michaelmas Term* (II. iii) in which Quomodo and his creatures angle for Easy the young heir. They work on his insecurity, his vanity, hope, guilt, friendliness and anger so that his emotional struggle finally delivers him, flapping weakly, on the bank. There the dramatic art is of a higher order

altogether compared with the *lazzi* of the early plays. In his last two
comedies, *A Trick to Catch the Old One* and *A Chaste Maid in
Cheapside*, this higher level of writing is sustained. The major *lazzi* are
prepared for more elaborately because the audience needs to know
more of the psychology of the protagonists if they are to appreciate the
conflicts. This may be illustrated by an analysis of Middleton's
technique in the early sequence where the Host deceives the *senex*
Lucre.

At first the Host appears to be a stock Jest Book type, and indeed he
represents himself as such to Lucre with complete success. He is,
however – as soon appears – actually a Middletonian wit and Coney-
Catcher, a more complex character altogether. Witgood the young
schemer recalls his past camaraderie with the Host and tells us he has
'rinsed the whoreson's gums in mullsack many a time' in good Jest
Book style; but the Host's attitude to their relationship turns out to be
less predictable:

> *Witgood* Comes my prosperity desiredly to thee?
> *Host* Come forfeitures to a usurer, fees to an officer, punks to an
> host, and pigs to a parson desiredly? why, then, la.   (I. i)

The host implies a different motivation in assisting Witgood – for him
it is just part of the civil war. Middleton is also insisting that his
audience attend to the characters as individuals rather than conventional puppets; the Host's role may be that of Vice for the moment, but
the possibilities are manifold, and he may turn on Witgood at any time
like any other predator, bawd, usurer or intelligencer. The dialogue
swarms with such implications and the now alerted audience can enjoy
the success of the Host's gambit with Lucre. Lucre relies on his prided
man-of-the-world's shrewdness in judging the Host to be of 'a good
blunt honesty'. The latter builds up this impression, makes Lucre
think he is being skilful in eliciting the information:

> *Lucre* What countryman might this young Witgood be?
> *Host* A Leicestershire gentleman, sir.
> *Lucre* My nephew, by th' mass, my nephew! I'll fetch out more of
> this, i'faith: a simple country fellow, I'll work 't out of him.
> [*Aside*]— And is that gentleman, sayst thou, presently to marry
> her?   (II. i)

In the phrase 'I'll work 't out of him' Middleton focuses the ironic
comedy of the situation; in fact the central interest in the sequence is

this study of character, and the soon doubled irony intensifies the
clarity with which Lucre is exposed as a vain man whose intelligence
succumbs to any appeal to self-love, and whose vigour, strength and
appetite drive him deep into folly. The Host contrives a story of
Witgood's wealth which causes Lucre to reverse the scornful criticism
made only moments earlier; the directness of this volte-face has a didactic clarity, and Lucre's lies in praise of Witgood betray Lucre's wholly
materialistic, obsessive greed:

Host Since your worship has so much knowledge in him, can you
resolve me, sir, what his living might be? . . .
Lucre Who, young master Witgood? why, believe it, he has as
goodly a fine living out yonder, — what do you call the place?
Host Nay, I know not, i'faith.
Lucre Hum — see, like a beast, if I have not forgot the name —
pooh! and out yonder again, goodly grown woods and fair
meadows: pax on't, I can ne'er hit of that place neither: he? why,
he's Witgood of Witgood Hall; he, an unknown thing!   (II. i)

Here the dialogue carries complete conviction as spoken English, and
at the same time it reveals the submerged thoughts busily swarming
beneath the surface. At the pause before Lucre's 'why, believe it'
Lucre has thought up the ploy of seeming forgetful about the property,
and at 'pooh' he decides to name Witgood Hall, judging it necessary to
impress the Host. Thus the Host, a detached, disguised trickster,
watches with amusement as Lucre, the duped would-be trickster, exer-
cises his art and reveals his greed. The Host concludes the demonstration by forcing Lucre to revile and condemn himself – the wicked
uncle – and the satiric-didactic aims of the sequence are fulfilled:

Host . . . trust me sir, we heard once he had no lands, but all lay
mortgaged to an uncle he has in town here . . .
Lucre Why, do you think, i'faith, he was ever so simple to
mortgage his lands to his uncle? or his uncle so unnatural to take
the extremity of such a mortgage?   (II. i)

A similar concern with subtler motivation is evident in the scene where
Hoard woos the Courtesan under the mistaken impression that she is
wealthy:

Courtesan Alas, you love not widows but for wealth!
I promise you I ha' nothing, sir.

> *Hoard*   Well said, widow,
> Well said; thy love is all I seek, before
> These gentlemen.   (III. i)

She points out Hoard's failure to take note of this statement at the end
of the play, emphasizing the patterned ironic construction of the plot
based on character; Hoard's greed once aroused, the Courtesan has
little difficulty in provoking him to marry her secretly.

The ridicule is directed with some invention and wit by Middleton;
at the moment where the Courtesan relinquishes Hoard's fictitious
rival, Witgood appears as the detached commentator:

> *Courtesan*   Is my love so deceiv'd? Before you all
> I do renounce him; on my knees I vow (*kneels*)
> He ne'er shall marry me.
> *Witgood* [*looking in*] Heaven knows he never meant it!   (III. i)

The manipulation of the two misers by the Courtesan for Witgood's
benefit is done by shrewd calculation of their psychology and admirable
timing of temptation. Lucre becomes desperate through repeated
rebuffs, finally commits himself:

> Widow, believe't, I vow by my best bliss,
> Before these gentlemen, I will give in
> The mortgage to my nephew instantly . . .
> Nay, more; . . . he shall be my heir;   (IV.i)

Hoard rejoices at this scene (on which he has eavesdropped) and this
very glee is turned against him by dashing his hopes, then deluding him
into thinking he has found a way out. Full of self-love at this achievement (as he conceives it) Hoard accepts all Witgood's debts in return
for Witgood's empty declaration of relinquishment of claim to the
Courtesan. Hoard's vanity and greed are emphasized in several places
to prepare for this scene. He declares his idea of love: 'to enrich my
state, augment my revenues, and build mine own fortunes' (III. ii).
Witgood has recommended Hoard to the Courtesan solely for his
acquisitive success: 'he's rich in money, moveables, and lands; marry
him' (III. i). Hoard early on reveals voracity, power and energy on the
scale of Volpone's:

> I'll mar your phrase, o'erturn your flatteries,
> Undo your windings, policies, and plots,
> Fall like a secret and despatchful plague
> On your secured comforts.   (II. ii)

At the point of his gulling, Witgood relinquishes the love of the Courtesan and, much more emphatically, claim to

> any of her manors, manor-houses, parks, groves, meadow-grounds, arable lands, barns, stacks, stables, dove-holes, and coney-burrows; together with all her cattle, money, plate, jewels, borders, chains, bracelets, furnitures, hangings, (IV. iv)

This long list of solid material wealth gives an impression of the very air being darkened by the mass of possessions. The comment on Hoard's attitude to love and marriage is memorable.

A Trick to Catch the Old One reveals the influence of Jonson's *Volpone*. Certain sequences are handled in an overtly schematic manner. The three creditors may be a pale imitation of Voltore, Corbaccio and Corvino: Middleton's dramatic style is very mannered here to emphasize their avarice and their absurdly predictable responses:

> *1 Creditor* I am glad of this news.
> *2 Creditor* So are we, by my faith.
> *3 Creditor* Young Witgood will be a gallant again now. (II. ii)

When Witgood flatters them their response is comparable:

> *Witgood* I may tell you as my friends.
> *1, 2 & 3 Creditors* O, O, O!

This farcical stylization prepares for the attempts of each creditor in turn to bribe Witgood privately, which is, again, reminiscent of the first half of *Volpone*. In addition to the three creditors there are Hoard's three gentlemen, who repeat the suit of Hoard to the Courtesan, and having done so they sue for credit with mechanical repetitiveness:

> *1 Gent* I was the first that moved her.
> *Hoard* You were, i'faith.
> *2 Gent* But it was I that took her at the bound.
> *Hoard* Ay, that was you...
> *3 Gent* I boasted least, but 'twas I join'd their hands. (III. iii)

Middleton uses the same style in the sequence where Hoard indulges his Faustus-like fantasy with the figures of the tailor, barber, perfumer, falconer and huntsman, treated as possessions, dancing like puppets to

his tune. The sequence (IV. iv) recalls indeed the less polished manner
of Comical Satyre, as do the ridicule sequences:

> *Lim* In your old age doat on a courtesan!
> *Hoard* Ha!
> *Kix* Marry a strumpet!
> *Hoard* Gentlemen!
> *O. Hoard* And Witgood's quean!
> *Hoard* O! Nor lands nor living?
> *O. Hoard* Living! ...
> *Hoard* Out! out! I am cheated; infinitely cozen'd!   (V. ii)

The Courtesan's repentant octosyllabics at the conclusion actually
echo *Cynthia's Revels* directly.

The psychological acuteness of Middleton's character drawing is
manifest in the villain-miser Hoard. As we have seen, Hoard has
an irrepressible animal vigour and lusty, crude high spirits. When
'winning over' the Courtesan, whom he believes to be rich, his
businessman's cynical sense of humour is undeniably infectious; the
Courtesan protests that she is poor, can offer nothing but love, and
Hoard guffaws at what he takes to be her naive scheming and
deception:

> Well said, widow,
> Well said; thy love is all I seek.

The same animal appeal informs his self-congratulatory outburst
'What a sweet blessing hast thou, master Hoard' which, for all its
crude materialist aspiration has an undeniable vigour and broad
humour. Of course such hubris invites a heavy dousing in ridicule, but
in the first place Middleton has given fully convincing life to that stock
conventional target of the satirists, the land-grabbing merchant-usurer.
It is a mark of Middleton's mature art that the sequence ridicules
Hoard's vanity, greed and folly while simultaneously revealing his
energy, courage and sheer animal gusto. It is a truthful portrayal which
stands up to the weight of irony, ridicule and moral censure without
losing life and psychological truth. In the event Hoard emerges as
perhaps a more convincing London citizen than the sentimentally
presented, Popular, and more famous creation of Dekker, Simon Eyre
the shoemaker. Hoard has the courage and the stature to stand up to
ridicule, to accept defeat and criticism; and having done so, he can find
his voice, and his manhood, again:

So, so, all friends! the wedding-dinner cools:
Who seem most crafty prove ofttimes most fools.

A Chaste Maid in Cheapside was written for the Popular stage between
1611 and 1613 and it is interesting to note what modifications
Middleton makes to the style and form of city comedy as he had written
it previously for Coterie audiences. Hoard, in the preceding play, had
by his very aggressive, ruthless materialism challenged the truth of
Dekker's character, the citizen shoemaker who becomes lord mayor
and in the process grows more and more the naively patriotic, loyal
tradesman rather than the politic, ruthless careerist we might expect.
The distinction of a deeper complexity in motive and character and
situation by Middleton gives his play an intellectual strength missing in
Dekker's. These qualities are manifest in *A Chaste Maid in Cheapside*,
though of course it does not take up the subject and form where they
were laid down by Middleton five years earlier.

It will be recalled that in chapter VII my discussion of *Westward Ho*
centred round the diffuseness which resulted from the reliance on
Popular conventions of play-making; there a series of scenes having no
common theme or purpose, directed towards building up no compre-
hensive picture or comment on society, was strung together merely by
the common presence of a set of city comedy characters. In Popular
comedy the characteristic looseness of articulation derives largely from
the playwrights' aim to present episodes purely for their comic
potential – anything goes, so long as the audience laughs, and if it does
not laugh the clowns will, likely as not, speak more than is set down for
them or 'will themselves laugh, to set on some quantity of barren
spectators to laugh too, though in the mean time, some necessary question of the play be then to be considered'. (*Hamlet*, III. ii.
40-4)

In *A Chaste Maid in Cheapside* the dialogue is frequently desultory
and loose, catching the inconsequentiality, the hack-work flavour of
Popular work, but its function differs. An example from early on in the
play may illuminate this technique.

The chaste maid herself, at the point where she is about to 'die'
delivers a pitiable cry which is sufficiently sloppy and sentimental, and
the half-suppressed echoes of earlier death speeches from famous plays
like *Romeo and Juliet* give it that characteristic ersatz flavour (familiar
from the romantic main plot speeches of Dekker in *Satiromastix* or
Westward Ho):

O, my heart dies! ...
Farewell, life! ...
O, bring me death tonight, love-pitying fates;
Let me not see tomorrow upon the world!   (IV. iii)

This has been preceded by such Popular Jest Book material as the jests of the Cambridge porter (I. i), the misunderstanding of the stage Welsh with Dekker-style 'mistaking of words' (IV. i) and the vulgar christening party scene (III. ii). When the chaste maid prepares to 'die' she sings a lament of sickly-sweet sentimentality, and her father responds to her death with predictably 'noble' rhetoric:

Yellowhammer   Take her in,
    Remove her from our sight, our shame and sorrow.
Touchwood Stay, let me help thee, 'tis the last cold kindness
    I can perform for my sweet brother's sake.   (V. ii)

and Touchwood Senior provides a lament in true Popular Act V style:

    What nature could there shine, that might redeem
    Perfection home to woman, but in her
    Was fully glorious? Beauty set in goodness
    Speaks what she was;   (V. iv)

Here we have exact and illuminating instances of Middleton's use of parody to make a strong positive comment on the characters who speak it. Middleton has not the least intention of presenting such sentimentality for its own sake. The speeches bear a weight of irony which is soon enough revealed. Moll's swan song is appreciated by her mother for its sweetness – her mother is more interested in its style than in the fact that she is apparently dying, and her father remarks with polite interest 'she plays the swan and sings herself to death'. The father is planning ahead at the very moment his daughter is being borne off dead on a bier, for what he calls 'our shame and sorrow' is in fact for him a financial scheme that has failed (she has not been well married off) so another scheme must be floated; he sets about planning:

Yellowhammer ... its our best course, wife ...
    T'absent ourselves till she be laid in ground.
Wife Where shall we spend that time?
Yellowhammer I'll tell thee where, wench:
    Go to some private church, and marry Tim
    To the rich Brecknock gentlewoman.   (V. ii)

'Naturally' his wife, bereaved as she is, cheers up instantly at this:

> Mass, a match;
> We'll not lose all at once, somewhat we'll catch.

In Act V. iv the funeral oration of Touchwood Senior is echoed by a mourner and then it is exposed as cant by the rising of the dead from their coffins, itself a parody of the stock Popular convention.[1]

Middleton's satire focuses on those characters for whom all human relationships are conceived of in terms of financial contract. This theme finds expression everywhere in the play, even in throw-away jests, as when Tim cries out:

> Thieves, thieves! my sister's stol'n! some thief hath got her:
> O how miraculously did my father's plate 'scape!
> 'Twas all left out, (IV. ii)

Tim's attitude to his sister is precisely the same as his attitude to the plate, and her father, Yellowhammer, regards his daughter as a marketable commodity (as I pointed out earlier). It is the financial concern of Touchwood Senior which prevents him fathering a family while it is precisely for financial and property reasons that Kix wishes for children. It leads Allwit to submit to the boorish domination of Sir Walter Whorehound, and drives him to prevent Sir Walter from marrying. One of the neatest ironies in the plot is that Allwits selfishly acquisitive motives produce a scheme by which the desires of Young Touchwood find satisfaction instead. In the christening party scene the real father, the cuckolder Sir Walter, wears the mask of Godfather (a savagely direct irony) and the titular father is dressed in one of the cuckolder's suits. This scene presents a microcosm of the comic world of Middleton, paying lip-service to Christian ideals but actually closely resembling that presented by the analysis of Thomas Hobbes.

Middleton presents in his mature comedies a moral and critical analysis of city society; his forceful purpose does not, however, deny the fuller human qualities in his villains. He presents with honesty and insight the vigour, the resilience, the human joys, fears and disappointments felt by characters who are condemned and satirized by the plays' design. At the centre of figures such as Quomodo, Lucre, Hoard, Whorehound and Allwit is their menace, their evil, their corrupting effect on society; but their threat is at once less sensational and more difficult to dismiss when we see what determination and intelligence they summon in pursuit of their prey. Middleton does not over-simplify the kind of liveliness from which the threat springs. Indeed he was, like Jonson, fascinated not only by their animal vitality but also by the sharp clarity with which they cut through convention and dogma to the thing itself. Certainly in the comedies Middleton does not hesitate to show that these figures are antipathetic to any Christian ethic; on the other hand it is his acknowledgement of Allwit's successful pragmatic policy which shows that Middleton is turning over the question 'why is this feasible if it is immoral?' It is out of this quarrel with himself that Middleton makes his art. Middleton's treatment of Allwit is powerfully ironic, the conclusion of the play manifestly condemns Allwit, and yet for Allwit financial and material success and enjoyment continue. He is not punished as even the brilliantly politic Volpone is punished. Allwit, like Jonson's Lovewit in *The Alchemist*, is perfectly adapted to his environment; he wins what he has and can keep it, as long as his wit holds out (to paraphrase Hobbes).

In the opening scene of *The Alchemist* three tricksters are discovered in conflict. Subtle claims to have made Face fit 'for more then ordinarie fellowships' when he was, beforehand, among 'broomes, and dust, and watring pots', while Face for his part claims to have raised Subtle from destitution at Pie Corner taking his 'meale of steeme in, from cookes stalls', looking 'piteously costive' with a pinched nose. Doll tries to halt the quarrel by reminding them that they must work together, and her cry immediately points up the continuity from Middletonian comedy to *The Alchemist*, and suggests the atmosphere of the play:

> Gentlemen, what meane you?
> Will you marre all? . . .
> Will you vn-doe your selves, with ciuill warre?   (I. i. 80-2)

Certainly Face, Subtle and Doll do not recognize what Hobbes was to call 'dominion'. If they do not war with one another it is so that they can war with men at large.

The three tricksters base their schemes on intelligent perception of their victims and manipulation of motive and temperament; their dupes are all greedy, the sin most familiar to the tricksters and therefore the best to control and direct in others. The chief dupe has the most powerful passion, the strongest fantasies of wish-fulfilment centring on a deep obsession with the Philosopher's Stone. The stone is the symbol of the absurdity and sterility at the heart of greed – in itself it is cold, dull, shapeless, unfeeling, dead – and with this of all things Sir Epicure expects to transform the world into a fairyland of riches.

The play's form reveals the same clarity and direct didactic purpose inherent in the symbol of the stone. The house deserted by Face's master is like the dukedom deserted by the disguised duke in earlier plays, and though Lovewit is only present at the conclusion his appearance fulfils the function of offering a detached, intelligent and critical view of people and events; Lovewit comments on the folly of the citizens and gulls exercised and exposed as a result of his absence. Face has performed the role of Vice, chief deviser of *lazzi* and *exempla* which satirize and ridicule Mammon, Ananias and Tribulation, the would-be gallant Kastril, Drugger the slow-witted tradesman, Lovewit's citizen-neighbours; and Jonson's survey includes the tricksters themselves, for Subtle and Doll receive harsh treatment in the catastrophe, though Face, by his wit and skill, escapes scot-free. Even here, the genre has precedents. Of course it must not be denied that the dazzling speed of the action and the complexity of the intrigue are complemented by the exhilarating fecundity in *lazzi* of Subtle, Doll and Face. At those moments where all three are thrown into a crisis which they must survive by instant action – as, for example, when Mammon arrives in the middle of Dapper's audience with the Queen of Faery in Act III. v – we are so interested in what will happen next, in what plan will be improvised, that we may well assume that the play depends altogether on surprise and the illusion of spontaneity.

The opening scene of the play, as I have already remarked, offers us satiric, epithetical descriptions of the rogues and of their careers; the quarrel elicits these Theophrastus-style 'characters' in an admirably dramatic manner:

Subtle You were once (time's not long past) the good,
     Honest, plaine, liuery-three-pound-thrum...
Face And your complexion, of the *romane* wash,
     Stuck full of black, and melancholique wormes,
     Like poulder-cornes, shot, at th'*artillerie-yard*...
Subtle   Cheater.
Face Bawd.
Subtle   Cow-herd.
Face   Coniuror.
Subtle Cut-purse.
Face   Witch.
Doll   O me!   (I. i. 15-16, 29-31, 106-8)

Doll, who makes them leave off quarrelling and submit to confession and correction, completes the *exemplum* form; its use by Jonson is ironic, for the rogues are thus brought back to the strait and narrow path of *crime*.

The scenes in which the aspirants Mammon, Drugger and the rest call at the house recall closely in form and function the scenes in *Volpone* where Voltore, Corbaccio and Corvino arrive, seeking news of their favour with Volpone and their chances of getting his wealth. Here Dapper's suit to the 'doctor' is taken up by Face with a great show of pessimism, and several attempts to attract the interest of the 'doctor' (Subtle) fail. The denials finally give way to some reluctant interest from Subtle, whose timing is admirable; his final and regretful acceptance of Dapper's money is like Quomodo's technique of getting Easy to sign the bond in *Michaelmas Term*. The skilful gradations of the trickster's gullery, which conclude in Dapper's complete belief in the Queen of Faery, present not only a highly comic spectacle but also bring out with sharp clarity the essential kinship of Dapper and Sir Epicure Mammon, even though the tricksters would never dare to make quite such open fun of Sir Epicure to his face as they do of Dapper:

> *Face*   Did you never see
>   Her royall *Grace*, yet?
> *Dapper*   Whom?
> *Face*   Your aunt of *Faerie*? (I. ii. 148-9)

Just after this exchange Jonson brings home to the audience how easy it is to mistake Face for a cheeky cockney, to underestimate his tireless professional alertness for a chance of profit; so, just as Dapper's bliss seems imminent, Face stings him:

> Well then, away. 'Tis but your bestowing
> Some twenty nobles, 'mong her *Graces* servants;
>
> > (I. ii. 172-3)

The audience is brought back to an awareness of the tricksters' essential predatoriness and regains its detached critical attitude to *all* the characters, loving nobody too freely.

The tricksters have no difficulty at all in eliciting the folly, fantastic superstition and greed in Drugger and Mammon. Drugger's speeches are frankly contrived by Jonson to show off his folly; he and Mammon betray themselves through their comically inappropriate juxtapositions, jumbling mythical with domestic, magical with banal. Drugger ploddingly explains:

And I would know, by art, sir, of your worship,
Which way I should make my dore, by *necromancie*.
And, where my shelves. And, which should be for boxes.

(I, iii. 10-12)

This from Drugger may be set beside Mammon's claim to

haue a peece of JASON'S fleece, too,
Which was no other, then a booke of *alchemie*,
Writ in large sheepe-skin, a good fat ram-vellam.

(II. i. 89-91)

Subtle and Face ridicule Drugger with conspiratorial vigour:

Face He lets me haue good *tabacco*, and he do's not
Sophisticate it, with sack-lees, or oyle . . .
Nor buries it, in grauell, vnder ground . . .
A neate, spruce-honest-fellow, and no gold-smith . . .
Subtle Your chest-nut, or your oliue-colour'd face
Do's neuer faile: and your long eare doth promise.
I knew't, by certaine spots too, in his teeth,

(I. iii. 23-4, 26, 32, 46-8)

When Mammon makes his first appearance Surly acts as the detached, critical commentator on the whole scene, and as spokesman for truth, reason, custom. He detects trickery:

Mammon   In eight, and twentie dayes,
I'll make an old man, of fourescore, a childe.
Surly No doubt, hee's that alreadie.   (II. i. 52-4)

Such deflation is very amusing too:

Subtle Ha' you set the oile of *Luna* in *kemia*?
Face Yes, sir.
Subtle   And the *philosophers* vinegar?
Face I.
Surly We shall haue a sallad.   (II. iii. 99-101)

Yet Surly's didacticism here is unflinching:

Rather, then I'll be brai'd sir, I'll beleeue,
That *Alchemie* is a pretty kind of game,
Somewhat like tricks o'the cards, to cheat a man,

(II.iii. 179-181)

and when Surly sees Doll he exclaims, much like Fitzgrave at the 'music school' (*Your Five Gallants* II. ii) 'Hart, this is a bawdy-house! I'll be burnt else' (II. iii. 226). Surly's plan to test the tricksters by disguising as a Spaniard, unmasking to expose them in full career, is another instance of the disguised-duke plot-form; one such plot is acted out within another in *The Alchemist* because Surly's didactic role actually fails, for the first time in city comedy.

In the sequence where Subtle, Face and Doll attempt to gull the 'Spaniard' (Surly in his disguise) Jonson provides a supreme instance of the comic ridicule convention of the genre when the rogues impudently inspect the foreigner:

> *Subtle* 'Slud, he do's looke too fat to be a *Spaniard*.
> *Face* Perhaps some *Fleming*, or some *Hollander* got him
> In D'ALVA'S time . . .
> *Surly Gratia*.
> *Subtle* He speakes, out of a fortification.   (IV. iii. 28-30, 32)

The fact that Surly dislikes ridicule makes him as comic as the tricksters whom he deceives:

> *Face*   Cossened, doe you see?
> My worthy *Donzel*, cossened.
> *Surly*   *Entiendo*.
> *Subtle* Doe you intend it? So doe we, deare *Don*.
> Haue you brought pistolets? or portagues?
> My solemne *Don*? Dost thou feele any? [*Face feels his
>   pockets*] . . .
> You shall be sok'd, and strok'd, and tub'd, and rub'd:
> And scrub'd, and fub'd, deare *Don*, before you goe.
>   (IV. iii. 39-43, 97-8)

The tricksters have the gleeful boisterousness of their ancestors in Comical Satyre; and when their target Surly takes off his disguise he is revealed as the Presenter, explaining, judging, in the convention of the role:

> Lady, you see into what hands, you are falne;
> Mongst what a nest of villaines! . . .
> I am a gentleman, come here disguis'd,
> Onely to find the knaueries of this *Citadell*.
>   (IV. vi. 1-2, 8-9)

Surly's satiric ridicule of Face and Subtle is unsparing, his threat of 'a cleane whip' recalls the sternness of Comical Satyre correction, the severity of Jonson's purpose there.

Surly has thoroughly outwitted the tricksters and has all the evidence needed to expose them. At this moment it seems that nothing can save Face and Subtle; but quick thinking produces a masterstroke, and the entry of Kastril the roaring boy (momentarily everyone had forgotten about him) is perfect because his sole characteristic is given a situation in which it can be useful. Next Drugger appears (the Marx Brothers frequently used this comic effect – cf. the sequence in *A Night at the Opera* where, one after another, about twenty-eight people on diverse errands all enter the tiny cabin already filled by Groucho's luggage) and he is told that Surly intends to steal the widow; he begins roaring too, and at this climax of noise and struggle Jonson effects one of the most memorable entrances in comic drama with Ananias, who intones his jargon greeting ('Peace to the household') with unintended aptness. Subtle points out to Ananias the abominable presence of a 'Spaniard', and thus defeat is turned into victory, the dominant follies of the gulls being directed full at Surly who can do nothing against this stream of insane hostility. The tricksters successfully alter and combine the three separate schemes of deception (on Drugger I. iii and II. vi, on Ananias II. v, III. i and III. ii, and on Kastril III. iv and IV. ii) and the new *lazzo* serves not only to outwit Surly but also to expose the folly of the gulls.

The scene is superbly effective not only because of the close succession of surprises, the sudden entrances of widely contrasting, absurd figures, the violent reversal for Surly, but also because the dupes are all seen together on stage for the first time and they do not realize what they have in common, nor that the tricksters have brought about a climax of ridicule directed towards them while they display their extreme 'humours':

Surly　　　　　Why, this is madnesse, sir,
　　Not valure in you: I must laugh at this.
Kastril　It is my humour: you are a Pimpe, and a Trig,
　　And an AMADIS *de Gaule*, or a *Don* QUIXOTE.
Drugger　Or a Knight o'the *curious cox-combe*. Doe you see?
Ananias　Peace to the houshold.
Kastril　　　　　　　Ile keepe peace, for no man.
Ananias　Casting of dollers is concluded lawfull.

Kastril Is he the Constable?
Subtle   Peace, ANANIAS.
Face No, sir.
Kastril   Then you are an *Otter*, and a *Shad*, a *Whit*,
    A very *Tim*.
Surly   You'll heare me, sir?
Kastril   I will not.
Ananias What is the motiue?
Subtle   Zeale, in the yong gentleman,
    Against his *Spanish* slops —
Ananias   They are profane,
    Leud, superstitious, and idolatrous breeches.

(IV. vii. 37-49)

After this the audience may feel that a little calm will follow, but almost before the actors have got their breath back Jonson devises a further shock – Lovewit, Face's master, owner of the house, returns. The disguised duke has returned to unmask folly, to judge and to restore order.

Act V begins with a short sequence exposing the slow-wittedness of the citizen neighbours, which prepares us for Face's brazen outfacing and ridiculing of their truthful account of events. Face here proceeds exactly in the manner of Voltore, pleading to the court in *Volpone* IV. vi. Face appeals that the events are too absurd to be credible, and gives weight to this by his 'disguise' of sober, dutiful butler. He directs all the force of the accusations of Surly, Mammon and the rest back on their own heads, claiming they suffer from absurd delusions. Lovewit provides the audience with an alternative viewpoint from which the events of the play do indeed appear drunken fantasies and apparitions. The appeal to the norm enhances Jonson's achievement, of course, as well as giving richness to the situation; he is directing us to the completeness of his art. With every turn Face contrives new traps for his impassioned enemies. The cool Machiavel wins the approval of the 'judge' himself. The righteous but wild protests of Kastril and Ananias swamp the more reasonable analysis of Surly, making their claims seem ridiculous; they complete their own gullery:

Kastril You will not come then? punque, deuice, my suster!
Ananias Call her not sister. Shee is a harlot, verily.
Kastril I'll raise the street.
Lovewit   Good gentlemen, a word.

Ananias Sathan, auoid, and hinder not our zeale.
Lovewit The world's turn'd *Bet'lem*.
Face　　　　　These are all broke loose
　　Out of S.KATHER'NES, where they vse to keepe,
　　The better sort of mad-folkes.　　　　　(V. iii. 50-6)

Dol and Subtle have meanwhile planned to ditch Face in true city
comedy style:

Subtle　　　　Soone at night, my DOLLY,
　　When we are shipt, and all our goods, aboord,
　　East-ward for *Ratcliffe*; we will turne our course
　　To *Brainford*, westward, if thou saist the word:
　　And take our leaues of this ore-weaning raskall,　(V. iv.74-8)

and they look forward to unlocking the trunks of spoil 'And say, this's
mine, and thine, and thine, and mine – ' (V. iv. 91). Face has,
however, foreseen this eventuality, his self-interest, cunning and
efficiency being a match for theirs. Warning them to run for it, Face
announces the end of their partnership with a legal metaphor; their
particular social contract to protect each other from each other's fear
and greed is now broken:

　　　　　　　　　　　　　　　　here
　　Determines the *indenture tripartite*
　　Twixt SVBTLE, DOL and FACE.　　　　　(V. iv. 130-2)

Hobbes had conversations with Ben Jonson, it is recorded.
　　Face the comic Machiavel is highly adapted to his environment and
acutely aware of its springs of motivation, while his master, Lovewit,
triumphs where even Volpone failed. Jonson acknowledges the
practical possibility that such a team, materialist and opportunist, can
go on thriving indefinitely in Jacobean London; Lovewit and Face (not
Carker and Dombey) win the urban civil war.
　　The play utilizes the conventions of city comedy to present an analysis of the varying follies to which men are driven by greed. The three
tricksters wield the bait and contrive a series of *exempla* exposing the
essential ridiculousness, futility and sterility of human greed. The
success of Face is in itself an ironic comment on the total dedication of
his urban society to acquisitiveness: Face is the ideal citizen, from one
point of view. The first and seemingly conclusive unmasking of the
conventional 'disguised duke' – in the form of Surly – actually fails for

the first time in the history of the genre to bring folly and wrongdoing to order. The old-fashioned morality, as embodied in the plot-convention and the character Surly, can no longer control and dominate the new kind of criminal and Coney-Catcher. When the second judge, Lovewit, appears, he also at first commands respect for his obviously conventional role. Then it dawns on the audience that he is really a superior kind of city gentleman – a smooth operator with a quick mind whose eye is always fixed on the main chance; and though the other fools, hypocrites and maniacs are judged and ridiculed in conventional fashion, he and his servant evade punishment. Jonson himself is conscious that their victory is, if not moral, yet convincing.

IX

'BARTHOLOMEW FAIR'
AND
'THE DEVIL IS AN ASS'

CITY COMEDY AT THE ZENITH

The final 'sting' in *The Alchemist* comes when Face turns away from the play-world to deliver the Epilogue; in his dramatic character he asks for mercy from the audience of Londoners, 'you, that are my country'. This ironic equivocation invites them to recognize their essential kinship with the gulls in the play, so that then they will see how the 'indenture tripartite' uniting the rogues in their improvised *lazzi* corresponds to the real contract binding on the King's Men. At the Globe, rather than Lovewit's house, the players induce audiences to part with their money in exchange for some quick-change artistry and hot air. What is *The Alchemist* in performance, after all (goes the implication) but an improvised ironic version of familiar London life? It utilizes only the simplest props, everyday dress (with a few shabby and skimped costumes such as Dol's faery dress or Subtle's doctor's gown), no elaborate scenes or machines, and only one special effect. That one effect, furthermore, as if to drive the irony home, is used to disperse all the concentrated hot air: for when the imaginary alchemical projection explodes with a bang, the gulls are left with nothing while the rogues have all the money. Even the division of the spoils is parallel to the Elizabethan players' routine when an acting company broke up. Face's sheer effrontery makes the audience good-humouredly acknowledge their folly and the wit of the play's comic analogy of city life, so busy with ephemeral noise and activity, where speculations based on credit are liable to burst and where robes and furred gowns, solemn officials and professional men, strive to dignify the pursuit of gold.

Bartholomew Fair has an epigraph on the title page, a quotation from

Horace, in which this line of thought is developed. In this play too Jonson presents the coalescence of satiric play-world and reality as a refined form of didactic irony: the lines from Horace, *Epistles* II. i,[1] run as follows:

> If Democritus were still in the land of the living, he would laugh himself silly, for he would pay far more attention to the audience than to the play, since the audience offers the more interesting spectacle. But as for the authors of the plays, he would conclude that they were telling their tales to a deaf donkey.

Bartholomew Fair begins with an Induction presenting a spacious and lively survey of attitudes to poetry and the theatre, but Jonson gives first place to the views of the Stage-Keeper, an obstinate, complacent philistine, who remembers Tarlton and has a profound scepticism about the new-fangled ways of these modern 'Master-*Poets*' with their 'absurd courses'. He advises the audience that the playwright has not hit the humours of the Bartholomew birds – 'he do's not know 'hem' – and has actually refused to incorporate the Stage-Keeper's suggestion for a comic scene: that he should present a punk with her stern upward, to be soused with water by 'my wity young masters o'th *Innes o' Court'*. Jonson gets his chance to reply at once in the contract, read out by the scrivener, to be agreed between the audience at the Hope on Bankside and the author. In that contract Jonson insists that he is not concerned with five and twenty, or thirty years ago, the time of Hieronimo or Andronicus, but with the present, October 1614, with a familiar place in the city of London, Smithfield, on the occasion of the annual fair on 24 August (we will note, in the play itself, distinct allusions to hot weather, flies, summer fruit, and dog-killers 'in this month of August').

In the Induction Jonson goes out of his way to acknowledge the absurd element in his austerely ambitious programme to educate and elevate his audience, for while he admits the irony of having to court the approbation of the 'vnderstanding Gentlemen o' the ground', in the play itself he deliberately accommodates the Popular comic spirit: elements of fairground entertainment, diverse low comic characters, farce routines and dense local allusions are allowed much freer play than in any previous comedy. Jonson gives full licence to Aristophanic wit – he spares nobody, including himself – so that through the broad panoramic farce a truly ancient saturnalian spirit is aroused. Jonson brings all the resources of his mature mastery to bear on a problem he

failed to solve in 1599–1601: how to write a masterpiece while
virtually dispensing with a strong main plot and one or two major
protagonists. It is the consciousness that he was attempting something
still original, experimental and difficult at this mid-Jacobean time that
explains Jonson's insistence, in the ostensibly old-fashioned Induction,
that his play *Bartholomew Fair* is not to be judged by Popular
Elizabethan criteria which have 'stood still, these five and twentie, or
thirtie yeeres'. Jonson will not pretend to be unambivalently pleased
with their open Popular stages 'as durty as *Smithfield*, and as stinking
every whit'.

Although *Bartholomew Fair* presents a wide and initially confusing
variety of London types for the audience's inspection, they belong to
distinct groups (whose progress through the fair and the day's time-
span is clearly exhibited) and, as individuals, they compose an extensive
gallery of representative citizens. The emphasis on London is obvious
in the innumerable allusions to local trades and activities: the coney-
skin woman of Budge Row, the cunning man in Cow Lane (and the
other in Moorfields), the grocer in Newgate Market, the dog-killer in
the month of August, the seller of tinder-boxes, the feather-makers of
Blackfriars, the rag-rakers in dunghills, the mouse-trap man, the dyer
of Puddle-wharf, the marrow-bone man, the sellers of cream at
Tottenham – not to mention lean playhouse 'poultry', privy rich
whores, porters, puppet-show men, pretenders to wit at such taverns as
the Three Cranes, Mitre or Mermaid. Yet London is also the capital
city, and there we find representatives of the whole nation: Whit, the
bawd, is Irish; the members of the Watch are Scots and Welsh (Bristle,
according to Wasp, stinks of leeks, metheglin and cheese); there is a
Northern clothier and a Western man, besides Busy, the ex-baker of
Banbury, and Cokes, a country visitor from Harrow. The
concentration of activities implied by a city is fleshed out by teeming
references to different kinds of food and drink, clothes, manufactured
goods, and tradesmen's tools, many of which are shown in use. The
performance requires practicable fairground booths and properties and
a complete puppet show, and demands to be judged for its verisimilitude; the Smithfield location is supported by many references to details
of the area, its court of Pie-Poudres, and the history of the fair itself.

Evidently, then, Jonson offers the annual fair as an ironic microcosm
of the whole kingdom, and Justice Overdo's farcical endeavours to act
the wise magistrate have their allusive parallels, among others, to
Shakespeare's Duke in *Measure for Measure* and thence to King

James I himself, who is addressed directly in the Prologue and Epilogue which Jonson wrote for the play's Court performance.[2] Clearly, the whole point of *Bartholomew Fair* the play, like the real event, is that it is overcrowded, drawing in people of all sorts from far and near and concentrating diverse activities which are normally pursued in widely separated locations. From the outside the form of the whole is clear, its beginning and end fixed by dramatic or civil law, but in the middle of the press of people there is an impression of confusion and excess; indeed this is one of the cardinal delights of Jonsonian comedy at its best, where there is an exuberant feeling of marvellous copiousness, of extravagantly prodigal expenditure of energy, wit, invention, colour, sensations of all kinds. So much, indeed, is happening so quickly that it is inevitable that the spectator will miss many good things; but the complete confidence that what he is missing is as good as what he observes and enjoys produces a wonderful sensation of buoyant well-being. An allusion here, a minor episode there, may pass too quickly to be caught, but the spectator knows that when he finally catches up with it there will be savour in it (like the allusion to Apicius by Sir Epicure Mammon in *The Alchemist*).[3]

The deliberate impression of local confusion reaches truly surrealistic heights which challenge the play's basic structure, that of a clear, firm and trenchant critical comedy presenting a carefully graduated range of vice and folly with appropriate chastisement and correction. Jonson is concerned with both individual and communal needs for self-expression in relation to the constraints of law and order, and this design at its simplest is apparent in the first scene, which begins with a wedding licence being brandished, and in the play's final scene, featuring the Puritan Busy's denial of the authority of the licence given by the Master of the Revels to the players. Love and art, simply enough, open and close the play's thematic design. It will be appropriate to develop this point a little further in order to help clarify the special sense in which it is possible to speak of Jonson's plotting in *Bartholomew Fair*.

The figure of the Puritan Zeal-of-the-Land Busy appears at first wholly comic from the accounts given of him, especially Littlewit's, who says he found him 'fast by the teeth, i' the cold Turkey-pye i' the cupbord, with a great white loafe on his left hand, and a glasse of *Malmesey* on his right'. Yet Dame Purecraft's account of his activities reveals his ambition in darker kinds of fraud, 'making himselfe rich, by being made *Feoffee* in trust to deceased *Brethren*, and coozning their

heyres, by swearing the absolute gift of their inheritance'; and this
evidence of his zealous appetite must be taken into account when Busy
is seen denouncing fairs and May-games, wakes, and Whitsun ales.
Busy's dogma, which is so extravagantly enacted in his speech, opposes
the whole social and legal hierarchy of the nation, denying its
terminology and replacing it, indeed, with a mad restricted jargon, the
very genius of the grotesque, in which eating cooked pork becomes 'the
publike eating of Swines flesh, to professe our hate, and loathing of
Iudaisme, whereof the brethren stand taxed', or wherein the Fair's
booths become 'the tents of the wicked', and even a Proctor is a 'claw
of the *Beast*'. When in the stocks, Busy calls the Watch ministers of
darkness, curses the sound of Horace and Persius, 'those superstitious
reliques, those lists of Latin, the very rags of *Rome*, and patches of
Poperie'. The would-be apocalyptic strain in Busy's language reaches
one bathetic climax when he attacks the stall full of gingerbread men
and speech gives way to 'sanctified noise'! If Busy is one of the madmen
in the play, we must yet note that his brand of madness has its own kind
of mechanical perfection. In Busy himself it is not curable, and perhaps
only in the specially festive atmosphere of Jonsonian comedy is it so
easy to dismiss the threat of such radical political rhetoric and its
purposefully infectious potential. Here at any rate even a fool as
absolute as Littlewit cottons on to the party line as an easy and useful
key to doing as one likes, as when he notes that the glutted Busy is
'purified', or advises his wife of the correct procedure among the
'brethren' for being allowed an otherwise incorrect feast of roast pork.

By contrast, Grace Wellborn is a victim of the contemporary law
relating to wards which allowed the right of guardianship to be bought
by any man. Grace's wardship has been bought by Justice Overdo and
he insists on marrying her to his brother-in-law, the idiotic Cokes.
Cokes may be absurd, but marriage in earnest to him – even with the
intermittent diversion of adulterous affairs – is something painful to
contemplate, and Grace is right to be ironic about her situation. She
seizes the chance of escaping Cokes when the theft of his marriage
licence gives her the opportunity, and she decides to abide by the
random decision of the next person she meets as to which of the two
available gallants she should marry instead of Cokes. As it happens, by
chance and by the playwright's design, this decision falls to Troubleall,
a familiar local institution, an ex-officer of Overdo's court of Pie-
Poudres, dismissed by Overdo and gone mad, now obsessively insisting
on a warrant signed by Overdo before executing even the simplest

action. Grace and Troubleall, these two proto-Dickensian victims of the law, the Busy the determined subverter of the law, constitute the ground base of the play's critical theme: each of them pursues an individual line through the dramatic action and sheer chance determines any meetings or connections between them. At the same time, if we step back, we can see that Jonson interweaves their lines with those of others to constitute, in effect, a multiple intrigue plot fitting each person to his deserved fate. The frame of order achieved by the laws of intrigue plotting licences the leisurely, detailed development of virtually self-sufficient exemplary episodes, just as the play's central informing critical ideas licence its anarchic comic dialects and its explosive farce; thus Comical Satyre's didactic episodes 'in suspension' are tactfully supported by causal plotting, in which each significant phase of the action is marked by a hilarious physical fight on the stage, at once exposing and chastising folly and serving to bring separate lines of action together, at first complicating, finally resolving all the individual actions, offering two totally contradictory perspectives, one orderly, the other chaotic.

In an important, though qualified sense, *Bartholomew Fair* may be said to be composed of a series of 'humour' demonstrations, and the exemplary form requires a Presenter. In accord with the ambitious copiousness of the play, Jonson provides three main Presenters, Justice Overdo, Quarlous and Winwife, but he also supports the critical design by proliferating minor quarrels, debates and conversations in which characters comment on one another's trade secrets, personal habits, manners and morals, with memorable particularity and eloquence. Certain preliminaries are disposed of in Act I establishing the groups of visitors to the fair: Proctor Littlewit and his wife, Dame Purecraft and Busy (Puritan citizens), Cokes, Grace Wellborn, Mistress Overdo and tutor Wasp (with Gentle pretensions), and Quarlous and Winwife (young gallants). Jonson makes very thorough use of the conventions of city comedy. Thus Act II, set in the fair itself, begins with the soliloquy-oration of Justice Overdo, disguised as Mad Arthur of Bradley. The disguised-duke convention is completely inverted here, as Jonson's dialogue insists: 'They may have seene many a foole in the habite of a Justice; but never till now, a Jusice in the habit of a foole' (II. i. 7-9). Overdo declares that his ambition is to rival the assiduity of a certain Wise Magistrate[4] who would go disguised into every alehouse, down into every cellar, inspecting weights and measures, taking the gauge of custards 'with a sticke; and their circumference, with a thrid; weigh the loaues of bread on his middle-finger', for 'hee would not trust his corrupt officers; he would do't himselfe'. The mounting absurdity of these detailed, finicky trivia reminds us of Nashe; and soon enough Overdo is beside himself at overhearing Ursula's lesson to Nightingale in the art of giving short measures of ale:

> Froth your cannes well i' the filling, at length, Rogue, and iogge your bottles o' the buttocke, Sirrah, then skinke out the first glasse, euer, and drinke with all companies, though you be sure to be drunke; you'll mis-reckon the better, and be lesse asham'd on't.   (II. ii. 96-100)

Overdo reacts to this with ludicrously exaggerated censure, as he does in marking Leatherhead's jibe at Joan Trash that her gingerbread is made of rotten ingredients. These minor dishonesties among the fair's booth-holders are keyed to the prevailing abrasive but routine bargaining, in hyperbolic invective and low abuse, shared by the fair people. Overdo's ineptitude as Presenter-Judge is ironically confirmed when Ursula good-naturedly greets the disguised Justice – 'what new Roarer is this?' – and her condescending hospitality fits the facts: 'Bring him a sixe penny bottle of Ale; they say, a fooles handsell is lucky'.

As Overdo the Presenter moves on through the fair his complete ineptitude as a judge of people is exhibited, at first simply, when he is taken in by the fair appearance of Edgworth the cutpurse and sanctimoniously moralizes 'What pitty 'tis, so civill a young man should haunt this debaucht company', then more fully, when the team of ballad-singer and cutpurse use Overdo's puritanical sermon as a cover under which to steal Cokes's purse. Thus Overdo's canting sermon is shown to correspond in effect to Busy's dialect, no more than an elaborate cover for gullery and theft. At the same time, the puritanical ideas in the sermon are shown to be characteristic of the demented ravings of Mad Arthur of Bradley: Wasp quite reasonably believes Overdo to be an accomplice of the cutpurse, and Jonson's satire finds Overdo's stereotyped prejudices intolerable, so that his boisterous drubbing from Wasp appears thoroughly deserved as well as humorously predictable; this is in fact the first of a whole series of corporal punishments and public humiliations in Comical Satyre style which Overdo must undergo in the play. The episodes involving the cutpurse dramatize Coney-Catching pamphlet material, and Jonson deliberately imitates the moralistic, naive tone of Robert Greene in poor Overdo, who like Greene has a 'black book' in which these 'enormities' are to be recorded – indeed it was just Greene's style to over-dramatize some minor abuse like Ursula's technique for giving short measures of ale. Yet although these episodes had been made conventional in pamphlets before the 1590s were out, they are made new in Jonson's wonderful low prose, which inspires in them a vitality worthy of Thomas Nashe himself. It is significant that two years later, in 1616, Jonson's revised version of *Every Man in His Humour* appeared, its new setting in London presenting a triumphantly refreshed, local yet fantastic prose world.[5]

Overdo is a farcically obvious parody of a Presenter; the other two Presenters, Quarlous and Winwife, by comparison have wit, judgement, and understanding, so that their progress through the fair constitutes, on the whole, a straightforward fulfilment of the Presenter role, reinforcing the direct exemplary function of the diverse episodes in which characters display their humours, or in which instances of social and moral abuse are exhibited. Jonson is content to employ a didactic form here which recalls the Comical Satyres in its complete simplicity, and indeed it seems as if he is deliberately insisting on the comparison. In such instances as the first appearance of Wasp and Cokes, the two gallants provide a detached standpoint and then amuse themselves by coining witty comparisons, in which Wasp is a pretty insect and Cokes looks like 'one that were made to catch flies, with his Sir *Cranion*-legs'. Next they encounter Ursula the pig-woman; their superior air of detachment is exaggerated further as they exercise their wit at her expense:

> *Quarlous* Nay, shee is too fat to be a *Fury*, sure, some walking Sow of tallow!
> *Winwife* An inspir'd vessell of Kitchin-stuffe!
> *Quarlous* She'll make excellent geere for the Coach-makers, here in Smithfield, to anoynt wheeles and axell trees with.

Ursula is at first prepared to deflect such jests, but with the encouragement of Knockhem she soon finds the temptation to quarrel irresistible, and her blood once up, she erupts in splendid rage. The outcome is not so simply accounted for as Quarlous seems to think, for though Ursula may be as greasy as a pig on a spit, as violent as any tavern-roarer, and as big as an ox, there is some wit in her assessment of the gallants as thin-blooded, snotty-nosed, avaricious and lecherous. Quarlous resorts to intellectual sneers ('I finde by her *similes*, she wanes a pace') and well deserves a drubbing with Ursula's scalding-pan which both gallants only just avoid when Ursula falls into her own cooking fire. The precision of Jonson's wit in devising action and dialogue here achieves a Rabelaisian degree of inspired fantasy. Ursula calls for the nearest emollients to treat her scalded leg and these turn out to be (of course) cream and salad oil, as used to dress cooked pork. Knockhem the horse courser examines her blister – as big as a 'Windgall' – and prescribes the white of an egg, a little honey and pork fat, so that it is hard to tell whether he is concerned with a peasant's sympathetic magic or a cook's recipe. The fair-people live in their own absurd rival to the educated man's world, but it has its own consistent internal logic which refuses to separate human and animal. Ursula is described in terms of horses, bears and whales as well as pigs; from her booth are dispensed food, drink and sexual satisfaction, while basic bodily functions are relieved within. These simple symbolic associations of her booth are made graphic by such episodes as the conversion of the wives of the Judge and Proctor to prostitution there, and perhaps even more explicitly by Quarlous's action, who strips Troubleall of his clothes and leaves him in the booth while he goes to find Dame Purecraft and marry her in the disguise. Troubleall's final appearance, naked except for Ursula's scalding-pan held before him for modesty's sake, fuses these Rabelaisian associations of Ursula's booth with unaccommodated man, Adam, the instinctive appetites for food and sex, and the need to reconcile them with the law. The naked Troubleall, modesty preserved by the pan, replaces the graphic image of the puppet Dionysus who refutes the Puritan challenge by lifting up his clothes to reveal that he has *no* sex. A comically fallen Adam is better than a wooden puppet, and both are better than a hypocritical Puritan on the rampage.

It is evident from this design that Jonson extends the function of the role of Presenter by testing it, so to speak, to destruction. Though they have wit, both Quarlous and Winwife succumb to the prevalent humour of quarrelling, universal in the fair; they succumb also to the temptation to hearken after the flesh, and these two instincts bring them face to face, swords drawn, in dispute over Grace Wellborn in Act IV. iii. Resolution comes by the action of mad Troubleall himself and Quarlous when in disguise as the madman. The right true end of love is folly.

In discussing *Every Man in His Humour* earlier in this book (see chapter IV, p.54) I argued that the characters' distorted psychology and their colliding schemes of personal self-assertion, as they struggled with the obstinate facts of their surroundings, gave the spectacle of folly an unexpected but convincing authority as a mirror of the world, so that the tension between communal and personal needs and values comes to seem a source of inevitable instability, a stubborn social fact.

In *Bartholomew Fair* Jonson presents society as a quarrel at every level of exchange, from economic and social commerce to speech itself. The play offers an extraordinary range of voices, accents and rival styles of speech, from the jigging veins of rhyming mother wits in the puppet play to the tradesmen's cries in the fair itself, from the ballads sung by Nightingale to the curses of ramping Alice, the low cockney of Knockhem and Ursula, the Irish of Whit, the Scots of Haggis and the Welsh of Bristle, all the way up (or down) to the educated witty discourse of the young gallants and the supremely solipsistic discourses of Overdo and Busy. Busy, very properly, is put in the stocks beside the foolish Justice and the ungovernable tutor, so composing a memorable tableau. An exact equation is established between education, the law and religion in the commonwealth in this ironic version of a traditional emblem[6] of the perils of anarchy.

Yet of course *Bartholomew Fair* is no mere piece of Tudor didacticism, and locking Busy in the stocks only serves to fuel his apocalyptically flaming appetite for the attack on puppet actors – instead of gingerbread men – in Act V. Wasp the tutor, by contrast, being a professional disciplinarian, knows how to elude punishment and does not hesitate to do so, substituting a hand for a foot in the stocks and easily escaping. Between Busy, who denies the very existence of the stocks and will not admit to the physical fact of his detention, and Wasp, who slips out of them, sits Overdo, for whom the real process of education has begun (he learns for the first time of his responsibility for Troubleall's madness and expresses true regret) but Overdo remains ludicrous in his pompous exaggeration of his situation, citing Horace and Persius where just a little common sense would fill him with proper shame. Jonson ensures that Overdo remains ridiculous (unlike Kent in the stocks in *King Lear*) because Overdo has much to learn yet. Overdo's wife, as the audience knows, is experiencing a parallel humiliation, having got drunk and then been attacked by ramping Alice for trespassing on her pitch – after all Mistress Overdo does bear all the marks of a high-class whore in her citizen's tuff-taffeta and velvet! In this (for her) unnerving crisis Mistress Overdo gives in to Knockhem who recruits her as one of his own whores, and the imminent puppet show promises customers and good profits. The play's lines of action are drawn together with seemingly effortless and accidental coincidence, yet each line is lucidly exemplary in itself, and the characters collected together at last represent, though unconsciously, a wonderfully intricate counterpoint of mutual reproof, arranged under the simple scheme of comic unmasking. Overdo, once free of the stocks, reasserts himself as disguised-duke Presenter: 'cloud-like, I will breake out in raine, and haile, lightning, and thunder, upon the head of enormity' (V. ii. 4-6).

As the many characters of *Bartholomew Fair* assemble to make the audience for the puppet play, the real spectators in the Hope theatre may recognize an ironic if hilarious mirror image of themselves. Jonson's characters, representative members of the commonwealth, are shown to have surprising and paradoxical interconnections. The fair people, the Puritan citizens, the tutor, the preacher, the Justice – they all in a sense shout their wares, have their specialized sales talk, obey society's market forces and its rules of commerce. Alice the prostitute may be almost worn out in the service, whereas young Grace becomes an independent adult for the first time on this day; but Grace says herself she was 'bought'[7] by Overdo, though she is in no ordinary sense a whore. Mistress Overdo and Win are on show in their new profession of prostitution, a fact which casts a retrospective irony on their attitudes to marriage and property-owning respectability. As for the men, Quarlous has his new wife, worth £6000, and Grace's inheritance passes from the control of Overdo only to fall under the control of Winwife. Busy is a blatant cheat, but we may recall Quarlous regretting that he did not spend another year at the Inns of Court so as to become a politic pick-lock of the law,[8] and we have watched Wasp actually unlock himself from the stocks. Edgworth's minor thefts on his own poor account contrast to the really important theft he undertakes for the gallants, giving the lasting benefit of a prosperous, respectable marriage to Winwife and Grace. Thus the conventional identification of crime with mainly the lowest classes is shown to be a convenient social myth. It preserves the status quo and allows of much manoeuvring and negotiation, a Jacobean version of modern *sottogoverno*.

Jonson's depiction of society in this play is too wittily profound to exemplify any simple moral, and the comic ritual releases truly elemental Dionysiac forces, the instinctual drives of life itself. The annual fair coincides with a wedding feast, both occasions being traditionally inseparable only in the jaundiced eyes of the law from unwelcome drunkenness, fighting and sexual licentiousness. Seen in isolation, Cokes's career exemplifies the old proverb 'A fool and his money are soon parted', and in the simplest way. Yet Jonson's design relates the figure of Cokes in doublet and hose with the naked Troubleall and the puppet Dionysius as a triple farcical image of unaccommodated man, and sets that image against the puppet play itself, a wry symbol of European culture's unbroken relation to ancient Greece where the festival of Dionysius fused art and religion in a supreme ritual.

Strategically placed at the beginning of Act V, the puppet master's discourse on market forces in the professional theatre stresses (though with burlesque effect) the thematic importance of the puppet play in Jonson's own great comedy of contemporary Jacobean London. Hence Leatherhead notes 'Your home-borne proiects proue euer the best, they are so easie, and familiar, they put too much learning i' their things now o' dayes'. Leatherhead gives an account of his best get-pennies, almost guaranteed to drive a Puritan into apoplexy, and even to test James I's well-known moderation: '*Sodom* and *Gomorrah*; with the rising o' the prentises; and pulling downe the bawdy houses there, vpon *Shroue-Tuesday*; but the *Gunpowder-plot*; there was a get-penny!' (V. i. 9-12).

The puppet play is written in the primitive jog-trot of pre-Marlovian Tudor drama,[9] through which Jonson salutes as he also mocks the clumsy, reactionary style of Popular hacks such as Heywood and the other Red Bull rogues, pandering to an audience taste which equates drama with fairground curiosities such as the '*Bull* with the fiue legges, and two pizzles' or the 'dogges that daunce the Morrice'. When Jonson recommends that English writers treat the ancients as guides, not commanders, he does not mean to approve primitive hackwork doggerel fit only for puppet-plays:

> *This while young* Leander, *with faire* Hero *is drinking,*
> *and* Hero *growne drunke, to any mans thinking!*
> *Yet was it not three pints of Sherry could flaw her,*
> *till* Cupid *distinguish'd like* Ionas *the Drawer,*
> *From under his apron, where his lechery lurkes,*
> *put loue in her Sacke. Now marke how it workes.*

> (V. iv. 289-94)

Jonson senses that he must defend the whole of drama against its philistine enemies, and enters into the spirit of the thing with wonderful exuberance, once he licenses himself to stand shoulder to shoulder with the Littlewits and their serene imbecility. To this puppet-show playwright it is as if Marlowe's dazzling artistry with the heroic couplet in *Hero & Leander* were yet to be written, or as if one were to read Nashe's wonderful burlesque of that fable in *Lenten Stuffe* as a simply straightforward low comedy. All the same, half reluctantly, Jonson acknowledges that simple popular amusement has its own ancient tradition, springing ultimately from the same impulse for play, festivity and art which informs the greatest art of Rome and Greece. It is granted a key place in his play and its defence of art. (Nevertheless Jonson will still expect understanding spectators to recall how the great Terence himself, in his time, had reason to complain of audiences so base that they preferred jugglers and tight-rope walkers to his subtle comic art.)[10]

Seen in these terms, the puppet play forms an entirely appropriate thematic focus for the play's climax, provoking Busy to attack it, with a vigour that out-Stubbes Stubbes, as idolatry, scurrility, licentiousness, profanity – its actors vagabonds of no true calling, their costumes vanity and pride, their female impersonations abomination. The puppet's answer is a simple gesture – and an Aristophanic joke. It lifts up its costume to flaunt its no-sex. Busy is dumbfounded at last. Yet Overdo, on the contrary, can contain himself no longer:

> It is time, to take Enormity by the fore head, and brand it; for,
> I haue discouer'd enough.   (V. v. 125-6)

Overdo confidently proceeds, according to convention, as if this were the end of Middleton's *Your Five Gallants* (indeed his moralistic attempt to unravel the action also has its sly allusive glances at the Duke in *Measure for Measure*). Yet here in Act V of *Bartholomew Fair* the Presenter role cannot hope to impose itself on the action. The effects of intoxication on Mistress Overdo have their spectacular outcome: still dressed in her prostitute's outfit, she calls for a basin to be sick into, a farcical sort of catharsis for herself, and, consequently, for her husband also. Only now that they are fully purged can a truly Roman saturnalian feast be proposed. The play ends, and for the spectators too it is dinner-time in their real city of London; thus the fusion of the play-world and the real world is lightly acknowledged in its last line, as Cokes proposes to have the rest of the play 'at home'.

When Jonson's ironic burlesque of himself as the puppet-master and playwright is dwelt upon, and when we perceive in Overdo's petty censoriousness something of Jonson the literary reformist, we may recognize one final truly unexpected unmasking – of Ben Jonson himself – as play-world and real world coalesce. The humility with which

Jonson reconciles the Popular and educated traditions of comedy in this play is reflected in Overdo's final change of heart. In both cases confession of folly does not involve sacrifice of principle but, on the contrary, the achievement of more magnanimous, humane wisdom in action. This accords with Sir Philip Sidney's conviction that the end of all earthly learning is virtuous action. So, finally, the public poet Ben Jonson himself confesses his folly and, feasting us (though at our own expense, too) he realizes the ancient ritual of comedy, an individual release which is also a social reconciliation.

The Devil Is an Ass contrasts with *Bartholomew Fair* by relying on a firm, fast-moving and strongly articulated main action; if the earlier play is the climax to the experiments in Comical Satyre, then *The Devil Is an Ass* is the terminal point in Jacobean city comedy, the modified, Italianate form developed by the interrelated experiments of Middleton, Marston and Jonson. The satiric tone is harsher than in *Bartholomew Fair*, and links the play with Jacobean predecessors such as *Volpone* or *Michaelmas Term*. The intelligence and wit displayed locally in dialogue and handling of situations show Jonson at the height of his powers, and his thorough reliance on the conventions of the genre merely serves to emphasize the imagination and invention with which he creates fresh, living drama. In any event, it is perhaps to enrich the meaning of the word 'convention' if we apply it to the line of aspiring wealth seekers, Volpone, Mammon and Meercraft, and their Middletonian brothers Falso, Quomodo, Hoard and Yellowhammer.

Jonson begins this last great play with an Induction in Hell, the purpose of which is to initiate a plot which once more follows the disguised-duke pattern. The role of Presenter and Commentator is given this time to a devil, whose aim is the exact reverse of the conventional Presenter: instead of observing, exposing and correcting folly and vice, the devil's aim is to initiate and spread vice and iniquity. This ironic inversion of the convention emphasizes the fact that it is a convention: and having openly reminded the audience of the old Morality play origins of Jacobean satiric city comedy, Jonson makes a further satiric point by suggesting that Medieval Christianity and its drama are old-fashioned and neglected, not only because of atheism and fashion 'nowadays' but because

> they are other things
> That are receiv'd now upon earth, for *Vices*;

Stranger, and newer: and chang'd every houre ...
And it is fear'd they have a stud o'their owne
Will put downe ours. Both our breed, and trade
Will suddenly decay, if we prevent not.
Unlesse it be a *Vice* of quality,
Or fashion, now, they take none from us ...
They have their *Vices*, there, most like to *Vertues*;
You cannot know 'hem, apart, by any difference:

(I. i. 100-2, 108-12, 121-2)

The devil's work:

the laming a poore Cow, or two?
Entring a Sow, to make her cast her farrow?
... sowre the Citizens Creame 'gainst Sunday   (I. i. 8-9, 19)

becomes as naive and petty as the traditional butt for Jonson's ridicule, Popular taste. This is an illustration of the lifelong conflict in Jonson's art between his classically educated, serious, exacting critical mind, his determined reforming zeal and innovatory achievement in drama on the one side, and his Elizabethan, Popular inheritance in comic technique, language and mood, his traditional religious faith, his sympathy with rogues, tavern roarers, pig-women, Jest Books and Balladry on the other. In *The Devil Is an Ass* we do indeed find, as Jonson implies, the old conventions in new guise, up-to-date Jacobean villains who run rings round a character from the old Morality drama; but the Morality play conventions persist, it is only that the Prodigal and the Vices have reversed roles.

The main theme of the play consists in the outwitting of the gulls Fitzdottrel, Pug the disguised devil, and Lady Tailbush, by the Coney-Catchers led by Meercraft and by the sane gentlemen Wittipol and Manly. The ridicule of Fitzdottrel is a main feature of the first half of the play, and is carried in sequences exposing innate foolishness as well as in *lazzi* devised by the rogues and gentlemen. These wits combine to outwit Fitzdottrel in Act IV, though their interests clash in the crisis of the action, where the two prizes, Fitzdottrel's wife and his wealth, bring the persons of the play together before the eye of justice, sanity and order. The Presenter, Pug the disguised devil, entirely fails to spread vice and becomes instead the victim of more skilful agents of ill will, proper city comedy types. His career as a Present-Vice concludes with the Chief Devil's appearance, judging his actions and ridiculing his folly, which we have witnessed in the preceding *exempla*, and taking him away from the city.

Meercraft is introduced by one of his creatures and enters accompanied by another (supposed to be a servant from a lady appealing for Meercraft's services), while directing his self-advertising remarks to two other creatures. It is only after all these preliminary ploys (which recall those of Quomodo in *Michaelmas Term*) that Meercraft deigns to attend to his actual target Fitzdottrel. Even then he hooks him in obliquely:

> *Meercraft* . . . [*to Fitzdottrel*] But you must harken, then.
> *Ingine* Harken? why Sr, do you doubt his eares? Alas!
> You doe not know Master *Fitz-dottrel*.
> *Fitzdottrel* He do's not know me indeed. I thank you, *Ingine*,
> For rectifying him.
> *Meercraft* Good! Why, *Ingine*, then [*he turnes to Ingine*]
> I'le tell it you. (I see you ha' credit, here,
> And, that you can keepe counsell, I'll not question.)
> Hee shall but be an undertaker with mee . . .
> Hee shall not draw
> A string of's purse. I'll drive his pattent for him.
> We'll take in Cittizens, *Commoners*, and *Aldermen,*
> To beare the charge, and blow 'hem off againe,
> Like so many dead flyes, when 'tis carryed.
> The thing is for recovery of drown'd land,
>
> (II. i. 29-36, 40-5)

Here Jonson refines even on the swift, irresistibly confident decisiveness of the rogues deceiving Mammon in *The Alchemist*; specifically to be remarked here is the aside to Ingine 'I see you ha' credit, here' – this to his own accomplice! – and the simile which fits the act so perfectly and conveys Meercraft's real ruthlessness: 'like so many dead flyes'! When he moves in on his victim Meercraft's aim is to 'blind with science' of course, and he does so by being absolutely specific about figures and details of engineering; here Jonson's poet's eye for the sharply observed physical detail strengthens his portrayal of a highly intelligent confidence trickster. Jonson's sardonic portrayal of Meercraft's projects works through subtle inflation, for the fantasies, like those of Volpone, Mammon, and their ancestor Tamburlaine, are composed of real material: in the present case Meercraft's project for draining the fens is wholly feasible, and the basic logic of the bottle ale project too is sound – and present day industrialists might not laugh at a technique of saving

> in cork,
> In my mere stop'ling, 'bove three thousand pound,
>   (II. i. 92-3)

This satire has several layers. In direct dramatic terms, Jonson is emphasizing the skill of Meercraft who here brilliantly varies the Mountebank's stock technique. Meercraft's imagination builds up a series of projects so diverse, in such quick succession, that it seems there is a limitless number of opportunities for technology, for industrial development and investment; indeed, Meercraft implies, nothing is impossible. Industry, Meercraft tells his prey, is an actual, unromantic, existing Philosopher's Stone. Thus in Meercraft Jonson gives us the alchemist all over again, so that he can satirize a different manifestation of the folly induced by greed.

Meercraft's list of projects is significant in another respect. Meercraft's excited sales-talk produces a whole jumble of totally unrelated schemes, so bizarre in their variety and relative sizes as to appear absurd, even though each might in itself be reasonable. This, Jonson implies, is the way man applies the logic of science – in treating dog skins! It is no doubt because of Jonson's own reluctant acknowledgement of the power of modern science that Meercraft's projects are in the main feasible (for example, fen drainage, the fully mechanized mass production and bottling of ale, the manufacture and sale of forks). The skilful use of capital in industrial investment surely is the nearest actual substitute man has found for alchemy. But if Jonson conveys the excitement of aspiration, yet the satiric form determines his presentation of Jacobean scientific and commercial ventures. Ironic pattern is dominant.

It is a complex irony when Fitzdottrel privately consults the supreme cozener Meercraft and also sees fit to warn Pug the devil to beware of

> old croanes, with wafers,
> To convey letters. Nor no youths, disguis'd
> Like country-wives, with creame, and marrow-puddings.
> Much knavery may be vented in a pudding,   (II. i. 163-6)

Pug's soliloquy, commenting on the naive warnings of Fitzdottrel about 'policy', show the devil even more innocent than the gull; Jonson uses the conventional role of commentator to reflect ironically on the character who fills it, and emphasizes Pug's innocent ineptitude in the immediately subsequent sequence. There, all Pug's efforts at Machiavellian seduction are brushed aside by Mistress Fitzdottrel as the obvious play-acting of a hired tempter. She calls out to the imagined husband:

> Come from your standing, doe, a little, spare
> Your selfe, Sir, from your watch, t'applaud your *Squire*
> That so well followes your instructions!   (II. ii. 130-2)

This double irony is a witty reversal of the stock city comedy sequence in which the trickster demonstrates the evil in a character for the benefit of disguised or concealed, detached witness-commentators. Mistress Fitzdottrel, knowing her husband's enthusiasm for new plays, including Ben Jonson's *The Devil Is an Ass* (see I. iv. 21) naturally assumes she is involved in a conventional *exemplum*, a vice demonstration from the genre. This is a subtle and effective use of the old Comical Satyre fashion for witty infringements of the dramatic illusion.

The irony of Pug's presence in the role of Presenter-Commentator emerges again when the love scene between Wittipol and Mistress Fitzdottrel is interrupted by Fitzdottrel, who then beats his wife. Pug suddenly realizes that in hindering the lovesuit he has behaved morally, strictly against his brief from Hell. He continues this course by behaving like a country gull, being simultaneously cozened of a ring and taken in by a whore. The conventional episodes of the genre make Pug look ridiculous, one after another – Jonson's virtuoso handling of the genre is imaginative and sharply enforces the satiric point: Pug's career as Vice actually turns out to be the stock role of gull, the butt of ridicule and *lazzi*.

As Meercraft moves through the play he comes into contact with a wide range of city life; as in *Bartholomew Fair*, Jonson is eager to include as much of London as he can, though here his approach is more analytic, and the focus is on the working of industry, courtiers' monopoly distribution, patent medicines, sharking tradesmen and money-lenders, the sale of honours, legal corruption and property swindles. If *Bartholomew Fair* absorbs the subject matter and style of Comical Satyre, *The Devil Is an Ass* clearly enough gives brilliant dramatic life to the main subjects and characters of mature city comedy, conventional in the plays of Middleton, Marston and Jonson from 1602-7. Indeed Jonson seems to be recalling the atmosphere of

Middletonian comedy in the *lazzo* of the ring, beginning with the
dialogue between jeweller Guilthead and his son, a dialogue which is
overtly expository, gesturing towards clichés of Middletonian plot such
as the cycle of rich tradesman cozening landed gentry, going to live in
the country, seeing his children grow up as gentry, the young prodigals
coming to the city 'with their lands on their backs', and being cozened
of their inheritance by city sharks, Coney-Catchers and tradesmen in
their turn. Other cliché situations discussed are equally Middletonian
in their insistence on the 'war of every man, against every man';
Guilthead warns his son

> Wee must deale
> With *Courtiers*, boy, as *Courtiers* deale with us.
> . . . . There,
> Nothing is done at once, but injuries, boy:
>
> (III. iii. 4-5, 12-13)

Meercraft shows himself a really skilful businessman, quick thinking,
devious, technically knowledgeable in a way familiar from Middleton's
Coney-Catching money-sharks:

> I must ha' you doe
> A noble Gentleman, a courtesie, here:
> In a mere toy (some pretty Ring, or Jewell)
> Of fifty, or threescore pound (Make it a hundred,
> And hedge in the last forty, that I owe you,
> And your owne price for the Ring) He's a good man, Sr . . .
>
> (III. ii. 2-7)

However when Meercraft is opposed by Everill, a rogue of some
experience, he reveals his kinship with Volpone and Face; indeed the
argument is resolved in just the way of Face and Subtle. It needs
teamwork to win the urban civil war:

> *Everill* . . . I have, now,
>   A pretty tasque, of it, to hold you in
>   Wi' your *Lady Tayle-bush*: but the toy will be,
>   How we shall both come off?
> *Meercraft* Leave you your doubting.
>   And doe your portion, what's assign'd you; I
>   Never fail'd yet.   (III. iii. 220-5)

Similarly Meercraft's final *lazzo*, the attempt to cozen Fitzdottrel of his estate, is in its detail reminiscent of the deed-signing in *Volpone* and *Michaelmas Term*, and in its form conventional to the genre in its middle period. Manly, the upright, unwaveringly moral gentleman, survives uncozened and unridiculed here, in sharp contrast to Surly in *The Alchemist* but exactly like the approved norm of conduct in city comedy of the 1602-7 period; in fact Manly's role is wholly and plainly didactic, his comments are to be relied on and it is he who delivers the judgement and the moral homily which is to be learned from the *exemplum* provided by the play.

The conclusion similarly recalls the more rigidly didactic form of city comedy in its middle years in the hands of Middleton. The final *lazzo* is disrupted by the Keeper of one of the London prisons, and the news he brings of the departure of Pug back to Hell causes Fitzdottrel to unmask his own feigning and the lies of the lawyer, and Manly steps in to complete the moral judgement; his terms are notably serious, unrelenting, moral and severe:

> Sir, you belie her. She is chaste, and vertuous,
> And we are honest. I doe know no glory
> A man should hope, by venting his owne follyes,
>
> > (V. viii. 151-3)

and though the criminals are not directly punished, they are recommended to corrrection:

> Let 'hem repent 'hem, and be not detected.
> It is not manly to take joy, or pride
> In humane errours   (V. viii. 168-70)

The ironic treatment of rogues in city comedy corresponds to the growing power and success of merchants, lawyers, and parliamentary opposition in Jacobean England. The comic and satiric potential in drama of attitudes of ruthless materialism is memorably exploited in the plays of Marlowe, and we may recall that T. S. Eliot called Jonson Marlowe's legitimate heir. It may help to focus the relationship by noticing that much Jacobean comic spirit is apparent already in the curt retort of Tamburlaine's lieutenant Techelles to a vanquished opponent:

> *Theridamas* Doost thou think that *Mahomet* will suffer this?
> *Techelles* Tis like he wil, when he cannot let it.

When Jonson completed *The Devil Is an Ass* two decades had passed since he first embarked on his campaign to make English stage comedy conform in principle and practice to the noblest classical example and Renaissance theory. Here, in his last undisputed masterpiece (a strict critical comedy) he ironically salutes the outmoded Tudor Morality and reworks the most popular elements from the city comedy of Middleton, his pupil and rival in the art. This self-consciousness advertises Jonson's concern to acknowledge in *The Devil Is an Ass* the evolution of the genre – which he does through the polarization of old and new dramatic form and old and new social attitudes. The rustic gull's career of Pug the devil highlights the fast-moving, ruthless cynicism of London in 1616. Jonson shows a city recognizably modern in its alienation: capital, technology, fashion and crime are dominant, and its new tough secular language has a confidence which bodes ill for the opponents of materialism. It is both ironic and natural that Restoration audiences should have so esteemed Jonson; Dryden, commenting on his popularity on the Restoration stage, observed that in design and language Jonson's comedies needed little alteration to be fully understood.

Critical comedies set in the city continued to be written after Jonson's zenith passed, notably by Brome and Massinger; the theatres were closed in 1642 and only reopened in 1660. Howard's play *The Committee* (1662) is a point of transition; after the Restoration the satiric treatment of city types and themes is used to ballast the sexual wit-comedy of manners demanded by the class-conscious audiences. If a terminal point for the history of city comedy motifs in English stage comedy is to be sought, perhaps Gay's *The Beggar's Opera* (1728) provides it.

In the present study I have placed a selective emphasis on the essential features of the genre as exhibited in its best plays, so that a reader may recognize a city comedy when he sees one. I do not believe that Brome or Massinger extend the resources of city comedy or alter its mode, nor that they provide much fresh insight into the underlying sources of tension, instability and change in seventeenth-century England. After the theatres were closed at the beginning of the Civil War the power of the idea of theatre continued to be recognized, not least in the way Andrew Marvell in 'Upon Appleton House' depicted the struggle in terms of the scenic transformations of a Court masque.

Retrospectively in *Samson Agonistes* Milton pours scorn on the Philistine rulers of Restoration London and their paltry idea of theatre, and his great tragedy dramatizes the failure of the English revolution in terms that were to be reaffirmed in later revolutionary times by Blake. Puritan opposition to the stage throughout the seventeenth century, however bitter, always acknowledges the power of drama in the culture. It is this acknowledgement, surely, which is expressed in the fierce irony of the decision to execute Charles I, the 'royal actor', on an open-air wooden stage in Whitehall, using the facade of the Banqueting House as tiring house. Thus Inigo Jones's design for a very different kind of theatre, exclusive, indoor, lavish, spectacular, absolutist, is reversed, and for one day the unworthy scaffold again presents a memorable scene.

APPENDIX

A MINOR GENRE:
THE CONEY-CATCHING PAMPHLET

The qualities of liveliness, vigour, flexibility, and strongly Anglo-Saxon vocabulary, characterize good Elizabethan low prose. These qualities manifest themselves in the drama, but they also account for much of the attractiveness of non-dramatic writing about low life. Although a pamphlet is not so overtly shaped by the requirements of artistic convention as a play, it must be shaped carefully, especially when the writer seeks to appear the mere reporter of directly observed event. There was, of course, no Elizabethan Henry Mayhew, no deliberate attempt at sociological study in the modern sense. Many of the writers under discussion here were also repertory playwrights who made a living – rarely a good one – from their pens. It is certain that the boom in low-life pamphlets in the late 1590s attracted such writers because of the financial rewards. As a consequence it seems reasonable to examine their work in literary terms: if they wrote to entertain and attract readers, they should be judged accordingly. In any case, at least enough emphasis has been placed on the documentary value of their work, and not enough on its relation to dramatic comedy.

John Awdelay and Gilbert Walker wrote the first important narratives of low life printed in sixteenth-century England. Neither work is a straightforward account of direct observation; yet Awdelay's *Fraternitie of Vagabonds* was perhaps the most influential work of all. It follows the German *Liber Vagatorum* of 1510, which was partly based on manuscript accounts of criminal trials at Basle. Awdelay follows the tripartite form of the pamphlet and reproduces the classes of vagabond and many of their tricks. This attempt to add an official air to the work with formal classifications also involved a restriction on the intensity of moral indignation that could be expressed: as a result, the prose style itself is hamstrung. Moreover, Awdelay lacks a sense of narrative timing, fails to point up his key line and dissipates the interest in his material, for example in the anecdote[1] of the Patriarke Co. A more basic failure is his inability to visualise a scene and indicate its dramatic development:

They thus ticklying the young man in the eare, willeth him to make as much money as he can, and they wil make as much as they can, and consent as though they wil play booty against him. But in the ende they so use the matter, that both the young man leeseth his part, and, as it seemeth to him, they leesing theirs also, and so maketh as though they would fal together by the eares with this fingerer, which by one wyle or other at last conveyeth himselfe away, & they as it were raging lyke mad bedlams, one runneth one way, an other an other way, leaving the loser indeede all alone.

(Ibid., p.9)

It is valid to analyse Awdelay's work in these terms because the anecdotal nature of his material demands compression, a sense of timing, apt vocabulary, perhaps the dialogue form if it is to be effective. It is these qualities we find in the best anecdotes of the early Jest Books, e.g. " 'I hope better' quoth Bolton, when his wife cried 'come in, cuckold' ' ". Walker's *Manifest Detection of Dice Play* is by contrast a sophisticated piece, fusing explanation of tricks with anecdote within a frame of moral comment. Walker's pamphlet is in the dialogue form, the victim of trickery standing for the reader in the following manner:

> *M.* Thus give they their own conveyance the name of cheating law; so do they other terms, as sacking law, high law, figging law, and suchlike.
>
> *R.* What mean ye hereby? Have ye spoken broad English all this while and now begin to choke me with mysteries and quaint terms?[2]

The experienced M. has a firm attitude to vagabonds, but the freshness of expression gives some vitality to his rehearsal of a 'nowadays' lament:

> Now, such is the misery of our time, or such is the licentious outrage of idle misgoverned persons, that of only dicers a man might have half an army, the greatest number so gaily beseen and so full of money,
>
> (Ibid., p.34)

Walker's pamphlet form gives coherence to the material, and discussion of moral and social themes emerges naturally from the conversation of the two characters M. and R. He takes care with detail, his prose rhythms imitate those of speech and his narrative control gives clarity to the subject matter.

> *M.* So long as a pair of barred cater-treys be walking on the board, so long can ye cast neither 5 nor 9, unless it be, by a great mischance, that the roughness of the board, or some other stay, force them to stay and run against their kind; for without cater-trey ye wot that 5 nor 9 can never fall.
>
> *R.* By this reason, he that hath the first dice is like always to strip and rob all the table about! (Ibid., p.39)

The clarity of this didacticism may be the explanation for its choice as a model by the authors of *A Notable Discovery of Coosnage* and of *Mihil Mumchance*, both of whom plundered it extensively.

The rational clarity of Walker is not characteristic of prose writing designed for quick sales, however; and in Harman's *Caveat for Common Cursetors* the sensationalism starts the mainstream of development in low life narrative.

The *Caveat* is an expansion of the *Fraternitie*. The expansion takes the form of anecdote, comment and emotional colouring; much of the latter is effected by a clumsy scattering of adjectives, word pairs and crude alliterative fustian:

> their drowsey demener and unlawfull language, pylfring pycking, wily wandering.[3]

and against this tale of evil is set the familiar positive symbol always siezed by the popular dramatist at a loss for a sentimental conclusion for a sequence:

> the Queenes most excelent maiestye, whom god of his infinyte goodnes, to his great glory, long and many yeares make most prosperously to raygne over us.   (*Harman*, pp. 21 – 2)

Harman is nothing if not effusive. But the crude style conceals some surprisingly shrewd modifications which point towards a successful formula for popular pamphlet writing.

To each of the terse and ineptly phrased 'characters' in Awdelay Harman adds illustrative material, usually Jest Book style anecdotes; and though many of these may be traditional some seem freshly conceived. Thus in the episode of Genyngs we find

> The boye that so folowed hym by Water, had no money to pay for his Bote hyre, but layde his Penner and his Ynkhorne to gage for a penny
>   (Ibid., p. 54)

and even a sociologist could scarce forbear to cheer when he reads

> he relented and plucked out another pursse, where in was eyght shyllings and od money; so had they in the hole that he had begged that day xiij shillings iii pens halfepeny.

The earnest moral approach of Harman – or, to look at it another way, his emphasis on the sensational wickedness of his subjects – leads him to tedious tumidity in style. Superlatives are used too generously, as, typically, here:

> *most* subtyll people: the most part of these are Walch men, and wyll *never* speake, unlesse they have *extreme* punishment, but wyll gape, and with a *marvelous* force wyll hold downe their toungs doubled.   (Ibid., p. 57)

It is characteristic of such narratives to insist on the amazing villainy which is being unmasked. It is, however, also in the interest of these writers to make trickery attractive and crime glamorous; if there is comedy to be found they do not ignore it. In the following example Harman invites his readers to enjoy, vicariously, the pleasures of knavery, and then to enjoy the pleasure of self-righteous condemnation of it. Here a parson, robbed by rogues who make him promise to spend twelve pence at the inn, arrives at the inn and asks after them:

> 'Which two men?' quoth this good wife. 'The straungers that came in when
> I was at your house wyth my neighbores yesterday.' 'What! your nevewes?'
> quoth she. 'My nevewes?' quoth this parson; 'I trowe thou art mad.' 'Nay,
> by god!' quoth this good wife, 'as sober as you; for they tolde me faithfully
> that you were their uncle...I never saw them before.' 'O out upon them!'
> quoth the parson; 'they be false theves.'   (Ibid., p.40)

The main body of Elizabethan narratives of low life is of interest primarily for
technical and stylistic developments, for although a large number of narratives
have survived, the writers are strikingly economical in their use of material,
and the coat made by Awdelay is turned and turned again. The first famous
Coney-Catching pamphlet, for example, *A Notable Discovery of Coosnage*
(1591), owes heavy debts to Awdelay, Walker and Harman, and actually
paraphrases Harman in the following passage:

> Yet, Gentlemen, am I sore threatened by the hacksters of that filthy faculty
> that if I set their practises in print, they will cut off that hand that writes.[4]

The *Notable Discovery* is no less interesting in technique for this, for here is
coined the phrase 'coney-catching', a most useful device for unifying
somewhat diverse material and a brand name easily remembered by the public.
The style is lively, the dialogue has point, speed and verisimilitude in rhythm
and vocabulary:

> So they shuffle and cut, but the verser wins. 'Well,' saith the setter, 'no
> butter will cleave on my bread. What! not one draught among five. Drawer, a
> fresh pint. I'll have another bout with you.'   (Ibid., p. 127)

By this date of course developments in dramatic writing were occurring with
mounting speed: it is no coincidence that the best effects here are gained in
dialogue.

The Second Part of Coney-Catching, registered in the same month, assumes
knowledge of the first and refers to it several times, particularly the self-
dramatization.

> [they will] cut off my right hand for penning down their abominable
> practices...But...I live still, and I live to display their villainies.[5]

The reader is addressed as an old friend, a valued, right-thinking citizen: he is
courted as the spectator is courted by the Prologue speaker in the theatres.
Greene was a repertory playwright and one of the great talents of such writers
was in the adaptation of diverse material to the conventional structure of
Popular plays. Situation comedy and sequences of melodrama are the basis of
low-life narrative episodes and it would have been natural for Greene to handle
such material with the same skill and freedom he used as a dramatist. The

Coney-Catching pamphlets, seen in this light, appear not as reprehensible attempts to deceive a gullible public or gullible historians, but as narratives written within a convention analogous to the conventions of stage comedy. The second pamphlet shows Greene establishing conventions, for example in the manner of introducing episodes: 'a gentleman, a friend of mine, reported unto me this pleasant tale of a foist' (p. 167) and providing familiar and specifically located settings: 'their (nips' and foists') chief walks is Pauls, Westminster, the Exchange' (p. 162). This latter convention is particularly significant, for it seems likely that it directly influenced the location, in contemporary London, of sequences in city comedy and before that in Shakespeare's later histories *Henry IV* and *Henry V* (though there the date is ostensibly over a century earlier).

What Greene does is to appear personally knowledgeable, expanding the briefer remarks of Walker with dramatic imagination, adding details of geographical setting and physical appearance of the characters, occasionally using Jest Book anecdote, and enriching the whole with racy and fast-moving dialogue.

In *The Third Part of Coney-Catching* the material is thin, and Greene's interest seems taken up by technique; thus an obvious and crude Merry Tale is dressed up in obligatory criminal robes: 'the carders receive their charge, the dicers theirs, the hangers-about-the-Court theirs'[6] and the action is set in 'St Laurence Lane' or 'the conduit in Aldermanbury'. Yet an episode he would have related in five hundred words in the *Notable Discovery* is here spun out to nearly two thousand, and the writing lacks edge. Greene does explore the convention of erecting pseudo-classifications of criminals, as the quotation (above) indicates, but with little conviction: he is 'cashing in' on earlier success. This is no less true of the *Disputation*[7] published also in 1592, full of rogue slang and classifications which may be traced back to Awdelay in most cases. Here Greene adds a fictional criminal biography, the latest fashion in low-life narrative, probably resulting from the translation of the picaresque novel *Lazarillo de Tormes* in 1586.[8] Greene's biography of the whore Nan is little more than crude anti-woman complaint, while his *Black Book's Messenger* is really a Jest Book given continuity by the presence of the hero Ned Browne in each episode, as in the anonymous collections *Scoggins Jests* and *Tarltons Jests*. Greene at any rate shows his versatility in incorporating such techniques under the 'Coney-Catching' label, in order to attract as many readers as possible.

It is not to the point here to establish how far Nashe's loose biography of *Jack Wilton, or the Unfortunate Traveller*, diverges from the strict picaresque novel; but it *is* to the purpose to note that as a fictional biography of a rogue it appeared two years after Greene's. The disparity between Greene's failure and Nashe's success in the form marks the difference in talent between the two writers; but it also marks the difference between the markets for which they were written: *Jack Wilton* is a long work, and written with care as well as boisterous energy.

The life of the rogue *Jack Wilton* has usually been discussed as an example of early experiment in the novel form – a somewhat double-edged compliment to say the least. In the present group of prose narratives, on the other hand, Nashe's work is so dazzling a triumph it almost stifles discussion, drawing all the oxygen to feed its own vigour. Nashe has a sophistication which derives partly from Martin Marprelate, but is far beyond the grasp of Robert Greene. Here is the tapster, for example:[9]

> he was an old servitor, a cavelier of an ancient house, as might appeare by the armes of his ancestors, drawen verie amiably in chalke on the in side of his tent dore.

More centrally important in this discussion is Nashe's marvellous facility in rendering, through choice of detail and appeal to the visual imagination, actuality of setting:

> for comming to him on a day, as he was counting his barels and setting the price in chalke on the head of them, I . . . tolde his *alie* honor I had matters of some secrecy to impart unto him, if it pleased him to grant me private audience. With me, yong *Wilton*, qd. he, mary, and shalt: bring us a pint of syder of a fresh tap into the three cups here, wash the pot: so into a backe roome hee lead me, where after he had spitte on his finger, and pickt of two or three moats of his olde moth eaten velvet cap, and spunged and wrong all the rumatike drivell fro his ill favored goats beard, he bad me declare my minde, and thereupon hee dranke to mee on the same.

Nashe gets his effects through specific attention to detail – 'wash the pot', 'a fresh tap'. His careful physical geography and his dramatist's eye for telling gesture only emphasize his fertile visual imagination and superb skill in verbal artifice. But joined to these is the admirably sustained pose of youthful humorous contempt – 'if it pleased him to grant me private audience' – and finally the extraordinary sensitivity to rhythm and to vocabulary ('rumatike drivell').

Nashe's imagination is fecund, and his flexible syntax suits his perpetual alertness to the possibilities of absurdity in what he writes as he writes it. His satiric attitude to his surroundings and his fellows fixes his work in physical detail only to make highly sophisticated patterns, striking out new combinations in witty incongruity. Thus a piece of dialogue may be based on indecorous mixture of literary and social styles:

> Not to make manie words, (since you will needs knowe,) the King saies flatly, you are a myser and a snudge, and he never hoped better of you. Nay, then (quoth he) questionles some Planet that loves not Syder hath conspired against me. (Ibid., p. 215)

But immediately Nashe substantiates the broad outline with physically visualized detail in which he follows the train of absurd thought to its conclusion:

the King hath vowed to give *Turwin* one hot breakfast onely with the bungs that he will plucke out of your barrells.

In fact, even when he carries an idea to completely fantastic lengths, the sheer accuracy of detailed observation makes the reader reluctant to dismiss the fantastic artifice. Here description of a heat-wave brings us closer to the physical stuff of Elizabethan London than all Greene's pamphlets put together: his pose of confident assertion and flat statement ('I have seen') are more convincing than the less absurd and certainly more credible fictions of lesser pamphleteers:

> Felt makers and Furriers, what the one with the hot steame of their wooll new taken out of the pan, and the other with the contagious heat of their slaughter budge and connieskinnes, died more thicke than of the pestelence: I have seene an old woman at that season, having three chins, wipe them all away one after another, as they melted to water, and left hir selfe nothing of a mouth but an upper chap . . . Masons paid nothing for haire to mixe their lyme, . . . it dropped off mens heads and beards faster than anie Barber could shave it. (Ibid., p. 229)

To examine the extant narratives which follow those discussed here is to learn nothing significant about the development of low-life narrative – it had been absorbed into the drama. The same conventions are followed, the same incidents recur, reproduced from the narratives of Greene, Walker, Harman, Awdelay: they even recur in Richard Head's *English Rogue* of 1665. One exception to this is the justly famous *Gull's Horn Book* in which Dekker shows the beneficial influence of Jonson and the early Jacobean vogue for dramatic satire, though his characteristic yeomanlike distaste for bitter satire preserves the tone of Nashe in what is in fact a parody of the pseudo-didactic low-life pamphlet. Plainly the parody indicates that the material, if not in dramatic form, is *vieux jeu* now:

> Short let thy sleepe at noone be,
> Or rather let it none be.

Sweete candied councell, but theres rats-bane under it: trust never a Bachiler of Art of them all, for he speakes your health faire, but to steale away the maidenhead of it: *Salerne* stands in the luxurious country of *Naples*, and who knowes not that the *Neapolitan* will (like *Derick* the hangman) embrace you with one arme, and rip your guts with the other?[10]

Only an Elizabethan pamphleteer like Dekker could so deftly parody its essential style.

NOTES

I CITY COMEDY AS A GENRE

1. Admirable general surveys of the comedy of the period to which I am indebted are Una Ellis-Fermor, *The Jacobean Drama* (London, 1936), L. C. Knights, *Drama and Society in the Age of Jonson* (London, 1937), O. J. Campbell, *Comicall Satyre and Shakespeare's Troilus and Cressida* (San Marino, California, 1938), Alfred Harbage, *Shakespeare and the Rival Traditions* (New York, 1952), M. C. Bradbrook, *The Growth and Structure of Elizabethan Comedy* (London, 1955). On dramatic conventions I learned much from M. C. Bradbrook, *Themes and Conventions of Elizabethan Tragedy* (Cambridge, 1935); on satire, from O. J. Campbell, op. cit. and Alvin Kernan, *The Cankered Muse* (London 1959). On individual dramatists the essays of T. S. Eliot on Jonson (1919), Middleton (1927) and Marston (London, 1934) contain the seeds of the best subsequent critical discussion. The term 'city comedy' is closely identified with Jonson, Marston and Middleton by M. C. Bradbrook, *The Growth and Structure of Elizabethan Comedy* (London, 1955), chapter 9. See also my Select Bibliography.
2. *Meditations on a Hobby Horse* (London, 1963), p.67.
3. *Discoveries* 2476-8 in *Ben Jonson*, ed. C. H. Herford and P. and E. Simpson (Oxford, 1925-52). All quotations from Jonson are taken from this edition. All quotations from Shakespeare are taken from the edition by Peter Alexander (1951).
4. 'Commerce and Coinage' in *Shakespeare's England* (London, 1917), vol. I, p.340.
5. See E. H. Gombrich, *Art and Illusion* (London, 1962), chapter 2, for many admirably clear examples of the importance of the schema to any representation in art, supporting Wölfflin's famous remark that all pictures owe more to other pictures than they do to nature: the artist must always catch a motif within the network of a schematic form.
6. See David M. Bevington, *Tudor Drama and Politics* (Cambridge, Mass., 1968).

7. The heavily insistent beat of these lines approaches self-caricature, though Asper seems to have Jonson's essential approval. See my discussion of the play below in Chapter IV.

8. *Brecht on Theatre*, trans. John Willett (London, 1964), p.161.

9. Ibid., pp.14-15.

10. See Harbage, op. cit., *passim*, or W. A. Armstrong, 'The Audience of the Elizabethan Private Theatres' (*RES*, 1959); more recently, an intelligent and well-written study of Coterie drama is Arthur C. Kirsch, *Jacobean Dramatic Perspectives* (Charlottesville, Va., 1972). The fashionable satiric style at the children's theatres need not have excluded all but the most intellectually and socially privileged spectators, and there is still no hard evidence that it did so (*pace* several recent articles by Michael Shapiro and others). Jonson's lines to Fletcher on *The Faithful Shepherdess* in 1608 suggest a far from exclusive social composition of the audience and scarcely overwhelming entrance price:

> *Gamester*, *Captaine*, *Knight*, *Knight's man*,
> *Lady*, or *Pusil*, that weares maske, or fan,
> *Velvet*, or *Taffeta* cap, rank'd in the darke
> With the shops *Foreman*, or some such brave sparke,
> That may judge for his *six-pence*

11. See John Peter, *Complaint and Satire in Early English Literature* (Oxford, 1956).

12. The relation of Jonson's early comedies to non-dramatic satire is studied in Campbell, op. cit. The Italian settings of these plays allow for ironic allusive comment on London but the language and social assumptions often dissolve the distinction between Italy and England. Jonson's revised version of *Every Man In* has an explicit and densely detailed London setting: see J. W. Lever's parallel-text edition in the Regent's Renaissance Drama series (London, 1971) which has succinct discussion of Jonson's revisions.

13. See my Appendix for a study of Coney-Catching pamphlets.

14. *Thomas Nashe* (London, 1962), p.24.

15. Bernard Harris in his New Mermaid edition of *The Malcontent* (London, 1967) notes that two extra scenes (I. viii. and V. i.) were added for the King's Men; the scenes involve Passarello, the only new role added for the Globe performance. Other minor additions were probably made to compensate for the absence of songs usual in performances by the children's companies. For further discussion of the play's transfer to the Globe see G. K. Hunter's edition in the Revels Plays (London, 1975). On the subject of acting styles at Blackfriars and Paul's there has been much debate: see G. K. Hunter, *John Lyly* (London, 1962) and his editions of Marston's *Antonio* plays in the Regent's series (London, 1965); R. A.

Foakes, 'John Marston's Fantastical Plays' (*PQ*, 1962) and *Shakespeare, the Dark Comedies to the Last Plays* (London, 1971). Further books and articles are listed in the Select Bibliography.

16. Peregrine Books edition (London, 1962), p.148.
17. Ibid.
18. In the final paragraph of *Leviathan*, ed. Michael Oakeshott (Oxford, 1946), p.467.

II A FOUNTAIN STIRR'D

1. L. Stone, *The Crisis of the Aristocracy, 1558-1641* (Oxford, 1965), p.368.
2. Hobbes, *Leviathan*, part I, chapter 11.
3. 'Of Usury' in *Works*, ed. Spedding, Ellis and Heath (1861), vol. VI, p.475.
4. Cited by Peter, op. cit., p.85.
5. Penguin edition (Harmondsworth, 1961), pp. 188-9.
6. Stone, op. cit., p.535.
7. Ibid.
8. G. R. Elton, *England under the Tudors* (London, 1962), pp.224-5.
9. Julian Cornwall, 'English Population in the Sixteenth Century', *EHR* (1970). See also Harry A. Miskimin, *The Economy of Later Renaissance Europe 1460-1600* (Cambridge, 1977), chapter 2. Elton, in his second edition of *England under the Tudors*, adds a chapter of Revisions (1972) in which he accepts the importance of population growth and rejects his earlier emphasis on the effect of imported Spanish silver as a cause of inflation.
10. *Inflation in Tudor and Stuart England* (1969), p.47.
11. Cf. Elton, op. cit., pp.224-38.
12. Ibid., p.232.
13. Ibid., p.362.
14. Vol.I, p.378.
15. Ibid., p.353.
16. Nef, op. cit., vol.I, pp.175-6.
17. J. U. Nef, 'Technology and Industry 1540-1640', *EHR* (1934); Miskimin, op. cit., chapters 4 and 6.
18. Stone, op. cit., pp.346-52.
19. *Voyages*, Everyman Library (London, 1962 edition), vol.VIII, p.60.
20. *Tudor England* (Harmondsworth, 1950), p.286.
21. (1904), p.188.
22. See L. Stone, *An Elizabethan: Sir Horatio Pallavicino* (Oxford, 1956), and A. F. Upton, *Sir Arthur Ingram 1565-1642* (Oxford, 1961). These two subjects present an arresting contrast to the indulgent portraits of merchants as folk heroes in Popular chronicle plays such as Heywood's *If*

You Know Not Me You Know Nobody, Part II or Dekker's *The Shoemakers' Holiday*, or the non-dramatic narratives of Deloney.

23. See R. Ashton, *The Crown and the Money Market* (Oxford, 1960).
24. *Tudor England*, p.288.
25. *Religion and the Rise of Capitalism*, pp.181-2.
26. Stone, *The Crisis*, pp. 530, 544, 546.
27. *Elizabethan Government and Society*, ed. S. T. Bindoff et al.. (London, 1961), p.176.
28. See above, n.22.
29. 'Myddelton of Tower Street' in Bindoff (ed.), op. cit., cf. n.27.
30. *Drama and Society in the Age of Jonson* (London, 1937), p.83.
31. *England under the Tudors*, p.256.
32. See *Queen Elizabeth and Her Times* (1838), especially pp.164-6.
33. Everyman edition (London, 1956), p.81.
34. Ibid., p.82.
35. Stone, *The Crisis*, p.273.
36. Ralph Dutton, *The English Country House* (London, 1962), p.35.
37. Elton, op. cit., pp.257-8.
38. *Brideshead Revisited*, revised Penguin edition (Harmondsworth, 1962), p.8.

III THE APPROACHING EQUINOX

1. Ashton, op. cit., p.176.
2. 'Of Seditions and Troubles', edn. cit., vol.VI, p.406.
3. M. A. Judson, *The Crisis in the Constitution* (1949), p.36.
4. Ibid., p.42.
5. W. Notenstein, *The Winning of the Initiative by the House of Commons* (London, 1924), pp.47-8.
6. Ibid., p.50.
7. Judson, op. cit., p.142.
8. Ibid., p.127.
9. Ibid., pp.154-5.
10. Ibid., p.280.
11. Notenstein, op. cit., p.43.
12. Judson, op. cit., p.159.
13. Ibid., p.75.
14. Cf. pp.490-5.
15. See G. P. V. Akrigg, *Jacobean Pageant* (London, 1962).
16. Elton, op. cit., p.465.
17. 'Of Great Place' in *Works*, ed. cit., vol.VI, p.400.
18. Notenstein, op. cit., p.26.
19. *Calendar of State Papers Venetian (CSPV)* (1603-7), no.341.
20. Notenstein, p.49, note.

21. *CSPV*, no. 440.
22. L. Stone, 'The Inflation of Honours 1558-1641', *Past and Present*, XIV (1958).
23. See *CSPV*, no.55: 'no Englishman, be his rank what it may, can enter the Presence Chamber without being summoned, whereas Scottish lords have free entree of the Privy Chamber' (dated May 1603).
24. Stone, 'The Inflation of Honours'.
25. C. R. Mayes, 'The Sale of Peerages in Early Stuart England', *Journal of Modern History*, XXIX, (1957).
26. Garrett Mattingly, *Renaissance Diplomacy*, Peregrine edition (London, 1965), p.247.
27. Ibid., p.248.
28. Miskimin, op. cit., p.178.
29. J. P. Kenyon, *Stuart England* (London, 1978), p.37.
30. John Summerson, *Inigo Jones* (Harmondsworth, 1966), p.134.
31. Kenyon, op. cit., p.73. See also J. W. Lever, *The Tragedy of State* (London, 1971), *passim*.

IV TO STRIP THE RAGGED FOLLIES OF THE TIME

1. See also Ernst Schanzer, *Shakespeare's Problem Plays* (London, 1963), for a discussion of the ironic mode in *Julius Caesar*.
2. See the convenient anthology, *Dr. Johnson on Shakespeare*, ed. W. K. Wimsatt (London, 1969), p.62.
3. Preface to Greene's *Menaphon*, ed. Arber (1880), p.9.
4. Sidney, *An Apology for Poetry*, ed. Shepherd (Manchester, 1973), p.137. This is orthodox Renaissance theory, as the editor notes. See also Madeleine Doran, *Endeavours of Art* (Madison, Wi., 1954), pp.105 ff., and notes.
5. For Self-wise-seeming schoolmasters see Sidney's own Rhombus in *The Lady of May*, and Shakespeare's Holofernes. Ascham, *The Schoolmaster*, refers to a traveller 'returned out of Italie worse transformed'. Sidney may have seen *commedia dell' arte* troupes in Venice in 1574: see K. M. Lea, *Italian Popular Comedy* (Oxford, 1934), vol.I, p.262.
6. Quotations are from the edition by H. J. C. Grierson (1912).
7. *The Plays of George Chapman*, ed. T. M. Parrott (London, 1913, reprinted 1961).
8. See viii. 185-251.
9. *Every Man In*, ed. J. W. Lever (London, 1971), Intro., p.xiv.

V MARSTON AND THE COURT

1. Quotations from *The Dramatic Works of Thomas Dekker*, ed. Bowers, 4 vols. (Cambridge, 1953-61).
2. This is to reverse the view proposed in the first edition of this book (London, 1968).

174   *Jacobean City Comedy*

3. *Antonio and Mellida*, ed. G. K. Hunter (London, 1965), IV. i. 224-6.
4. Quotations from *The Plays of John Marston*, ed. H. Harvey Wood (Edinburgh, 1938).
5. This is the view of Philip J. Finkelpearl, *John Marston of the Inner Temple* (Cambridge, Mass., 1969), pp.175-7.
6. Cf. G. K. Hunter's edition, Intro., pp.xlv-xlvi.
7. Cf. Bernard Harris's edition, Intro., p.xxxii.
8. G. K. Hunter's edition, Intro., p.lxxi.
9. *The Fawn*, ed. Gerald A. Smith (London, 1964), Intro., p.xi. Finkelpearl argues for 1606 (op. cit., p.223, note).
10. Cf. A. W. Upton, *PMLA* (1929); Finkelpearl, op. cit., pp.220-37.
11. See M. W. Beresford, 'The Common Informer', *EHR* (1957).
12. See David M. Bergeron, *English Civic Pageantry 1558-1642* (London, 1971), p.66. This book gives admirably detailed accounts of shows and of the individual contributions of Munday, Dekker, Middleton, Heywood, Squire, Webster and Taylor, besides a useful general history of the subject.

VI MONEY MAKES THE WORLD GO AROUND:
THE CITY SATIRIZED

1. See R. C. Bald, 'The Chronology of Thomas Middleton's Plays', *MLR* (1937); David George, 'Thomas Middleton's Sources: A Survey', *N&Q* (1971); David J. Lake, *The Canon of Thomas Middleton's Plays* (Cambridge, 1975), and the conclusions of editors of individual plays in modern editions in the following series: New Mermaid, Regent's Renaissance, Revels, Fountainwell.
2. Thomas Middleton, *The Phoenix*, II. ii. 80, 81, in the edition of *The Works of Thomas Middleton* by A. H. Bullen (1885) from which all quotations from Middleton's plays are taken.
3. See Alan C. Dessen, 'The 'Estates' Morality Play', *SP* (1965), and 'Middleton's *The Phoenix* and the Allegorical Tradition', *SEL* (1964).
4. *Your Five Gallants* IV. v; cf. *Every Man Out* IV. vi. 72-118.
5. Machiavelli, *Mandragola*, trans. Frederick May and Eric Bentley, in *The Classic Theatre*, ed. Eric Bentley (1958), vol. I.
6. Marston, *The Dutch Courtezan*, ed. Peter Davison (Edinburgh, 1968).
7. See Mario Praz, *The Flaming Heart* (New York, 1958), chapter 4, 'Ben Jonson's Italy'. Praz remarks that in *Volpone* 'the Venetian local colour is rendered with such an accuracy as to leave behind any other contemporary dramatist fond of picturesque allusion' (p.170).
8. Machiavelli's Induction to *The Jew of Malta* in *The Works of Christopher Marlowe*, ed. C. F. Tucker Brooke (1910).

VII CONVENTIONAL PLAYS 1604-7

1. Jonson, *Discoveries* 2472-3.

2. ' ...they were in perpetual financial straits even with high prices for admission. The only possible explanation is slim attendance', (p.45).
3. *The Plays of Thomas Dekker*, ed. F. T. Bowers, (4 vols. Cambridge, 1953-61). All quotations from Dekker's plays are from this edition.
4. I here correct my statement in the first edition, where I described the wives as actually adulterous.
5. John Day, *The Ile of Gulls* (1606), sig. A2^v.
6. Quoted from A. H. Bullen's edition of *The Works of John Day* (1881).
7. *Dodsley's Old English Plays*, 4th ed. (1874-6, reprinted C. W. Traylen 1964).
8. For the allusions to James, see Ian Donaldson, *The World Upside Down* (Oxford, 1970), chapter 3, or William Blissett, 'Your Majesty is Welcome to a Fair' in *The Elizabethan Theatre IV* (London, 1974). C. R. Baskervill, *MP* (1908) conjectured allusions to episodes in the life of Sir Thomas More. On this see also Douglas Duncan, *Ben Jonson and the Lucianic Tradition* (Cambridge, 1979), pp.217-8.
9. See F. J. Fisher, 'London as a Centre of Conspicuous Consumption in the Sixteenth and Seventeenth Centuries', *Trans. R. Hist. S.* (1948).

VIII MIDDLETON AND JONSON

1. See M. C. Bradbrook, *Themes and Conventions of Elizabethan Tragedy*, p.121, n.

IX *BARTHOLOMEW FAIR* AND *THE DEVIL IS AN ASS*:
CITY COMEDY AT THE ZENITH

1. Translation from G. R. Hibbard's edition of *Bartholomew Fair* (London, 1977), p.2.
2. Jonson's epilogue addressed to James takes advantage of the happy atmosphere of the conclusion to persuade the king not to take offence at the comedy's licence, and to protect the author and players from the disapproval of others at Court.
3. Marcus Gavius Apicius, a gourmand of the early Roman Empire, inherited a huge fortune. He spent half of it in ten years on gourmandizing, then it struck him that he might outlive his remaining £75,000 and be forced one day to eat frugally, so he promptly committed suicide! A collection of recipe books attributed to him contains some of the recipes referred to in Sir Epicure's speech in *The Alchemist* II. ii. See *Apicius, Cooking and Dining in Imperial Rome*, edited and translated by J. D. Vehling, (1936, reprinted 1977), and notes in the edition of *The Alchemist* by F. H. Mares (London, 1967), II. ii. 72-87. Apicius is recognized by Sir Epicure as a heroic example in his life as in his letters.
4. On the 'Wise Magistrate' tradition see J. W. Lever's introduction to his edition of *Measure for Measure* (London, 1965), pp.xliv-li.
5. See Jonas Barish's study of this version in his *Ben Jonson and the*

Language of Prose Comedy (Cambridge, Mass., 1960).

6. The emblem 'Justice in the Stocks' is reproduced by T. W. Craik (from Flettner's woodcut of 1525) in *The Tudor Interlude* (Leicester, 1958).

7. Cf. III. v. 273-4.

8. Cf. III. v. 277-80

9. Herford and Simpson, in a note to V. iii. 7, observe that the 'motion' is twice described as an 'Interlude', and comment that Jonson took, as the starting point of his burlesque, Richard Edwardes, *The Excellent Comedie of two the moste faithfullest Freendes, Damon and Pithias* (1571).

10. The play in question was Terence's *Hecyra*: see W. Beare's account of Terence's career in *The Roman Stage* (London, 1964), and my own introduction to Congreve, *The Way of the World* (London, 1971), pp.xii-xiii. Congreve associates his own career with those of Jonson and Terence.

APPENDIX

1. Awdelay, 'The Fraternitie of Vagabonds', ed. F. J. Furnivall, *E.E.T.S.* (1869), p.6.

2. Walker, 'A Manifest Detection of Dice Play', ed. A. V. Judges in *The Elizabethan Underworld* (London, 1930), p.35.

3. Harman, 'The Caveat for Common Cursetors', ed. F. J. Furnivall (op. cit. of *E.E.T.S.*).

4. ?Anon, 'A Notable Discovery of Coosnage' in Judges, op. cit., p.122.

5. Greene, 'The Second Part of Coney-Catching' ibid., p.151.

6. Greene, 'The Third Part of Coney-Catching' ibid., p.182.

7. Greene, 'A Disputation &c.' ibid., pp.206-47.

8. This fashion and its possible connection with *Lazarillo de Tormes* is discussed by F. W. Chandler in *The Literature of Roguery* (1909), vol. I.

9. *The Works of Thomas Nashe*, ed. R. B. McKerrow, corr. F. P. Wilson (Oxford, 1958), vol.II, p.211.

10. Thomas Dekker, 'The Gull's Hornbook', ed. G. Saintsbury in *Elizabethan and Jacobean Pamphlets* (1892), pp.226-7.

SELECT BIBLIOGRAPHY

This is a highly selective list: it contains (a) a selection of those works published before 1967 which (with one or two trifling exceptions) I read or consulted when I was writing this book, the first edition of which was published in 1968; (b) works published in 1967 or later which are materially relevant to critical debate or literary history, or, in the case of historical studies, which are essential further reading for the non-specialist student of the period.

Many of the works listed here have excellent bibliographies, and I have marked a number of these with an asterisk. The reader in search of further guidance can consult the annual review of criticism and scholarship in *The Year's Work in English Studies*, the Renaissance Drama issue of *Studies in English Literature*, and, for History, *The Annual Bulletin of Historical Literature*. A full, unselective list of publications, including dissertations, is presented in the annual MLA Bibliography.

Excellent modern editions of single plays contain important contributions to critical appreciation as well as scholarship, and readers are recommended to consult all the available editions of a particular play in the following series: *Fountainwell Drama Texts*; *The New Mermaids*; *Regent's Renaissance Drama*; *The Revels Plays*; *The Yale Ben Jonson*. The standard edition of the complete works of Jonson remains that of C. H. Herford and P. and E. Simpson; there is no modern complete edition of either Marston or Middleton, though their major comedies are available in modern single-play editions.

A. THE HISTORICAL BACKGROUND

Aikin, Lucy (1822) *Memoirs of the Court of King James the First* (London).
Akrigg, G. P. V. (1962) *Jacobean Pageant* (London: Hamish Hamilton).
Ashton, R. (1960) *The Crown and the Money Market* (Oxford: Oxford University Press).
____. (1979) *The City and the Court, 1603-1643* (Cambridge: Cambridge University Press).
Aylmer, G. E. (1975) *The Levellers in the English Revolution* (London: Thames & Hudson).

Beresford, M. W. (1957) 'The Common Informer', *EHR*.

Bindoff, S. T. (1950) *Tudor England* (Harmondsworth: Penguin).

———. (ed.) (1961) *Elizabethan Government and Society* (London: Athlone).

Braudel, Fernand (1973) *Capitalism and Material Life 1400-1800* (London: Fontana).

Butterfield, H. (1962) *Origins of Modern Science* (London: Bell).

Dickens, A. G. (1964) *The English Reformation* (London: Batsford).

*Elton, G. R. (1962) *England Under the Tudors*; revised and amplified 1972 (London: Methuen).

Fisher, F. J. (1948) 'London as a Centre of Conspicuous Consumption in the Sixteenth and Seventeenth Centuries', *Trans. R. Hist. S.*

Gardiner, S. R. (1883-4) *History of England 1603-42* (London).

———. (1893) *History of the Great Civil War* (London).

Hexter, J. H. (1963) *Reappraisals in History* (London: Longman).

Hill, Christopher (1961) *The Century of Revolution* (London: Nelson).

———. (1940) *The English Revolution 1640* (London: Secker & Warburg).

———. (1958) *Puritanism and Revolution* (London: Secker & Warburg).

———. (1967) *Reformation to Industrial Revolution* (London: Weidenfeld & Nicolson).

———. (1972) *The World Turned Upside Down* (London: Maurice Temple Smith).

Judson, M. A. (1949) *The Crisis in the Constitution*. (Rutgers University Press).

Kearney, Hugh F. (1964) *Origins of the Scientific Revolution* (Harlow: Longman).

*Kenyon, J. P. (1978) *Stuart England* (London: Allen Lane).

Lever, J. W. (1971) *The Tragedy of State* (London: Methuen).

Mattingly, Garrett (1955) *Renaissance Diplomacy* (London: Cape).

Mayes, C. R. (1957) 'The Sale of Peerages in Early Stuart England', *JMH*.

Miskimin, Harry A. (1977) *The Economy of Later Renaissance Europe 1460-1600* (Cambridge: Cambridge University Press).

Nef, J. U. (1934) 'Technology and Industry 1540-1640', *EHR*.

———. (1940) *Industry and Government in France and England 1540-1640*, (New York, NY: American Philosophical Society).

Notenstein, W. (1924) *The Winning of the Initiative by the House of Commons* (London).

Outhwaite, R. B. (1969) *Inflation in Tudor and Stuart England* (London: Macmillan).

Pearl, V. (1961) *London and the Outbreak of the Puritan Revolution* (Oxford: Oxford University Press).

Pocock, J. G. A. (1975) *The Machiavellian Moment* (Princeton, N. J.: Princeton University Press).

Raab, Felix (1964) *The English Face of Machiavelli* (London: Routledge & Kegan Paul).

Russell, Conrad (ed.) (1973) *The Origins of the English Civil War* (London: Macmillan).

Stone, Lawrence (1956) *An Elizabethan: Sir Horatio Pallavicino* (Oxford: Oxford University Press).

_____. (1965) *The Crisis of the Aristocracy 1558-1641* (Oxford: Oxford University Press).

_____. (ed.) (1965) *Social Change and Revolution in England 1540-1640* (London: Longman).

_____. (1958) 'The Inflation of Honours 1558-1641', *Past and Present*, xiv.

Tawney, R. H. (1926) *Religion and the Rise of Capitalism* (London: John Murray).

Trevor-Roper, H. R. (1950) 'The Elizabethan Aristocracy: An Anatomy Anatomized', *EHR*, 2nd ser. 3, 279-98.

_____. *The Gentry: 1540-1640*, *EHR Supplements* 1, n.d.

_____. (1967) *Religion, the Reformation and Social Change* (London: Macmillan).

Unwin, George (1904) *Industrial Organization in the Sixteenth and Seventeenth Centuries* (London: Cass).

Upton, A. F. (1961) *Sir Arthur Ingram 1565-1642* (London: Oxford University Press).

B. EARLIER SIXTEENTH-CENTURY TRADITIONS

Altman, Joel (1978) *The Tudor Play of Mind* (Berkeley, Calif., University of California Press).

Bentley, Eric (1946) *The Playwright as Thinker* (New York, N.Y.: Harcourt Brace Jovanovich).

Bergeron, David M. (1971) *English Civic Pageantry* (London: Edward Arnold).

Bevington, David (1962) *From 'Mankind' to Marlowe: Growth of Structure in the Popular Drama of Tudor England* (Cambridge, Mass.: Harvard University Press).

_____. (1968) *Tudor Drama and Politics* (Cambridge, Mass.: Harvard University Press).

Brecht, Bertolt (1964) *Brecht on Theatre*, trs. John Willett (London: Eyre Methuen).

Chandler, F. W. (1909) *The Literature of Roguery* (London)

Craik, T. W. (1958) *The Tudor Interlude* (Leicester: Leicester University Press).

*Harner, James L. (1978) *English Renaissance Prose Fiction, 1500-1660* (London: G. Prior)

Herrick, Marvin T. (1960) *Italian Comedy in the Renaissance* (Urbana, Ill.: University of Illinois Press).

Hibbard, G. R. (1962) *Thomas Nashe* (London: Routledge & Kegan Paul).

Lea, K. M. (1934) *Italian Popular Comedy* (Oxford).
Nicoll, Allardyce (1937) *Stuart Masques and the Renaissance Stage* (London: Harrap).
——. (1963) *The World of Harlequin* (New York, N.Y.: Cambridge University Press).
Oreglia, Giacomo (1968) *The Commedia dell' Arte*, trans. L. Edwards (London: Methuen).
Praz, Mario (1958) *The Flaming Heart* (New York, N.Y.: Doubleday).
Summerson, John (1966) *Inigo Jones* (Harmondsworth: Penguin).

C. JACOBEAN COMEDY AND DRAMATIC TRADITION

Bradbrook, M. C. (1955) *The Growth and Structure of Elizabethan Comedy* (London: Chatto).
——. (1976) *The Living Monument* (Cambridge: Cambridge University Press).
——. (1969) *Shakespeare the Craftsman* (London: Chatto).
——. (1978) *Shakespeare, the Poet in His World*. (London: Weidenfeld & Nicolson).
——. (1935) *Themes and Conventions of Elizabethan Tragedy* (Cambridge: Cambridge University Press).
Brown, Arthur 'Citizen Comedy and Domestic Drama', in Brown and Harris, *Jacobean Theatre* (q.v.)
Brown, John Russell, and Bernard Harris (eds.) (1960) *Stratford-upon-Avon Studies 1: Jacobean Theatre* (1960); *2: Elizabethan Poetry* (1961); *9: Elizabethan Theatre* (1966).
Campbell, Oscar James (1938) *Comicall Satyre and Shakespeare's Troilus and Cressida*, 1st edn (San Marino, Calif.: Huntington Library).
Doran, Madeleine (1954) *Endeavors of Art: A Study of Form in Elizabethan Drama* (Madison, Wi.: University of Wisconsin Press).
Ellis-Fermor, Una (1936) *The Jacobean Drama* (London: Methuen).
Empson, William (1935) *Some Versions of Pastoral* (London: Chatto).
Farnham, Willard (1936) *The Medieval Heritage of Elizabethan Tragedy* (Oxford: Blackwell).
Freeburg, V. O. (1915) *Disguise Plots in Elizabethan Drama* (New York N.Y.: Blom).
Gombrich, E. H. (1962) *Art and Illusion* (London: Phaidon).
——. (1963) *Meditations on a Hobby Horse* (London: Phaidon).
*Harbage, Alfred (1952) *Shakespeare and the Rival Traditions* (Bloomington, Indiana: Indiana University Press).
Harris, Bernard (1961) 'Men Like Satyrs', in Brown and Harris, *Elizabethan Poetry* (q.v.).
Hibbard, G.R. (ed.) *The Elizabethan Theatre*: IV (1974), VI (1978) (London: Macmillan).

Hibbard, G.R. (1978) 'Love, Marriage and Money in Shakespeare's Theatre and Shakespeare's England', in Hibbard, *The Elizabethan Theatre VI* (q.v.).

Kernan, Alvin (1959) *The Cankered Muse: Satire of the English Renaissance* (London: Yale University Press).

Kirsch, Arthur C. (1972) *Jacobean Dramatic Perspectives* (Charlottesville, Va.: University Press of Virginia).

*Knights, L. C. (1937) *Drama and Society in the Age of Jonson* (London: Chatto).

*Leggatt, Alexander (1973) *Citizen Comedy in the Age of Shakespeare* (University of Toronto Press).

*Levin, Richard (1971) *The Multiple Plot in English Renaissance Drama* (Chicago, Ill.: University of Chicago Press).

Lynch, Kathleen M. (1926) *The Social Mode of Restoration Comedy* (New York, N.Y.: Octagon).

*Peter, John. (1956) *Complaint and Satire in Early English Literature* (Oxford: Oxford University Press).

Salingar, L. G. (1967) 'Farce and Fashion in "The Silent Woman" ', *Essays and Studies*, New Series xx, 29-46.

____. (1974) *Shakespeare and the Traditions of Comedy* (Cambridge: Cambridge University Press).

Spivack, Bernard (1958) *Shakespeare and the Allegory of Evil* (New York, N.Y.: Columbia University Press).

Welsford, Enid (1935) *The Fool: His Social and Literary History* (London: Faber).

Wilson, F. P. (1945) *Elizabethan and Jacobean* (Oxford: Oxford University Press).

____. (1969) *The English Drama, 1485-1585*. Oxford History of English Literature, vol. 4, part I.

Wright, Louis B. (1935) *Middle-Class Culture in Elizabethan England* (Ithaca, N. Y.: Cornell University Press).

D. THE DISGUISED DUKE TRADITION AND *MEASURE FOR MEASURE*

*Lever, J. W. (ed.) (1965) *Measure for Measure* (London: Methuen).

Miles, Rosalind (1976) *The Problem of Measure for Measure* (London: Vision Press).

Stevenson, David L. (1959) 'The role of James I in Shakespeare's *Measure for Measure*', *ELH*.

E. ACTING COMPANIES, STAGES, AUDIENCES

Armstrong, W. A. (1959) 'The Audience of the Elizabethan Private Theatres', *RES*.

Bentley, G. E. (1941-68) *The Jacobean and Caroline Stage*, 7 vols, (Oxford)

_____. (1971) *The Profession of Dramatist in Shakespeare's Time* (Princeton, N. J.: Princeton University Press).

Bradbrook, M. C. (1962) *The Rise of the Common Player* (London: Chatto).

_____. (1978) 'Shakespeare and the Multiple Theatres of Jacobean London', *The Elizabethan Theatre*, VI.

Chambers, E. K. (1924) *The Elizabethan Stage* (Oxford: Oxford University Press).

Foakes, R. A. (1962) 'John Marston's Fantastical Plays', *PQ*.

_____. (1971) *Shakespeare, the Dark Comedies to the Last Plays* (London: Routledge & Kegan Paul).

_____. (1978) 'Tragedy at the Children's Theatres after 1600', *The Elizabethan Theatre*, VI.

Gair, Reavley (1978) 'The Presentation of Plays at Paul's: The Early Phase, 1599-1602', *The Elizabethan Theatre*, VI.

George, David Y. (1978) 'Another Elizabethan Stage', *Theatre Notebook*.

Gibbons, Brian (1968) 'Unstable Proteus: Marlowe's *Tragedy of Dido*' in Brian Morris (ed.) *Christopher Marlowe, Mermaid Critical Commentaries* (London: Benn).

Harbage, Alfred (1941) *Shakespeare's Audience* (New York, N. Y.: Columbia University Press).

Heywood, Thomas (1612) *An Apology for Actors.*

Hillebrand, H. N. (1926) *The Child Actors* (Urbana, Illinois: University of Illinois Press).

Hodges, C. Walter (1968) *The Globe Restored* (London: Oxford University Press).

_____. (1973) *Shakespeare's Second Globe* (London: Oxford University Press).

Hosley, Richard (1975) 'The Blackfriars Theatre' in *The Revels History of Drama in English*, vol. III, part 3, chapter 4.

_____. (1978) 'A Reconstruction of the Fortune Playhouse', *The Elizabethan Theatre*, VI.

Hunter, G. K. (1962) *John Lyly: The Humanist as Courtier* (London: Routledge & Kegan Paul).

Neill, Michael (1978) 'The Audience of the Caroline Private Theatres', *SEL*.

Nicoll, Allardyce (1931) *Masks, Mimes and Miracles: Studies in the Popular Theatre* (New York, N. Y.: Cooper Square).

Salingar, L. G. (1968) 'Les comédiens et leur public en Angleterre de 1520 a 1640', in *Dramaturgie et societé*, ed. Jean Jacquot (Paris: C.N.R.S.).

Sisson, C. J. (1972) *The Boar's Head Theatre* (London: Routledge & Kegan Paul).

Smith, Irwin (1964). *Shakespeare's Blackfriars Playhouse* (New York, N. Y.: New York University Press).

Southern, Richard (1973) *The Staging of Plays before Shakespeare* (London: Faber).

Wickham, G. (1969) *Early English Stages 1300-1650* (London: Routledge).

F. BEN JONSON

Bacon, Wallace (1956) 'The Magnetic Field: The Structure of Jonson's Comedies.' *HLQ*, XIX, 121-53.

Barish, Jonas (1959) 'Bartholomew Fair and its Puppets', *MLQ*, xx (March) 3-17.

———. (ed.) (1963) *Ben Jonson: A Collection of Critical Essays* (Englewood Cliffs, N. J.: Prentice-Hall)

———. (1960) *Ben Jonson and the Language of Prose Comedy* (Cambridge, Mass: Harvard University Press).

———. (1953) 'The Double Plot in *Volpone*', *MP* 51, 83-92.

Baskervill, Charles Read (1911) *English Elements in Jonson's Early Comedy* (New York, N. Y.: Gordian Press).

Baum, Helena Watts (1947) *The Satiric and the Didactic in Ben Jonson's Comedy* (Chapel Hill: University of N. Carolina Press).

Beaurline, L. A. (1969) 'Ben Jonson and the Illusion of Completeness', *PMLA*, LXXXIV, 51-9.

Blissett, William (1968) 'The Venter Tripartite in *The Alchemist*', *SEL*, VIII, 323-34.

———. (1974) 'Your Majesty Is Welcome to a Fair', in *The Elizabethan Theatre*, IV.

Bradbrook, M. C. (1973) 'Social Change and the Evolution of Ben Jonson's Court Masques', *Studies in the Literary Imagination*, (Atlanta, Ga.).

Champion, Larry (1968) *Ben Jonson's 'Dotages': A Reconsideration of the Late Plays* (Lexington, Ky.: University Press of Kentucky).

Cope, Jackson (1965) '*Bartholomew Fair* as Blasphemy', *Ren.D.*, VIII, . 127-52.

Davison, P. H. (1963) '*Volpone* and the Old Comedy', *MLQ*.

Dessen, Alan (1964) '*The Alchemist*: Jonson's "Estates" Play.' *Ren.D.*, VII, 35-54.

———. (1972) *Jonson's Moral Comedy* (Evanston, Ill.: Northwestern University Press).

———. (1964) '*Volpone* and the Late Morality Tradition,' *MLQ*.

Donaldson, Ian (1968) 'Jonson's Tortoise.', *RES*, 162-6.

———. (1970) *The World Upside-Down* (Oxford: Oxford University Press).

———. (1971) '*Volpone* Quick and Dead', *Essays in Criticism*.

Duncan, Douglas (1979) *Ben Jonson and the Lucianic Tradition* (Cambridge: Cambridge University Press).

Empson, William (1968-9) 'Volpone', *The Hudson Review*.

———. (1969-70) 'The Alchemist', *The Hudson Review*.

184 *Jacobean City Comedy*

Enck, Jon (1957) *Jonson and the Comic Truth* (Madison, Wi.: University of Wisconsin).

Greenblatt, Stephen (1976) 'The False Ending in *Volpone*', *JEGP*.

Hamel, Guy (1973) 'Order and Judgment in *Bartholomew Fair*', *UTQ*.

Heffner, Ray (1954) 'Unifying Symbols in the Comedy of Ben Jonson', *English Institute Essays*.

Jackson, Gabrielle Bernhard (1968) *Vision and Judgment in Ben Jonson's Drama* (New Haven, Conn.: Yale University Press).

Levin, Harry (1943) 'Jonson's Metempsychosis', *PG*, XXII, 231-9.

Parker, R. B. (July 1970) 'The Themes and Staging of Bartholomew Fair', *UTQ*, XXXIX, 239-309.

Partridge, Edward B. (1966) 'Ben Jonson: The Makings of the Dramatist (1596-1602)' in Brown and Harris *Elizabethan Theatre* (q.v.).

_____. (1958) *The Broken Compass* (London: Chatto).

_____. (1957) 'The Symbolism of Clothes in Jonson's Last Plays', *JEGP*, LVI, 396-409.

Townsend, Freda (1947) *Apologie for 'Bartholomew Fayre': The Art of Jonson's Comedies* (New York, N. Y.: Modern Language Association).

Williams, Patrick (1978) 'Ben Jonson's Satiric Choreography', *Ren.D.* IX.

G. THOMAS HEYWOOD AND THOMAS DEKKER

Brown, Arthur (1962) 'Thomas Heywood's Dramatic Art.' *Essays on Shakespeare and Elizabethan Drama in Honor of Hardin Craig*, ed. Richard Hosley (New York: Columbia University Press).

Grivelet, Michel (1957) *Thomas Heywood et le drame domestique Elizabéthain* (Paris).

Jones-Davies, Marie-Thérèse (1958) *Un Peintre de la vie Londonienne: Thomas Dekker*, 2 vols (Paris).

Leggatt, Alexander (1973) *Citizen Comedy in the Age of Shakespeare* (University of Toronto Press).

H. JOHN MARSTON

Caputi, Anthony (1961) *John Marston, Satirist* (Ithaca, N. Y.: Cornell University Press).

Finkelpearl, Philip (1969) *John Marston of the Middle Temple: An Elizabethan Dramatist in His Social Setting* (Cambridge, Mass.: Harvard University Press).

Hunter, G. K. 'English Folly and Italian Vice: The Moral Landscape of John Marston' in Brown and Harris, *Jacobean Theatre* (q.v.).

Peter, John (1950) 'John Marston's Plays', *Scrutiny*, XVII (Summer) 132-53.

Schoenbaum, Samuel (1952) 'The Precarious Balance of John Marston', *PMLA*, LXVII (December) 1069-78.

Spencer, Theodore (1934) 'John Marston', *Criterion*, XIII, 581-99.

I. THOMAS MIDDLETON

Bald, R. C. (1937) 'The Chronology of Thomas Middleton's Plays', *MLR*, XXXII, 33-43.
——. (1933) 'Middleton's Civic Employments', *MP*, XXXI, 65-78.
——. (1934) 'The Sources of Middleton's City Comedies', *JEGP*, XXXIII, 373-87.
Barker, Richard Hindry (1958) *Thomas Middleton* (New York, N.Y.: Columbia University Press).
Chatterji, Ruby. (1965) 'Theme, Imagery, and Unity in *A Chaste Maid in Cheapside*', *Ren.D.*, VIII, 105-26.
——. (1968) 'Unity and Disparity: *Michaelmas Term*', *SEL*, VIII 349-63.
Davidson, Clifford (1968) '*The Phoenix*: Middleton's Didactic Comedy', *Papers on Language and Literature* 4, 121-30.
Dessen, Alan (1965) 'The "Estates" Morality Play', *SP*, LXII, 121-36.
——. (1966) 'Middleton's *The Phoenix* and the Allegorical Tradition', *SEL*, VI, 291-308.
Doebler, John (1965) 'Beaumont's *Knight of the Burning Pestle* and the Prodigal Son Plays', *SEL*, V.
George, David (1971) 'Thomas Middleton's Sources: A Survey', *N&Q*, New Series 18, 17-24.
Hallett, Charles (1971) 'Volpone as the Source of the Sickroom Scheme in Middleton's *Mad World*', *N&Q*, New Series 18, 24-5.
Heinemann, Margot (1980) *Puritanism and Theatre* (Cambridge: Cambridge University Press).
Lake, David J. (1975) *The Canon of Thomas Middleton's Plays* (Cambridge: Cambridge University Press).
Marotti, Arthur (1969) 'Fertility and Comic Form in *A Chaste Maid in Cheapside*', *Comp.D.*, III, 65-74.
Parker, R.B. (1960) 'Middleton's Experiments with Comedy and Judgement', in Brown and Harris (eds) *Jacobean Theatre*.
Schoenbaum, Samuel (1959) '*A Chaste Maid in Cheapside* and Middleton's City Comedy', *Studies in the English Renaissance Drama*, ed. J.W. Bennett *et al*. (New York, N.Y.: New York University Press).
Slights, William (1969) 'The Trickster-Hero and Middleton's *A Mad World, My Masters*', *Comp.D.*, III, 87-98.
Ure, Peter (1966) 'Patient Madman and Honest Whore: The Middleton-Dekker Oxymoron', *Essays and Studies*, New Series, XIX, 18-40.
Williams, Robert I. (1970) 'Machiavelli's *Mandragola*, Touchwood Senior, and the Comedy of Middleton's A Chaste Maid in Cheapside, *SEL*, X (Spring), 385-96.

INDEX

DATE DUE
